Behind the Mask

Behind the Mask
Nurses, Their Unions and Nursing Policy

Christopher Hart
MA, RMN, RGN
Regional Officer, Unison
Formerly Services Manager,
St Luke's Hospital, London

Learning Resources
Centre

Baillière Tindall

London   Philadelphia   Toronto   Sydney   Tokyo

Baillière Tindall   24–28 Oval Road
W. B. Saunders   London NW1 7DX

The Curtis Center
Independence Square West
Philadelphia, PA 19106-3399, USA

Harcourt Brace & Company
55 Horner Avenue
Toronto, Ontario, M8Z 4X6, Canada

Harcourt Brace & Company, Australia
30–52 Smidmore Street
Marrickville
NSW 2204, Australia

Harcourt Brace & Company, Japan
Ichibancho Central Building
22-1 Ichibancho
Chiyoda-ku, Tokyo 102, Japan

ISBN 0-7020-1674-8

Typeset by Columns Design and Production Services Limited, Reading

Printed and bound in Great Britain by Mackays of Chatham, Kent

Contents

Picture Credits

Plates I to XII: Mary Evans Picture Library.

Plates XIII and XX: Dan McPhee, *The Guardian*.

Plates XIV and XV: Gerry Weaser, *The Guardian*.

Plate XVI: E. Hamilton West, *The Guardian*.

Plates XVII, XVIII and XXI: Hulton Deutsch Collection.

Plate XVIIa: Kenneth Saunders.

Plate XIX: David Osborn, *The Guardian*.

Plate XXII: Mick Ridge.

Acknowledgements

Although my name appears as writer of this book, I cannot claim credit for all of the ideas presented here. As with all such ventures, the final product is a far more collective affair than might seem apparent. There are numerous people to thank and I will probably fail to credit some important ones. Nonetheless, I will start with the many full-time and lay officials from both the RCN and COHSE who kindly offered me their opinions and thoughts on any number of issues. Also the staff at the RCN library, Tom Morgan at the Mary Evans Picture Library, Jim Aindow at Hulton Deutsch and Gwen Christianson at *The Guardian*.

This book originally started life as a dissertation and I am indebted to my tutors for their encouragement and help, particularly Jaqi Nixon and Bob Skelton. Equally important were my fellow students. Mick Carpenter was of special importance. I am indebted to both his example and assistance, as I am to the constant ideas and inspiration provided by Ian Morton, who knows a few things about football, too. James Hicks always reminded me that the health service and its trade unionism don't begin and end with nurses; Eamon Pryle, Taunus Kemasang, Tony Stevens, John Durham and, especially, Adrian D'Aubney were all fellow travellers. I also have to thank the nurses at the Maudsley Hospital from May 1985 to March 1989 – especially those on Ward 6. They were a constant source of surprise and gratificiation. Thanks to the nurses in Bloomsbury's Mental Health Unit also, to Keith Jerrome and Michael Walker for the loan of their unpublished manuscripts; to John Andrews for his help with the photographs. A special thank you to my editor, Sarah James, who was a most skilful midwife in the process of delivering the final copy and Karen Gilmour, who nursed it through some sticky moments, not forgetting Jackie Curthoys – who's a Palace fan! There were many more but they shall have to remain anonymous. Last, but by no means least, Barbara, Nathan and little Jake, without whom ... This book is dedicated to the memory of my parents.

Introduction

In November 1937 a group of London nurses marched through the streets of central London. This was not terribly uncommon. Nurses would often be seen collecting money for their hospitals on flag days. It was different this time, however. These young women were carrying sandwich boards proclaiming their deep sense of grievance and their faces were masked. Those nurses remain nameless today, their identities hidden at the time for fear of victimisation, but their stand against nursing shortages, long hours of work and low pay was a historical turning point. Although a long tradition of radical nurses existed, they had been in the asylums and Poor Law institutions. From behind their masks, for the first time, general nurses from London's local authority hospitals had broken free of the traditions of self-sacrifice and unquestioning obedience that bound them and challenged the myths that created and perpetuated those traditions of vocation and subservience.

This book follows a strand of nursing history of which those LCC nurses were a distinct and vital example. For although they did not wish to be identified as individuals, they did want to be seen and to make their voice heard. In 1937, as at other crucial times in the history of nursing, those nurses had been 'invisible', unable to direct or even influence events and policy as they affected them and the work that they did. That invisibility extended to them as individuals and as an occupational group working within a rigid, hierarchical and often harsh structure designed to firmly control them and within a model of care that was largely the result of, and subservient to, a system dominated by the medical profession.

This book looks at how nursing has evolved as a wide and comprehensive occupation and service from its 'modern' origins in the mid nineteenth century through to the present day but focusing particularly on the role of the nurses' professional associations and trade unions. However, it is not an entirely straightforward history of events arranged in strictly chronological order. It asks questions not only about what happened but also why particular events occurred at a particular time: thus it concerns itself with nursing myth and tradition and attempts to place nursing history in a wider context. The first chapter concentrates on why nursing developed as it did, as women's work, as a vocation subordinated to medicine and what lay behind the drive to get nurses trained and registered. Chapters 2 and 3 examine the origins and progress of the professional associations and trade unions and question why it was that they sprang to prominence in the areas of health care they did – the former in the voluntary hospitals, the latter in the asylums and Poor Law institutions – the events that shaped their development and how, in turn, they influenced those events. A key element in this book is to explore the differences between the professional associations and trade unions which have nursing members. The Royal College of Nursing (RCN) has been chosen as the prime example of the former, the Confederation of Health Service Employees (COHSE) for the latter. The differences between the two types of organisation are vital to grasp if we are to develop any understanding of nursing itself and Chapter 4 concentrates on these. The issues that are fundamental to one are often not shared by the other. Far from it; the two are opposed to each other on as many issues as they are united. Why that is reveals much about the types of nurses who make up the wider workforce, their different aspirations and the struggle for dominance within nursing circles that is as old as nursing itself.

The absence of nursing unions and organisations in the many histories of nursing may be as much to do with the manner of telling the nurses' 'story' as anything else, with an emphasis on general nurses in hospitals, which offers little attention or insight into the work of nurses in other areas and their early adoption of trade unions (Carpenter, 1980). In these histories, the professional ethos and its values are often seen as vital elements, implying autonomy, independence and control over one's work, an apparent step away from the subservience and submissiveness suggested by the term '-

vocation' (Salvage, 1985: p. 90). Profession also implies status which, as we shall see, has been an important issue for many nurses. But the term 'profession' has got to be questioned. What does it mean? Certainly, its meaning must have different connotations in particular social circles and has undoubtedly changed over the years, for lawyers and doctors regard themselves as professionals and point to professional bodies that regulate and govern their work – but so do professional footballers. We even hear descriptions of 'professional thieves'. There are very precise sociological definitions of what constitutes a profession and although these vary slightly, nursing does not usually meet their criteria. But whether or not nursing is a profession is, perhaps, not the key question. What is more interesting is why it has been so important for nursing to be established as a profession and to what use the professional ethos has been put by its supporters. These issues are dealt with throughout the first half of the book but concentrated on in their modern context in Chapter 5, which looks at nurses and the work that they do. The terms profession and professionalism will be used in this book but only in the context of the meanings ascribed to them by particular associations or groups.

Is nursing in crisis? This was a question asked in 1919, in 1937 and at many other stages of its history. It is not a phenomonen of the 1980s or 1990s. It has also been a question posed at regular intervals about the National Health Service. Clearly, a crisis implies a short term, acute problem. Thus it is hard to see how such a definition can be applied to either nursing or the NHS. More, it has been a case of ongoing problems and tensions that periodically reach crisis point before being partially resolved and leaving the political agenda. These tensions have concerned nurses and other occupational groups within the health service, those who work in the health service and government and the role and functions of health care itself. Nursing has so frequently been a source of tension essentially because the role of the nurse is at the heart of the service. This has meant that nurses' work, status, pay and conditions have all been subject to the vicissitudes of the National Health Service, just as with its predecessors. In some respects nurses' fortunes could be said to reflect the wider passage of society itself, whilst their drifts to and fro across the political spectrum have also mirrored those of the wider electorate. Particularly in Chapters 7, 8 and 9, concerning specific policy developments in the 1980s, these issues are brought to the fore.

There are further problems in developing any history of nursing. Nurses are grouped together, not just in the public mind and in the potent myths and images that shape people's perceptions of them, but also in the way in which broad political policy is formulated. Yet they are a far from homogeneous group. And nurses as an occupational group are quite different from both midwives and health visitors.

There is inevitably a lot missed in any nursing history. Within the scope of this particular text it was impossible to give much attention at all to the work of midwives and health visitors, particularly given the importance of their respective roles and the traditions of the Health Visitors Association and Royal College of Midwives. It would also have detracted from the comparison between the aims and activities of a professional association and traditional trade union organising among the same group of workers. The book has focused more than originally intended on hospital nursing but this is an inevitable consequence of the domination of hospitals in health care provision and nursing; as such, they have been both the main battleground between the professional associations and trade unions and main source of membership. Some readers will inevitably take the view that particular themes have been left underdeveloped or ignored; this is, to an extent, a part of the process of reading, but there are also some points which could not be explored further without disturbing an already complex narrative. As stated in the acknowledgements, there were many people whose ideas, thinking and work have influenced this book; the mistakes and errors, however, are mine totally. I have also taken the unusual step of referring to nurses throughout the text using feminine pronouns when a generalised description is being given, even though I have been at pains to record that nursing is made up of men and women from all backgrounds. However, the large majority of general nurses have always been women and women still numerically dominate nursing, midwifery and health visiting, even if they are sorely disadvantaged and underrepresented at higher grades and in management. My decision, then, was partly for those reasons and partly rooted in nursing's history. Nursing was described as, and forged into, 'women's work'; when things went wrong in early nursing and, most notably, midwifery, it was women who had to shoulder the blame. Men made a rather late entry into nursing but when it has been appropriate I have identified their presence, as in the asylums or their early influence through the Society of Registered Male Nurses. I hope that my readers, my male nursing colleagues particularly, will understand my decision.

That hospitals have been described as ideological metaphors in which systems of control are constructed, which operate not simply to cure or to treat but to manage, to classify and maintain (Maggs, 1987: p. 177), perhaps gives us clues about the dominance hospital based nurses have exercised within nursing, including the importance of nursing's myths in achieving it. This is particularly so if it is accepted that the management of meaning, a process of symbol construction and value use, is then employed to create a legitimacy for the ideas, actions and demands designed to protect the interests of the dominant groups, both in nursing and outside it (see White, 1986 and Pettigrew, McKee & Ferlie, 1988). Lukes (1974) has argued cogently that one of the most sophisticated but least visible uses of power is that which suppresses potential issues and averts conflicts before they even get on the political agenda and these themes are explored more fully, particularly in Chapter 6.

The three policy initiatives featured in the latter third of the book are the Griffiths Report on general management and its implementation, clinical grading for nurses, midwives and health visitors and the White Paper, *Working for Patients*. Two of these involved major reorganisations of the health service, with the other aimed at pay but with a radical element of restructuring the staff involved. All were inextricably linked, not only to each other but to earlier policy developments around both service organisation and nursing practice. The consequences of those three policies rapidly dovetailed and have resulted in a major reshaping of nursing and the NHS. They will be shown to have been an attempt by the Conservative government to deal with the tensions in the NHS in a centrist and managerial manner. Although the Conservative government of the period were clearly driven by a strong antiprofessional, anti-public service ideology, there was an equally strong belief that there were disabling flaws in the health service and an apparently insatiable demand for expansion that could not be afforded. The Conservatives' strategy was – and is – to try to manage it more efficiently and effectively whilst containing spending. The control of nursing is as essential a part of this strategy now as it was in the 1930s (see Abel-Smith, 1960: p. 130).

For the nursing unions, the formulation of a response to these initiatives was an extremely complex one, revealing as much about their internal workings and interrelationships as *their* dominant ideologies; confounded by the problem of controlling their own diverse and potentially volatile nurse members and trying to forge a unified image out of the many differences.

There has also been a steady flow of events and developments attempting to muscle their way into the book almost on a weekly basis and drawing a line is decidedly difficult. Even as the last pages were being written, two events occurred that seemed to offer a comment on the many changes of the 1980s. The 'flagship of the new NHS', Guy's Hospital, is facing virtual closure and the Clothier Inquiry into the Beverley Allitt murders at Grantham and Kesteven Hospital in 1991 has just been published, making 'recommendations which have a national implication' but 'no criticism that might have national implications' despite many believing that 'Nurse Allitt's success as a killer was the direct result of the government's failure as a manager of the NHS – that she exploited a hospital which was underfunded, demoralised, and distorted by commercialism' (Davies, *The Guardian*, 12.2.94).

The protest of those masked nurses in 1937 has been almost totally expunged from the collective nursing memory/history books. They and many other radical nurses from different generations who have tried to exert influence and gain some control over the policies that govern their working lives have no place within the accepted image, the myth of nursing. Their meaning is not that of the image makers. Theirs is a history not just forgotten but hidden. Behind the mask of professional respectability, continually striving for status within a controlled and controlling hierarchical, rigid framework, lies a different history with its own meaning and importance. This book aims to get behind the mask by questioning the accepted myths and trying to understand nursing's hidden history.

Chapter 1

A nurse born and bred?
The making of the modern nurse

The history of nursing is so shrouded in myth and stereotype that it is difficult to disentangle its 'real' origins from those of popular perception. The Lady of the Lamp is familiar to all, as is the demure, innocently self-sacrificing young nurse in splendid uniform drawn towards Florence Nightingale's light. Together, they emerged to conquer the comic image of the Dickensian Sarah Gamps, the gin-sodden women, untrained and of ill repute, who had preceded them.

Myth, Stereotype and the Evolution of Nursing History

Whilst it may seem that those myths and stereotypes now have little resonance in the modern age one needs only to consider contemporary images of nurses. The overall perception is complex when examined in detail, encompassing a number of factors, but the modern nurse is still viewed as a direct descendent of Florence Nightingale. They are smart, disciplined young women, dedicated, with a strong sense of duty. The notion of self-sacrifice and vocation still weighs heavily on the keepers of the role (Salvage, 1985).

That Florence Nightingale is the one prominent nursing figure virtually everyone in Britain could name is significant enough. But when it is considered that her contemporary, Mary Seacole (see below), is virtually unknown, despite her prominence in the latter part of the nineteenth century, the issue of who has become important in nursing history, and why, can be seen to be all the more necessary to understand. If we are to begin to make sense of modern nursing, we must explore how those images evolved and what the factors were that so influence nursing's origins.

Equally, there are themes common in nursing history, notably the struggles over nurse training and registration. Whilst their significance should not be minimalised, they are almost inexorably linked to the development of nursing in the voluntary London teaching hospitals of the period and little else.

Through this process it becomes much more difficult to rescue from the archives those forgotten or excluded. Yet it is worth considering how and why people and events have been excluded from nursing's past. For whilst we can, to an extent, make up our own minds about historical characters presented to us, we are inevitably denied that opportunity with those hidden from view. This is not to suggest a conspiracy to conceal elements of nursing history which do not sit easily within an accepted version of events or those which contradict the current orthodoxy but one of the most effective uses of power is to decide what does and does not find its way onto the agenda for discussion. It is a more sophisticated exercise in control or power – precisely because it is the least visible – to keep things 'hidden', to suppress potential issues and avert conflict, not opening up issues for debate (Lukes, 1974). The process by which nursing history has evolved is no different from any other. Thousands upon thousands of documents exist chronicling the stories of nurses from all over the country. Many of them are mundane, repetitive and apparently lacking in noteworthiness. Yet they reveal how nursing practice developed in different hospitals, the activities of nurses at particular moments in time, including innovations, breakthroughs and the frustrations of those looking to make progress against the odds. When examined in detail they can reveal the painfully slow process by which thinking on certain issues developed, as well as the occasional great leap forward. But these facts have had to be dug out, examined, edited, interpreted, perhaps many times over. Then they have to be put together and presented in a coherent form. Inevitably they reflect the views of the author and the meaning they have attached to the historical facts as they saw them, just as those who originally recorded them may have attached their own meaning to what it was they were writing down.

Many nursing histories relate the facts as those in positions of power and influence originally set them down, telling what is largely their own story. Even when lesser known incidents are recorded they are often placed at the margins or only find a place in specialist publications that few will ever see. History rarely has room for losers, whose version of events goes largely untold (Carr, 1961). It has to be recognised that the evolution and triumph of nursing's myths are no accident. They have served a definite purpose.

Winners and Losers

Thus, in the process of myth or stereotype there are winners and losers. Not only is the predominant image one of young women, driven by a sense of vocation and self-sacrifice; they are largely young, white, Anglo-Saxon women from affluent backgrounds working in an acute teaching hospital. This ignores those nurses who do not fit this image who might have been working in mental health settings or with the elderly, providing care in the community as district nurses, health visitors or midwives. Many will be from different socioeconomic backgrounds, of different race or ethnicity and/or gender. These nurses and midwives are not only marginalised in the telling of the story but also the development of the service. How that is reflected in terms of influence on policy making will be examined later, but it poses a major difficulty for nurses, whatever their working background. For midwives, who do not even describe or think of themselves as nurses but are frequently labelled as such, it is particularly problematic. That they are often subjected to the same policy making processes has often meant that their needs have been overshadowed.

To talk of 'nurses' as a homogeneous group is a misnomer and those who regard them as such have, according to Trevor Clay, been taken in by their stereotype (Clay, 1987: p. 28). It is axiomatic that (even if they do not always seem to acknowledge this themselves) there are many things that nurses do have in common, whatever their background and area of work. But when nursing is viewed simply as an indivisible whole in this way it denies the differing groups their own identity and past, often with their own, mutually exclusive, specific objectives and the fact that they are, on occasions, in competition with one another. It also, of course, denies the importance of those different groups. That nursing is faced with such potentially powerful conflicts is difficult enough; that they are subsumed within this ill-fitting uniform only compounds the initial problem.

In this sense, the open competition and rivalry – if not outright hostility – between the different nursing unions and organisations are a truer reflection of the reality, with each having evolved in their own ways and possessing their own historical power base. By acknowledging and further exploring the differences, the way in which nurses have been socialised and the role of myth in that process, both as an influence and as a result of that socialisation, can be seen in its true context.

The Need for Nurses Begins to Emerge

References to nurses and nursing go back to biblical times and beyond. However, to trace the origins of today's nurses, it is necessary to look back to the mid nineteenth century, which saw the emergence of 'a body of skill and knowledge in the care of the sick which justified the division of labour – the emergence of the "nurse", carefully selected and systematically taught' (Abel-Smith, 1960: p. 1). Immediately the key factors can be discerned: selection, training and the division of labour.

Nursing is, then, defined by the process of selection, as much by which people were unable to become nurses as those who were. Those selecting their successors were, of course, nurses. And their intention was to 'reproduce' themselves, to select in their own likeness, ensuring the continuation of a certain tradition and culture within a given system. While the tech-nical necessities of training could easily be argued, there is no doubt that it was essential that if such a system, complete with its culture and values, were to survive and grow, nurses would have to be trained not just in technical and clinical proficiencies but also in how to be a nurse and what it meant to be a nurse.

In examining the division of labour, it is virtually impossible to discuss nursing without viewing it in relation to the medical profession. So much about this relationship is symbolised in the apparent innocence of that age-old children's game, doctors and nurses. The separation out of tasks, the distinct roles for the boy and girl, the power relationship and even the sexual undercurrents are all played out. The relationship is, in reality, extremely complex and it is not enough to argue that they are two separate occupational groups that have evolved differently for perfectly natural reasons; nor is it satisfactory to suggest that nursing is completely subordinated to medical practice, as will be explored later. The way in which health care is organised reflects contemporary social, economic and political structures; as it is a product of those structures, so it also exerts its own influence on them in an almost uniquely reciprocal relationship and, it can be argued, replicates them to a certain extent within its own internal institutions and systems. Nursing is thus inherently bound up within those structures and relationships.

The rise of the nurse occurred at a time that saw the increasing prominence and influence of doctors. This was in the context of the changes wrought by the Industrial Revolution. With the population doubling in the first half of the nineteenth century and then again by 1900, large numbers were migrating into ever expanding cities as rural employment declined rapidly, with enormous upheaval. Unemployment and poverty were growing at a catastrophic rate. Starvation wages were forcing families to send their children out to work in the cruellest of conditions. Public health and sanitation in the new cities was a cause for major concern. For those who had work, employers were cutting wages, knowing that lowly paid workers then had their wages made up out of the local rates. This money came from the poor rate, an early form of welfare, which had also doubled in less than half a century, costing £4 000 000 by 1800, rising to almost twice that before falling back slightly by 1834. Additionally, legislation meant that paupers had to return for their payments or relief to their own parish, who were then responsible for them but completely unable to meet the financial burden.

Growing pressure for reform as well as the need to alleviate the financial burden forced the government to act; the Poor Law (Amendment) Act 1834 abolished the old outdoor relief, a payment given to paupers outside of any institution (Plate IV). To discourage participation in the scheme, anyone entering any form of institution had to be in conditions less favourable than the poorest labourer outside. However, they had to work within the institution. Although they would not benefit themselves, this did bring in fresh sections of workers involved in profit making employment. The Act also laid out provision for the localised care of the poor, with parishes able to band together as 'unions' (Morton, 1989: pp. 339–42). Prior to this, parishes might have had their own poorhouses for administering what was known as indoor relief – an arrangement dating back to Elizabethan times – but after the 1834 Act important changes were made in response to the needs of the 'new' poor. The sick poor fell within the category requiring indoor relief, as did the very elderly, orphans and 'handicapped'. The expansion in numbers requiring relief meant that the old parish poorhouses were no longer adequate. Much larger buildings were needed. The workhouse was born.

Prior to 1834 there had been no discrete provision at a local level for the sick. The poor sick were often tended within the old poorhouse by other residents. Others would be cared for at home. Again, those who were very poor would apply for outdoor relief. The new workhouses, provided for by the Act, were originally supposed to have separate accommodation for the sick. But with the massive numbers going into them they could not fulfil their original role, even though to qualify for admission meant the person had to be destitute, owning no possessions whatsoever and with no means of support. Receiving relief then left the recipient disenfranchised for a further year and their destitution was thus complete (Plate II). Perversely, the entire family of someone in need of relief would be admitted to the workhouse. This was because of the conditions set upon the testing and was a direct means of wanting to control Poor Law costs, which still came out of local rates (White, 1978a: pp. 6–8). The family, particularly the young, would be put to work, even if that work was 'degrading and senseless', and on extremely low wages; some children would go through workhouse apprenticeships before being transferred to work in factories and mills in the north of England (Morton, 1989: p. 341). Significantly, cost was already a major factor in the provision of even this most limited welfare service. The governance of the workhouse was designed to minimise the expenditure of the poor rate; if that meant the sick must suffer with the rest, then so be it.

Despite the large numbers of sick in the workhouses there were few nurses. The majority of nursing care was still provided by other inmates. They would be given extra rations and clothes, sometimes a uniform, but were unskilled and received no pay. Contemporary articles and reports referred to their inferiority of character, agedness, uncleanliness, intoxication, illiteracy and promiscuity (Davies, 1980: p. 85). By 1861 there were around 50 000 sick in workhouses throughout the country, cared for in inadequate buildings, with poor diet and sanitation (Plate VII).

The wealthy would normally be cared for in their own home if they fell sick. In the nineteenth century, hospital admissions were still the exception as indicated in the census records for 1851, showing only 7619 patients resident in hospital. Again, their nurses would be mostly untrained, drawn from domestic servants, the most common occupation for women at the time. Even those nursing in the few contemporary voluntary hospitals were from a similar background, with no special training and experience. Hospital nurses were paid and often received free board, but the wages were extremely low, particularly outside London, often lower even than in the factories.

Doctors Fail to Have It All Their Way

Medical officers had carved out a pre-eminent role for themselves in the workhouse, as they had in the voluntary hospitals, where their control was even more well established. However, for doctors practising in the community, the situation they faced was evolving in an entirely different way. They were experiencing serious difficulties by the late 1800s as they tried to gain the same position of dominance as a professional group they had enjoyed in the hospitals and other institutions. The skilled working class of the latter half of the nineteenth century were forming themselves into trade unions to fight within the workplace and into friendly societies as a means of supplying mutual welfare aid for their members in order to combat the hated Poor Law. By 1893 the societies had a membership numbering 3.8 million, more than half the adult industrial male population. Medical benefits and sick pay were also being increasingly offered by the burgeoning trade unions, who were competing with the societies for members. Branches or lodges of each society actually employed their own medical officer, either following a vote of all members or following a tendering process. They were paid on the basis of a capitation fee – for each person under their care – usually given quarterly; their contracts might be determined by the branch or for fixed periods. The societies were keen to ensure that the doctor was there to benefit their entire membership and did all they could to limit the doctors' time with private patients and keep them under control. They also made provision for the poorer in the community who managed to stay above destitution level (Green, 1985).

There was no role for nurses in the friendly societies' system, although district nursing services were, by then, being set up and midwives had thriving practices, completely independent of doctors. Midwives, too, provided an obstacle to the medical profession's hoped for monopoly. They were self-employed and had no formal training; most were older women, married, often having learned their skills from their own mothers. Whilst some were well educated, as with nurses, standards were highly variable. Campaigns by groups of midwives for formal instruction in midwifery dated as far back as the early seventeenth century but to no avail.

Whereas the practice of 'normal' midwifery had been almost the exclusive province of women, with doctors only having a role in more complicated births, the nineteenth century saw the emergence of the man-midwife, doctors intruding into the woman's role. With doctors sharing much in the way of background and having achieved a higher social status, this almost inevitably resulted in their gradually providing care for the more wealthy families, thus receiving higher fees. The effect on midwives was to push them into concentrating their service on a poorer, often non-fee-paying clientele. With little sanitation and poor diet, having received hardly any education and with husbands on low wages, these women and their babies had a far greater mortality rate. Consequentially, with their service facing increasing criticism as the twentieth century approached, the calls for greater controls on midwives grew and they, too, were as often caricatured as Gamps as the emerging nursing population. However, any concern about infant mortality rates was not simply a case of altruism, sympathy for the working classes or about advancing the case for trained midwives; it coincided with Britain staking its claim as an imperial power.

Eugenecist theories about racial superiority were seriously debated and had support in influential circles while more and more middle-class women were remaining, by choice, childless at a time when the strength of the nation was being equated with the size and class of its population. Another consideration was that working-class women should be able to provide children – boys, naturally – who would grow to be fit enough to colonise Britain's growing empire and fight its wars. This was exemplified by the sense of moral outrage when it was discovered that, in 1899, out of every 1000 male applicants, 300 were not fit enough to fight in the Boer War. The 1902 Midwives Act was not the only result; even greater public health reform followed. War, in some instances, can be good for mothers and babies (Davin, 1978).

Thus it should be noted that during this period doctors did not enjoy a position of unchallenged superiority. They greatly resented the control exerted by the friendly societies, particularly regarding what they viewed as the low rates of pay, and fought against the system with increasing vigour as their power grew. In the field of child delivery they were competing against the midwives. Even in the voluntary hospitals all was not as it was to become: junior doctors and medical students were actually carrying out some patient care duties now regarded as quintessentially those of nurses.

A Diseased Society?

However, the demands of a rapidly expanding, industrialised and urban society were creating a market for health care. This involved moving away from the workhouse as a storehouse for the sick, where no curative treatments were effected. A side effect of industrialisation and the growth of science was to show that there was the potential for a curative response to some diseases, restoring health and, importantly for a market economy, productivity. The sick role was being inexorably transformed and appropriated, taken away from the family home and into the arms of the medical profession in their chosen setting, the hospital. The importance of the hospital in defining notions of illness and disease cannot be underestimated. To be admitted to hospital meant a decision being taken by a doctor based on an esoteric body of knowledge taught him by other doctors. Foucault described the hospital as a form of 'closed' system where the doctor could observe and experiment on the basis of a large number of patients. This so-called 'medical gaze' was turned upon the signs of sickness (Foucault, 1986). The decision to admit someone into hospital meant that they became a patient, 'sick, ill or diseased', requiring medical treatment as prescribed by the doctor.

At a time when it was trying to establish itself as a serious middle-class profession, medicine was also gaining more importance because of the legitimation it was willing to give to the cultural shift away from a reliance on religion to science in explaining the social order. With Darwinian concepts of a natural order and the 'survival of the fittest' being transplanted into the social and political order, the class and sexual relations that emerged as a result of the Industrial Revolution could be explained and justified (Doyal, 1979: pp. 141–8). Equally, to become sick meant becoming unproductive, dysfunctional and thus deviant. To be affected by illness meant adopting a changed role. To be healthy was normal and it was necessary to seek help to regain normality when 'affected'. That help, of course, came from the doctor. But if the doctors' role were to develop they would need to be freed up and have the time to expand their 'gaze' and practice. So the need for a new type of nurse became urgent.

The Search for a Better Woman

Many nursing historians cite Mrs Elizabeth Fry, better known as a prison reformer, as a key nursing pioneer of the early nineteenth century. Although there had been nurses in, for example, St Bartholomew's Hospital since the mid sixteenth century and Guy's from 1725, Mrs Fry's achievement was to be in providing *trustworthy* women of sound character, social class and efficiency as private nurses, to provide care for the affluent in their own homes. They also did some work in hospitals alongside the far less reputable nurses already employed within the institution. However, if their manner, attitude and character were considered a great improvement, the nursing care they delivered was of a similar nature, carried out upon the direct instruction of doctors, specific to their wishes. There were also a limited number of trained nurses from a number of holy orders such as St John's House, which was inaugurated in 1848. They, too, worked in hospitals whilst also supplying nurses for the wealthy in their own homes. Their hospital work was carried out according to medical wishes and within defined parameters placed upon them by both the medical model and the limitations of their training and numbers. Although marginal in terms of overall service provision at the time, they were to assume greater significance as a model for the future. As has been noted, the vast majority of nurses were, then, untrained and apparently of ill repute (Plate V).

An important account of early hospital nurses, however, entirely contradicts the 'Gampish' image. A surgeon at St Thomas' Hospital, John South, published a pamphlet in 1857 arguing that the overall standards of nursing were not as bad as they were publicly painted, defending their character and integrity. He described wards staffed by sisters who had tenure, lived in the hospital (often in rooms adjacent to their ward) and who were salaried; the nurses were more akin to ward maids, directly linked to the background of domestic servants. Their work was based on the duties of a domestic, but with some limited patient contact and nursing duties. A significant number were almost completely illiterate. Some would live in, but in poor, cramped conditions. The ward sister would spend 'the greater part of her day on the ward . . . [and] is more frequently up night after night,' he wrote. The matron was unlikely to be a nurse, but had an administrative and housekeeping role. A report in the London *Times* supported South's view: 'Hospital nurses have been much abused – they have their faults but most of them are due to want of proper treatment . . . scolded by matrons, sworn at by surgeons, bullied by dressers . . . they are what any women might be under these circumstances' (Abel-Smith, 1960).

Just as doctoring was a male domain, nursing was defined as women's work (Gamarnikow, 1991: p. 110). This was, again, no accident of history but resulted in its origins within the holy orders and domestic service. Now doctors were taking more people into hospital, particularly the wealthy who, rather than the apparently disreputable untrained nurse of popular myth, wanted the same class of woman to care for them as they had within their own homes. This went some way to creating the necessary conditions for changes in the type of nurses working in hospitals and their role in providing care.

Both doctors and nursing reformers wanted a 'better' standard of woman (Plate I). But the wages and image of the job precluded this. There was also the question of what work nurses would do. One consequence of the attempts to get more nurses from the higher strata of society was to create a public backlash against the 'Gamps' and for this reason the popular image of nurses pre-Nightingale has to be viewed with some skepticism. It was certainly important in shaping the image of the type of nurses needed to 'improve' the service, where breeding, character and social class were paramount qualities.

'Reform' was thus a development of the growth of nursing which, in turn, was following the expansion of medical practice. Its beginnings coincided with the arrival of Florence Nightingale, who was to take a key role; however, it became an immediate challenge to medical domination. Although never formally trained as a nurse, Nightingale became a national heroine as a result of her endeavours in the Crimean War. With the telegraph being used for the first time in war, the army had not developed a system of censorship. The public, originally supportive of the war, were outraged at the reports being sent home from Russia. Military blunders and horrendous conditions saw soldiers die unneccesarily in their thousands. Ms Nightingale estimated that 16 000 of the 25 000 British deaths could be attributed to failures within the military system (Morton, 1989: p. 352) She had gone out to the Crimea with a small group of nurses and her work contributed to reducing the death rate from 427 per 1000 to 22 per 1000 (Jolley, 1982: p. 28). That most potent of legends, the Lady of the Lamp, was born and helped her, upon her return to England, to raise £45 000 for a training school, which opened in 1860.

Struggling for Control

Rigorous discipline, supervision and character training were maintained throughout the one year training. It was also considered essential to break the hold doctors had over the nurses working on their wards. The aim was to institute a unified system of nursing, with its own hierarchy, rules and culture built around an occupational group loyal to itself above all else. Living in was considered part of the training and high moral character more important than education. But care of the sick and nursing duties, as opposed to domestic service, became the significant component of hospital nursing. A nursing hierarchy did begin to emerge, with trained nurses going on to become matrons. Nightingale provided an understanding about hospitals as institutions and their administrative requirements as well as the need for hygiene to prevent cross-infection or control the spread of sickness. This meant that nurses were able to make an impact on the organisational structure of hospitals and begin a symbiotic relationship with the medical profession built around the treatment and care of the sick. This was enhanced as some of Nightingale's nurses went on to become matrons, cajoled by her to be as ruthless in their pursuit of enhancing the nursing position within their own hospital environment as she was at a more strategic level (Abel-Smith, 1960: pp. 24–5). The new nurses required by the medical profession, able to assist them, were thus only obtained at a price, which was the challenge to doctors' control of nursing.

The nature of nurses' training became a key battleground. Some of the contradictions that still pervade nursing began to crystallise. Although it occurred against the background of an early nursing hierarchy, with nurses already receiving instructions from their own senior nurses, their training was still framed entirely by medical practice and led to the 'reformed' nurses' role being subordinated to a medical, male-defined model.

Theoretical training was limited; doctors were concerned that it should allow nurses enough knowledge of anatomy and physiology to act as informed assistants, but should not match that of doctors themselves. Even providing nurses with this limited knowledge was seen as subversive by some in the medical profession. A division of labour was developing but it was far from clear. The 'problem' was that the ward sister *translated* the doctors' instructions to junior nurses, delegating nursing tasks herself rather than the doctors doing it. And nurses began to develop a role as interpreters of medical instructions as the doctor could not be at the bedside, or even in the same ward, all of the time. This, coupled with the way in which nurses interpreted and filtered their observations (albeit ones normally prescribed by the doctor) before reporting them, gave the nurse an important discretionary power. Ms Nightingale was absolutely clear that it was the duty of the nurse to obey the medical officer or to see his orders carried out. But it was no longer that simple. As much as many doctors clearly disliked it, their medical interventions were becoming more distinct and precise, and given to a greater number of patients. They were thus increasingly dependent on the nurses remaining close to the patient and reacting to changes in a way they no longer could; in short, the doctor had to rely on the nurses' role, discretion and all, to ensure the success of his own.

The selection of nurses was not the problem for Nightingale it was for some others, such as Mrs Bedford Fenwick, who fervently believed in building a nursing service with an elite group of women, something she put into practice when matron at St Bartholomews Hospital. Ms Nightingale welcomed the notion of taking probationers from a variety of social and economic backgrounds; for her the emphasis was such that certain women were 'born' with the necessary characteristics to become nurses. Through her fame, the money that had allowed her to collect, her own extraordinary willpower and the right combination of external factors, middle-class, educated and well-bred women were now interested in becoming nurses. That there were not enough of these 'suitable women' available, was, therefore, not a problem of great significance for Nightingale. For while there would still need to be a reliance on the more respectable working-class women or middle-class women who needed to work to support themselves, this raw material, equipped with the right caring instincts, was to be moulded into the 'new' nurses. An essential part of the moulding process was to inculcate the new nurses with the cultural values, ethos and aspirations of the dominant class.

The image of the archetypal nurse was emerging. As much as being about what she was, it was also about a number of things she was not. She was not a Sarah Gamp. She was not poor, foul-mouthed or a drunkard. She was not a thief – essential to her wealthier patients – and nor was she promiscuous. The importance of this was not only in terms of nurses' reputations but also to ensure that anxious parents would let their daughters journey to London and reside in the hospitals.

They were caring, nurturing, feminine and, now, in growing numbers, trained. Willing to work long hours, they undertook menial tasks for very little pay, submitting themselves to the discipline and control of their seniors, both in their work and by living within the hospital. Off duty discipline was almost as strict as it was on the wards (Plate IX). More than merely display a willingness to subject themselves to such rigours, they were expected to make a virtue of it. Their work, even as their discretionary role grew, was carried out entirely in the context of the medical profession's needs, their knowledge base and their male view of the world. Thus was needed a degree of passivity and subordination to balance the active caring that was seen as essential to the 'good' nurse, combining the influences of domestic service, the military and the holy orders. Out of this grew class and gender relations, with a division of labour that mirrored a patriarchal Victorian society where deference, discipline and obedience were seen as paramount.

This image was already excluding many. The older, untrained nurses often still practised in hospitals, despite their alleged faults (although they were forced out wherever possible); those nursing within the workhouse, no matter how primitive the conditions; attendants in the lunatic asylums. The narrow focus of fame and attention needed to promote the new ideal forced the exclusion of other important individuals and the process by which progress in different fields of nursing had been made and there are indications that, for instance, 'the Nightingale Fund successfully appropriated the credit for developments which were occurring in many localities throughout the 1860s' (Dingwall, Rafferty & Webster, 1988: p. 65).

Mary Seacole – A Forgotten Heroine

There were those like Mary Seacole, who made a major impact in her day despite being faced with innumerable obstacles, but who were ignored by the next generation of nurses and nursing historians (Plate X). Mary was a contemporary of Florence Nightingale's and the two women bore some similarities. She was not a trained nurse but went out to the Crimea to care for the wounded and sick and was a national heroine upon her return. Like Florence, Mary became a woman of letters of some note, writing a bestselling account of her exploits, was feted by royalty and occupied a prominent place in London society. The difference was that she was black, from Kingston, Jamaica. She had considerable clinical experience, having learned her skills from her mother initially and then practised extensively in the Caribbean, nursing cholera and yellow fever victims and developing surgical skills, repairing gunshot and knife wounds in the wilder parts of Central America. Her mother had also left her a boarding house which gave her financial independence.

Denied official access to the Crimea because of her colour by both the War Office and Elizabeth Herbert, who was recruiting nurses, she travelled out under her own steam to the Crimea, actually meeting Florence Nightingale at the latter's hospital situated behind the lines at Scutari. Despite the shortage of nurses and Mary Seacole's vast experience, Nightingale told her she was not needed. She remained undeterred and set herself up as a 'sutler', providing canteen services for the military and using her 'British Hotel' as a base to establish herself as a nurse, forging out onto the battlefields, under fire, to dress wounds and care for the dying. The abrupt end of the Crimean War left her penniless and she returned to London in dire straits. However, her reputation was such that a fund was launched to support her and, by the time of her death in 1881, she was firmly established as a nurse in London whilst she also returned periodically to her native Kingston. However, Mary Seacole also had a tremendous understanding about the nature of disease, particularly cholera, and how to treat its victims. She recognised cholera was infectious – against contemporary thinking – and favoured isolation nursing as a technique. But despite her progressive ideas and knowledge, as well as her celebrity in society circles, there was still no place for Mary in the development of British nursing (Alexander & Dewjee, 1984).

It would have taken a great leap of the imagination to fit Mary Seacole into the new image of nurses. Although in no sense a political radical, her self-reliance, determination and an experience shaped separately from that of the medical establishment made her – apart from her colour and race – deeply subversive and, as such, outside the newly established order. It was this order and image that encouraged the 'lady-pupils' into an adapted form of 'training'; these women actually paid for instruction, although they were excused more menial duties. Often they did not complete a year's training and might not attend for the long hours of their probationer colleagues. They were, however, to be Nightingale's stormtroopers. From the Nightingale School the students mushroomed out, captured the role of matron for that of the trained nurse and followed their mentor's urgings to challenge the authority of the medical establishment and lay administration in the voluntary hospitals for control of the nursing service. It was not a battle to subvert the curative role of the doctor or even to put forward an alternative form of nursing independent of the medical model; it was a struggle about who should instruct nurses and about establishing a nursing hierarchy within its own department. By the end of the century, despite fierce criticism from doctors – and some of the older nurses – the new matrons had won.

> Over the nurses themselves the matrons wielded absolute power. This power was re-inforced by the para-military organization of the nursing staff and the rigid discipline imposed in the training schools. As Miss Nightingale said rather ominously 'no good ever comes of anyone interfering between the head of the nursing establishment and her nurses. It is fatal to discipline.' The control of the matrons over her nurses was to play a crucial role in future attempts to enrol nurses in professional organizations or trade unions.
>
> (Abel-Smith, 1960: p. 29).

So the Nightingale model expanded and its influence took hold. Women began to think about work to take them away from the home, with the possibility of moving up to a more senior post and a reasonable salary compared with other jobs to which they might be attracted. Nursing bacame fashionable with the young although Nightingale's view that women of all backgrounds and social classes might be able to become nurses was now to be overtaken. But if nursing had attained newfound respectability, it was still only in the voluntary hospitals. It was a different story in the workhouses and asylums.

'Progress' Brings the Asylums

It has already been argued that the growing power of the medical profession, within the context of industrialisation and an expanding, increasingly complex society geared to a capitalist economy, had ensured that 'illness' became the province of doctors. Psychiatry, it can be argued, concerned itself with a similar relationship between the individual and society but came to contain greater elements of social control and, in addition, medicalised another form of so-called deviancy.

Asylums date back as far as the thirteenth century, the most famous of those early institutions being the Bethlem Hospital, known colloquially as Bedlam. Early reformers such as Pinel and Tuke are often cited by historians of psychiatry as prime motivators in humanising its practice; Pinel unchaining the Paris lunatics and treating them with 'the restraint and kindness that *sickness* requires' (my emphasis) (Miller, 1962: p. 304), and Tuke instituting a benign regime of moral and religious treatment aimed at reproducing familial intimacy at his Retreat just outside York. The Retreat was relatively small and it was possible for Tuke to know all of the patients, to involve himself in all aspects of the life of the institution. These ideas were adopted by medical superintendents in other asylums. It was, however, recognised that if the chains were to remain off there would be a need for more attendants who would have the intention of advancing the recovery of those under their care, as opposed to their virtual imprisonment and control. Tuke and Pinel also established the authority of the physician in cases of mental disease. Prior to their work, confinement was generalised but was not in the province of medical authority. But, following on from the rules of the Retreat, admission was only complete upon the signing of a certificate by a medical person.

Again, the 'progress' of the nineteenth century shaped events in asylums, just as it had in other areas of the care and treatment for the sick. The new voluntary hospitals were concerning themselves with curative medicine and nursing that complemented this approach and conditions had altered materially within the hospitals to attract the right kind of nurse; the workhouse was increasingly the dumping ground for those with chronic or incurable problems and its nurses, such as they were, reflected this. In the asylums, the situation became even worse. There is a strong counter argument to challenge the accepted orthodoxy that saw Tuke and Pinel as great and benign reformers but, nevertheless, their practice was drowned by a growing population of what were, in effect, society's unwashed and unwanted, those whom the great majority of 'normal' citizens feared may 'infect' them with their insanity (Foucault, 1961).

The asylums were much less about the treatment of madness, but were involved in the isolation and exclusion of the most difficult and problematic elements of the disreputable poor. The earlier reputation for humane treatment and involvement of medical practitioners glossed over poor conditions and the fact that it was rapidly becoming clear that recovery or cure was not the treatment objective for many inmates. The prevailing political climate remained one of *laissez faire*; the attitude of government and many influential thinkers of the time being that the poor had brought about their own misfortune. The 'undeserving poor' was a common description of the army of paupers wandering the country in the eighteenth and, particularly, nineteenth centuries, a phenomenon not restricted to England but common to all the European capitalist economies (Foucault, 1986). Whilst the workhouse and asylum may seem, to modern sensibilities, oppressive and harsh, they were viewed as reforms by many contemporary figures and were more enlightened than some of the other solutions seriously put forward at the time, such as work camps where the destitute and their families would be incarcerated, only to work, producing goods for society, from the cradle to the grave.

As the numbers of poor and unemployed grew, so did the populations of the asylums and workhouses. Built in the latter half of the nineteenth century, the asylums (many of which were still housing patients until the final decade of this century) were expensive to build and maintain and, as with the workhouses, the control of costs was paramount. Again, in some instances the most able of the inmates were drafted to take control of the remainder. Work was an essential part of the regime, largely as a means of reducing overheads and generating income, taking a wide variety of forms.

With the late Victorian asylums far more akin to prisons than the workhouse (Plate VIII), the nurses or attendants working within them were almost as much prisoners as the inmates. Often from very poor backgrounds, often unemployed before working in the institution, the nurses were chosen as much for their strength as their compassion and caring; indeed, the appalling conditions and low wages made it almost impossible to recruit anyone other than those who could not get work elsewhere. Working in these massive institutions in isolated, rural settings for long hours (usually 10–12 hours a day at least), they would then sleep in rooms adjacent to the wards where they could be called upon as necessary as, in most asylums, there were no night staff. The attendants and nurses were subjected to the most rigorous and harsh forms of discipline and control by the medical superintendent, largely because they were not believed to be trustworthy (Carpenter, 1988).

No interest had been shown by nursing reformers to extend their work into the asylums. There were very few women working within them, although strong attempts were subsequently made to recruit women at the turn of the century and after. With almost all of the nurses from the lowest social classes, perhaps for different reasons, the reformers also viewed asylum nurses as having being born to their work. Training was virtually non-existent. Thus reform, such as it was, was to be much more directly linked to trade union activity.

Women Take the Blame Again

There was a powerful lobby, however, seeking reform of midwifery services and it was a movement very similar to that within nursing. Although there had been unsuccessful attempts to organise formal instruction in midwifery for over a century, an inquiry by the Obstetric Society of London in 1869 which revealed that many midwives were completely untrained increased the pressure. It was less publicised, however, that doctors were only responsible for three out of ten deliveries at most, as few as one in ten in some instances. The outcome of the results of the Society's inquiry was that it was the poor women's midwives who were to blame for the state of midwifery, as the poor were responsible for their own impoverishment. It is undoubtedly true that untrained and uneducated midwives were, in some cases, spreading infection and providing inadequate care for pauperised and working-class women but these were the prevailing social conditions of the time, legitimised by the state. With doctors vying for business with mid-wives, it is again, perhaps, no surprise that they were amongst those blackening the reputation of their female competitors. Yet the fact that they had successfully abandoned their limited role in taking charge of potentially difficult births and become 'man-midwife' to the wealthy, fee-paying families was to help shape the destiny of midwifery.

By 1872 the Obstetric Society had introduced an exam and diploma for midwives, but possession of this did not allow women to join the Society and, again, the dilemma of the medical profession was becoming apparent. They had opposed women becoming registered as medical practitioners (although by 1880 there were sixteen women on the register) but most doctors want-ed an improvement in overall standards. They did not wish to see midwives, as with nurses, gain improved status or authority but could not, in reality, do without their skills.

Those lobbying for policy changes that would lead to improve-ments in midwifery practice had another obstacle, the nature of which was diagnosed by Florence Nightingale, even if she did not make any suggestion about how it might be overcome. Referring to the need for midwifery training, she wrote:

> France, Germany and even Russia would consider it *woman-*slaughter to 'practise' as we do . . . It is true that in these countries everything is done by Government; with us by private enterprise. But we are not accustomed in England to hold private enterprise as lagging behind Government in efficiency.
>
> (Cowell & Wainwright, 1981: p. 16).

A group of midwives, all possessing the Obstetric Society's diploma and under the leadership of Louisa Hubbard and Zepharina Veitch, formed The Matron's Aid Society or Trained Midwives' Registration Society in 1881, later to become the College of Midwives and, subesequent to receiving its Royal Charter, the Royal College of Midwives (RCM). The one thing midwives had which allowed them to pursue their goals as an occupational group more effectively than nurses was unity. This was partly because of their smaller numbers and tight parameters surrounding their field of work, with the College of Midwives representing the majority of the practitioners. But while there were – and still are – significant differences about how to deliver their aims, once a dominant group had established itself that could exert a certain amount of political pressure, they were able to proceed without the mass of internal divisions that were to plague nurses.

The women involved were all from comfortable backgrounds, educated prior to their training in midwifery (most had also been trained at the British Lying-in Hospital in Endell Street as well as gaining their diploma) and, as a group, had support from some quarters of the medical profession. Their concern for the welfare of working-class women was well founded and grounded in experience.

As with their nursing counterparts in the late nineteenth century, they wanted to see improved standards; they believed that the way to achieve this was through control and regulation of the practice of midwifery. Formal training and registration would achieve this whilst also giving midwives greater status. Lectures were provided to certificated midwives and trained nurses by doctors sympathetic to the cause, although there was still stiff opposition to any attempt to improve the status and quality of midwifery from the profession as a whole. Nonetheless, it was becoming more organised. As more were joining the 'numbers of trained, intelligent, often highly educated women' nursing the sick, so Rosalind Paget, a leading figure in the Institiute of Midwifery, looked forward to the 'class of certificated midwives' increasing, until it would, in time, 'supercede the untrained woman' (Cowell & Wainwright, 1981: p. 18).

Early parliamentary bills seeking to introduce registration for midwives were lost, partly as a result of opposition by the medical profession but also, paradoxically, by some influential in nursing circles who were seeking joint registration (Bent, 1982: pp. 181–2). Circumstance was nonetheless to favour the midwives before the nurses. By 1902 the medical profession had largely thrown its now considerable weight into supporting registration for midwives. The outcry at unqualified midwives not using antiseptics or even soap and water, the dosing of mothers with gin and of infants being deliberately suffocated – all evidence presented to a select committee investigating the issue (Abel-Smith, 1960: p. 77) – was supplemented by the knowledge that registration would lead to midwives calling upon more medical assistance than they were in their untrained state. Besides, for reasons outlined above, for many doctors and medical officers in the latter part of the nineteenth and early twentieth centuries, the saving of infant life was becoming a matter of imperial importance. Rather than look at the problems of starvation wages, very limited public health measures and all of the other structural problems facing mothers, it was the women themselves who were blamed, both the mothers, and the midwives (Davin, 1978: pp. 10–15).

The Midwives' Act 1902 was set down to secure the better training of midwives and to regulate their practice, with a principal aim of protecting the public from bad practice. A Central Board of Midwives was established, with four of its nine members being drawn from the medical profession. Only one of the remaining five had to be a woman. There was no mandatory requirement to have any midwives at all on the board, although there were three amongst the founder members.

Thus the midwives succeeded in winning registration. The control they were able to exert over their work was limited, although with members on the board they now had some influence over future policy making. That was focused on establishing and maintaining a roll of certified midwives, with training and examinations being set up for incoming midwives. All with the qualification from the London Obstetrical Society or similar diplomas were automatically admitted but it was also necessary to admit those able to establish at least one year's practice who were, importantly, of 'good character' (Bent, 1982: p. 183). Those not certified, after 1910, were only supposed to practise under the direction of a doctor. The Act also placed clear limitations on what midwives could do and, effectively, ensured that they could not interfere with the medical profession's dominance.

The Coming of Controls and State Intervention

The Midwives Act 1902 designated county councils and boroughs as local supervisory authorities (LSAs) to have authority over midwives, generally supervising their work, keeping rolls, with power to suspend in cases of misconduct. They also appointed supervisors of midwives. This was only a small part of the legislation effecting change in health care provision. Much else of it was aimed at ensuring the nation's young could grow to usefully serve the motherland, but the Public Health Acts passed also had a wider purpose. In many ways the infectious diseases running rampant in the new city slums stood as a metaphor for the contaminating effects of poverty and social ills perceived to dwell within them. The middle classes especially feared cholera, of which there had been several epidemics in the 1830s and 1840s, just as they feared the social and political unrest of the working class which was fuelled by the dire conditions and poverty in which they found themselves (Doyal, 1979: pp. 142–7). It was also believed that the poor often became destitute through disease. Thus in 1848 the first Public Heath Act passed onto the statute books. Although it did not compel any town to enact public health measures, other than in the most extreme circumstances, and was roundly opposed by those with vested interests, e.g. slum landlords, sewage dealers, etc., by 1870 a public health service was emerging, with medical officers throughout the country. The subsequent Act of 1875 continued the improvements.

Concern about public health and, particularly, the rising infant mortality rate throughout the latter half of the century, whatever the motivation for it, cannot be underestimated. It fuelled a new branch of nursing, any number of ladies' societies and, ultimately, health visiting. Although the nursing of the wealthy in their own homes was a well-established practice, the concept of training nurses specifically for serving a community or district sprang from at least as early as the 1860s (Plate XI). One of its early proponents was William Rathbone, the uncle of Rosalind Paget. Rathbone and the nurses involved saw the benefits of having nurses able to go into people's homes and provide care for them there, knowing that in many cases the patient would not be able to get into hospital. They also recognised that this would require different skills and training, as well as a different attitude. Educated women of good character were still the issue; however, key distinctions were made from the qualities being bred into hospital nurses, such as discipline, subordination and deference.

District nurses were expected and encouraged to be able to use their initiative and exercise their personality to a much greater degree.

While district nursing was being established in Liverpool, in Manchester and nearby Salford a different approach was being taken by a Reform Association. The 'Manchester Model' involved middle-class 'ladies' collecting money (Plate III), giving lectures and supervising the work of the actual health visitors. These tended to be women from working-class backgrounds because they would identify with and be trusted by the women they were aiming to help, although this was not the model used elsewhere. Instead of nursing in the traditional sense, the Association's members were involved in distributing educative information. In a role that grew from municipal authorities' responsibilities for public health beyond sewers, drains and building structures, evolved the work of the sanitary inspector and, subsequently, health visitor (Davis, 1987).

Early health visitors were drawn from nurses, sanitary inspectors, teachers and even doctors. They had the responsibility of visiting every home where a child had been born, their role very much involved with looking at hygiene and sanitation, seeing to disinfection, watching over child rearing, feeding and some care of the mother. Again, if a child died from an infectious disease, a health visitor would be required to visit. The education of the mother and family continued (White, 1978: p. 133). Again, training was established as an issue very early on and a training course set up in the 1890s with Florence Nightingale's support (Plate XII). By 1908 it was decided by the London County Council that health visitors should possess medical degrees, the midwives' certificate or be trained as nurses. One common requirement was the possession of the health visitors' certificate. By 1915, with the number of working health visitors increased to 900, the infant mortality rate had fallen by 11%.

Health visitors lacked one thing their more traditional nursing or midwifery counterparts had and that was a past public image. There was no image of drunken, lazy, irresponsible or dangerous health visitors from which to escape. Perhaps that was one of the reasons there never had to be any massive drive to establish a respectable image that would secure lasting support and attract the right sort of women. As a result, it evolved more naturally in some respects but, because its focus was outside the hospital and dominant ideology of health care, it was already marginalised, particularly once infant mortality began to improve and public health legislation started to impact. One thing it did quickly establish for itself which was, again, different was its own association, initially known as the Women Sanitary Inspectors' Association. This was formed in 1896 and can be followed through its different incarnations to today's Health Visitors' Association (although the WSIA originally opposed 'health visitors' as a description of their work as local authorities were employing such women on lower wages than their counterparts employed as sanitary inspectors). With its members' different origins, their association immediately set out on a different path. With its members face to face with the reality of poverty, unemployment and social deprivation and their effects on people of all ages, the Association was far more radical than any of the other associations or even early nurses' unions. It registered as a trade union in 1918 and affiliated to the TUC in 1924, with its members often taking a key role in early major political issues, such as women's suffrage (Jerrome, 1993: pp. 114–15).

Times were indeed changing. The state was being drawn further and further into legislating on health issues. As the medical profession expanded so did nursing and midwifery and other branches of the service.

The class and social divisions apparent in the origins of health care were now increasingly pronounced. The voluntary hospitals, with their doctors and trained Nightingale nurses propelled by scientific and technological progress, were concerned with curing the (predominantly wealthy) sick. Here there was a triangular relationship patterned on a replication of the paradigm so important to Victorian England's deeply patriarchal society, that of the family. The doctor had the controlling, penetrative, dominant role of the father; the nurse was placed in the subordinate, nurturing role, managing not only the patient's anxiety but also that of the doctor and nurse herself; the patient even more passive, waiting to be acted upon. The whole 'sick episode', even the nursing care, was organised and controlled within a framework of medical beliefs and practice, which gave form and meaning to the patient's illness (Littlewood, 1991: p. 145 and Carpenter, 1991: p. 9).

This still left the poor, who were largely reliant on the friendly societies or the workhouse. From 1860, as reform spread through all aspects of nursing and midwifery, Poor Law nurses evolved from the inmates who had been working as pauper nurses. Their role was more concerned with providing long term nursing care for the chronically sick or disabled, the aged, paupers and those left behind by the process of industrialisation. Philosophical and practical differences began to emerge between these nurses and those advancing the case for highly trained and skilled nurses working in voluntary hospitals about whether or not specialised nursing skills were needed in caring for the long term sick and hospitalised; similar issues surrounded the work of nurses or attendants in the asylums. As some workhouses established infirmaries, the opportunity to provide better nursing care were taken advantage of and, overall, the standard of nursing care improved although it was always compared unfavourably to the hospitals. There were other cultural differences, especially about the nurses' relationship to their matrons and lay officials, but the refusal of Poor Law nurses to quietly acquiesce in the manner of their sisters in the voluntary hospitals did not endear them to their seniors. The improved image of nurses was due to the work of the 'anonymous' Poor Law nurses as much as those in the voluntary hospitals, against far greater difficulties than their counterparts faced and despite the continued place the workhouses occupied in the demonology of the poor. However, as their role was concentrated almost exclusively on caring rather than 'curing' and thus not rendering their patients 'productive' or useful for society and was given to those society valued the least – if not written off completely – it was inevitable that their work would remain undervalued (Carpenter, 1991: p. 24).

What was Won with Registration

As much as Nightingale had argued strongly in favour of women taking charge of nursing and away from the influence of men, she could not be regarded as a supporter of women's suffrage. Nor, interestingly, did she support the registration of nurses. Yet, nursing had been set upon a certain path and registration lay through the gateway at its end. Greater status for the work had been achieved through training and discipline although it was largely subordinated to medicine. The number of nurses was growing rapidly but there was still a need for more young women of the right sort. Moreover, those already trained and in positions of power wanted that power and status consolidated. Any number of other reasons were given, including protecting the patients from criminal nurses, regulating training and ensuring it was theoretical as well as practical.

Registration had been pursued since the late nineteenth century. Its leading proponent, Ethel Bedford Fenwick, a matron from the age of 24 who had given up working after marrying Dr Bedford Fenwick, was also a staunch supporter of the suffragette movement led by Mrs Pankhurst. For her, the nurse question was the women question (Abel-Smith, 1960: p. 66). But winning the battle for registration was also a way of securing nursing for middle-class women and excluding a large number of potential recruits who were not regarded as being suitable. To advance this line, the Bedford Fenwicks argued that nursing trainees should not be paid at all and probationers themselves should pay a fee for examination and registration. It was also desired that any woman who was not registered be prevented by law from nursing, as was the case with midwives as a result of the 1902 Act. Even for those whose views were not as radical as Mrs Bedford Fenwick's, it was clear that the low wages endemic in nursing – and unlikely to improve in the foreseeable future – would have to be compensated for by something, which meant that great emphasis had to be placed upon the enhanced status that registration would bring with it.

By now the medical profession recognised that it needed a great many more staff as the demands doctors were making upon nurses grew. But they initially opposed registration, believing that it would limit severely the number of women joining the service, thus causing intolerable shortages. They also wanted to ensure that nurses retained their place within the social order of hospital life, i.e. as the faithful recipients of the doctors' orders.

The issue split both nursing and medicine. Bills attempting to introduce registration were presented to parliament annually over the first few years of the century. However, despite their regular defeats, external events conspired to thrust forward the case for registration: the outbreak of war in 1914 saw nurses play a prominent part in the great struggle as literally millions of men died or were wounded. There were not enough trained nurses or male orderlies and female, untrained volunteers had to be enlisted; there were insufficient hospital beds and nurses for the civilian sick and, with no nationally co-ordinated service or system of organising nursing, accounts of contemporary events communicate a great sense of chaos. Partly as a means of addressing this, the College of Nursing Ltd was formed in 1916, coming into direct and often bitter conflict with the British Nurses' Association (BNA), later to obtain a Royal Charter and become the RBNA, an organisation of the self-styled 'elite of the profession', of which Bedford Fenwick was permanent president. This had been formed in 1887 after the break-up of a stormy meeting with senior members of the Hospitals' Association, designed to set up a nurses' wing of their organisation. The BNA had a general council, was committed to a three year training and state registration, objectives opposed by Florence Nightingale, particularly the extended training. However, the new reformers were at least united in their belief that nursing needed a greater scientific foundation and therefore needed a longer period of training.

Nursing was not the only occupation of women during the war. They played a major part in many facets of British society, not the least of which was their work on the land and in the munitions factories, both key areas in the war effort. They had gained a newfound confidence and organisation. After years of bitter, often contemptuous resistance to the suffragette movement, the Liberal government had to concede and give women the vote. This made registration, now supported by the vast majority of nurses if not the matrons outside London, inevitable. For the Conservative and Liberal parties, there was also the recognition that to deny nurses registration at this stage would almost certainly lead to unionisation and an alliance with the burgeoning Labour party, a longtime supporter of both women's suffrage and the nurses. It followed in 1919, the same year that the Ministry of Health was established.

Although Bedford Fenwick was not wholly successful in seeing her vision of registration through parliament, supporters of the

Act were able to consolidate the principles of elitism and status. Nursing was moving away from being purely vocational. Ironically, that part of the image, now having taken on mythic proportions, had to remain nonetheless (Plate XII). But now nurses had to be trained rather than bred. Breeding remained fundamental – after all, the drive for registration had been, in part, about purging nursing of its 'criminal' and recidivist element – but even the highborn required training.

The Bill itself had eventually been put forward by the government because of the bitter disagreements between the RBNA and College of Nursing, both of whom had presented their own Bills, the former to the House of Commons, the College putting theirs to the Lords. Both hoped to gain control over nursing and policy making through the passage of their Bills but lost out largely because of the opposition of the other organisation. The government also had to decide the future of huge numbers of war volunteer nurses, many with extensive experience. They were being inextricably drawn further into the affairs of nursing and policy making.

It was widely recognised that the Poor Law infirmaries represented the only attempt at a public hospital service (White, 1978: p. 111), especially since voluntary hospitals were being forced to take in more private patients because of financial difficulties. Yet this was not reflected by their influence on health care or nursing. Registration had long been a cause championed by the London teaching hospitals, whose strong connections with ruling politicians and the wealthy and influential were now cemented, and was much less well supported in the provinces. They had the majority of nurses present on the first General Nursing Council (GNC), and the majority membership from any nurses' organisation was overwhelmingly that of the College of Nursing. Doctors had also been placed on the Council by the Minister. Although the issue of who qualified as a trained nurse initially dogged the GNC and proved highly controversial, the door was opened for controlling the entry of women into nursing, the process of socialisation of nurses and, ultimately, nursing itself.

Chapter 2

Behind The Mask.
The growth of nursing trade unionism

An integral part of the myth of the 'modern' nurse was that trade unionism had no part in her world (Plate XIII). She would rise above all such material distractions as pay and conditions of service, glowing majestically as she tended the sick, who would be her one and only concern, finding her reward in spiritual contentment/improvement as she succumbed to the discipline of self-sacrifice.

Women, Nursing and the Early Trade Unions

The importance of the myth's potency was that it was used to recruit women who would, hopefully, be attracted by such an image; once recruited it was also used as an essential part of the socialisation process, the attempt to mould the workforce and control it. Cost and productivity were – as in any other occupation – always determining factors.

The very foundations of modern nursing, then, were antithetical to those of the burgeoning trade union movement. Nurses of power and influence, the trained nurses and new matrons, especially in the voluntary hospitals, were from a sharply differing background from many of those fighting to establish trade unionism. They were also, of course, women. Whilst some women were organising themselves along the lines of the early trade unions, this was rare in the nineteenth century. Employment for women outside the factories and service in the households of the wealthy was not common and there was no platform on which they could organise. Their place was very much regarded as within the home unless they were very poor, in which case they would work but most often in the isolated role of a servant, stuck in a factory or, worse, in the workhouse. As the century progressed towards the millennium the pressure upon them to bear children grew, particularly those in the middle classes. It was these women who were the most politically active, but that activity was directed more towards seeking to gain improvements in welfare institutions such as the workhouse, prisons, hospitals and public health. Their thinking was geared more towards the people using the service rather than those providing it, who were often condemned as part of the problem rather than victims of an oppressive system.

Moreover, when nursing proved to be an outlet for those with professional and career aspirations, their background, culture and experience usually took them in a very different direction to that of the trade union activists in their crafts and new industries. Indeed, those factors often alienated them from the concept of trade unions and their objectives. As nursing established itself this became the dominant culture of the service. Because they did not have a strong base in the workplace, the so-called 'lady' campaigners, those involved in more straightforward political struggles, often took up the case of women's suffrage. There were, of course, working-class women engaged in various political groupings and strikes; some broke away from the Amalgamated Society of Tailors to form the Independent Ladies' Tailors Union to fight for a shorter working week and went on strike in pursuit of their aims when the men wouldn't join them and, whilst not the most militant, Sylvia Pankhurst's East London Federation of Working Women was the most radical and politically astute. There was also a Women's Trade Union League which sought to fight for women workers' rights.

There was one other important factor. As in virtually every other sphere of Victorian life, the trade union movement was dominated by men, with relatively little understanding of the needs and aspirations of women. One occupational group – and probably the most powerful – that was an exception to this was nursing. It was singularly personified as women's work, with women now in charge, despite the continuing presence and domination of policy making by men from the medical profession. Its associations and professional organisations were similarly heavily influenced by men but women formed the wider membership and had senior female figures with whom they could identify. Thus, if the leading women in nursing went one way, the majority of them followed.

Invisible Forces of History?

That trade unionism was actively discouraged by the employer will come as no surprise; but for all of the reasons listed above it also became something to be frowned upon by many on the professional wing of nursing, even – perhaps particularly so – if they were members of one of the rival professional organisations. Equally so, where it existed, it had to be 'written over' or masked. An example can be gleaned from Cowie's chapter entitled 'Organised Labour' in *Nursing, Midwifery and Health Visiting Since 1900* (Allan & Jolley, 1982: p. 215). Writing about the growth of trade unions, Ms Cowie states:

> The prosperity of the 1850s and 1860s, resulting from the Industrial Revolution, perhaps induced in the employers an attitude of expansiveness, so that they felt able to accept that there should be joint negotiation on employment matters which had, in earlier years, been for their decision alone. Whatever the reason, trade union activity, combined with the social legislation passed by the Parliaments of the era, served to improve considerably the lot of wage-earners of the time.

Within that paragraph is a view of history as benign development, of understanding and co-operation that springs from the material conditions of the time. In the phrase, 'Whatever the reason,' there is a hint of invisible, mysterious and incomprehensible forces at work. Akin, perhaps, to the mysterious forces which shape the nursing service, enabling young women to become 'good' nurses? An entire history is rendered invisible unless we peer behind the mask of that apparently innocuous phrase, written for nurses by a nurse who was, at the time, the Director of Labour Relations at the Royal College of Nursing and who also held the position of staff side secretary on the Nurses' and Midwives' Whitley Council.

It is necessary to examine briefly the growth of trade unionism to place its development in nursing in context as well as considering how this growth was associated with wider reforms in British society which, in turn, led to further advances in nursing. For the work of those struggling for the development of nursing or reforms in the workhouses and hospitals – as was true of those reformers in factories, education or public health – did not occur, nor could have been successful, in a political vacuum.

'Forming Traditions of Mutuality . . .'

The nineteenth century began with a period of fierce political oppression. The Combination Acts of 1799 and 1800 were passed to ban the increasingly effective combinations – early organisations of workers in a particular trade or craft determined to improve their wages. A government concerned that the mood of revolution abroad could become popular in England was also, paradoxically, determined that its own *laissez faire* economic philosophy should not be undermined and thus intervened powerfully on behalf of the employers. It was also a period of widespread public disorder 'associated with the dislocations of war and price inflation' (Pelling, 1971: p. 24). The enclosure of fields to increase corn and other crop production in line with population growth had a number of significant side effects: it concentrated the profit in the hands of fewer, bigger landowners; along with the concomitant rise of industry, it ended village life as it had been known, robbing many of their traditional occupations. Women were particularly affected, seeing their work, such as spinning, separated from the household. The agricultural smallholders were reduced to labourers. Many were left destitute, pauperised.

The end of the Napoleonic wars only brought further industrial and agricultural depression. The struggle to achieve freedom for independent trade unions was closely but not exclusively wedded to that of the campaign for the vote, at that time denied to all but a privileged few. All demands for reform were severely repressed by an increasingly unpopular Tory government and, in 1819, a mass meeting of Manchester cotton operatives demanding manhood suffrage was dispersed by a cavalry charge which killed 11 people. Although government restrictions eased some years after the 'Peterloo Massacre', the first Reform Bill which gave, amongst other things, voting rights to some property owning males, was only passed in 1832 amidst an atmosphere of crisis and 'political agitation unparalleled in the history of Great Britain'. It followed a period during which the bourgeoisie feared the rise of the poor and working classes, widespread disease and epidemics – cholera especially – violence and economic depression. Above all was the recognition from the factory owners, shopkeepers and others of the middle classes that the country could no longer be held together by systematic social, economic and political repression (Trevelyan, 1959: pp. 455–76). The electorate was, nonetheless, only increased from 220 000 to about 670 000 in a population of 14 million and working class disillusionment was again rampant within two years.

Still, the right to negotiate a better wage, fewer hours (many – women and children included – were working a minimum of 60 hours weekly) and better conditions through a legitimate trade union were the principal aims. Some, such as the shortlived Grand National Consolidated Trades Union, merged from different unions, shared these but had as its 'great and ultimate object' the idea to 'bring about a different order of things'. With fears of revolution again stalking the government as strikes swept the country, six Dorset agricultural labourers – the so-called Tolpuddle Martyrs – were found guilty of administering unlawful oaths for seditious purposes and sentenced to seven years transportation to Australia as an example to all dissidents. Protests occurred throughout the country, the largest of which numbered 100 000 at King's Cross (this figure was not untypical for political protests of the time, an astonishing feat in an age with relatively poor communications and transport systems) (Morton, 1989: pp. 336–65). This was 1834, the year of the Poor Law Act.

The Grand National, from a peak of approximately 250 000 members, was effectively bankrupted because of the number of strikes it undertook and the fact that most of its members could not pay their contributions and organisation amongst trade unions generally was damaged. This was a lesson not lost on later trade union leaders.

The Reform Bill had created a problem for trade unionists, neatly summarised by E.P. Thompson:

It was the reformed House of Commons which sanctioned the transportation of the Dorchester labourers in 1834 ... and ... launched the struggle to break the trade unions ... Against the manifesto of the masters, the Yorkshire Trades Union issued its own: 'The war cry of the masters has not only been sounded, but the havoc of war; war against freedom; war against opinion; war against justice and war without justifying cause ... '

(Thompson, 1968: p. 908).

Yet through the setbacks and the failure of a more revolutionary type of trade unionism something else was emerging. Until the 1830s there was no group that could be identified as the 'working class.' There were the working classes, the poor, the destitute, the paupers but no unified whole. That evolved, bringing with it 'intellectual and libertarian traditions' and 'forming traditions of mutuality' through the process of struggle culminating in the Industrial Revolution. These traditions acquired a peculiar resonance in every aspect of English life to which nursing was to be far from impervious (Thompson, 1968: pp. 913–14).

The following years were spent consolidating the individual trade unions and fighting for members' rights; there was no unifying organisation at national level and little national leadership to speak of. Reform, or the seeking of an expansion of the franchise, was sought as unions recognised that if their members could vote they had the hope of seeing their aspirations secured in law, rather than having the law used against them. Although not regarded as criminal organisations, trade unions were still illegal since they were deemed to act 'in restraint of trade' when the second Reform Bill was passed in 1867. This extended the vote to working class men in towns; those in rural districts were enfranchised in 1884. The formation of a political party that could represent the interests of the working class was now a real possibility.

The continuation of legal difficulties and the possible loss of funds were contributing factors to the organisation of the first Trades Union Congress in 1868. By the time of the third Congress, in 1871, the Trade Union Bill effectively legalised trade unions. Defiance of the employer could still, nonetheless, bring harsh penalties. In December 1872, London gasworkers striking to prevent the victimisation of unionists were sentenced to 12 months' hard labour for breaking their contracts. A year later, the wives of striking agricultural labourers were sentenced to hard labour – 'admittedly, only for a few days – for "intimidation" of blacklegs' (Pelling, 1971: p. 74).

Within the mainstream of the early trade union movement, as has been noted, there was little room for women. The participation in early Trades Union Congresses by a few, relatively affluent women whose concern lay with the conditions of working women was not widely welcomed. It was believed that 'under the influence of emotion they might vote for things they would regret in cooler moments' (Pelling, 1971: p. 86).

Nurses Get Off to a Late Start

By the time nurses began to organise, the trade union movement had survived its initial ordeals and established itself as a major political and cultural force. That nurses were relatively slow in organising is, in some respects, unsurprising. They were a fractured group, with diverse backgrounds and different occupational aims. Certainly, many of the nurses working in the voluntary hospitals would not have identified with the working-class tradition and collective self-consciousness referred to by Thompson, particularly those in positions of influence and authority. The mostly untrained and poorly educated nurses working in the workhouses and asylums, physically as well as metaphorically cut off from the wider society, were almost as much a part of the institution as the inmates.

There was also some difference in the nature of the relationship with the employer. Without an obvious economic profit going into the hands of those in control, the 'envy' and unfairness factors were less keenly focused. In fact nurses and attendants knew that they were working in an environment that was cash starved; the voluntary hospitals were reliant on donations or income from private patients while the money for the asylums and Poor Law infirmaries came out of the rates, with the local authorities continually seeking to contain if not reduce it. In addition, in some respects, the conditions were even harsher for nurses than manual workers, particularly in the asylums. Control was a fundamental principle, inherent within the hierarchy, with loyalty, allegiance and subordination to the doctor first and then the senior nurses or matrons instilled in all nurses as part of their training. But, in turn, nurses were expected to play a part in the control of the patients, further wedding them to the process. The strict code of discipline was completely enmeshed within the nature of the work, while the rule about living in – often in rooms directly adjacent to the wards – meant that the long hours of the working day could, literally, be stretched into the even longer night. Indeed, at a time when trade unions were forcing legislative changes to reduce the average working week nurses, who were exempt from the Act, were still working between 70 and 90 hours. Whether trained or untrained, nurses could be disciplined without warning, both for breaches of conduct and issues relating to patients (still a factor today). Conditions were such that it was seen as impossible for a Cardiff nurse to justify her conduct in marrying without permission of the matron whilst on holiday, making any punishment wholly acceptable (*Nursing Mirror*, 8.10.1910). Inevitably, the knowledge that the nurses were caring for the sick and vulnerable helped employers retain their loyalty, even in such circumstances.

Never Together

From the outset, nurses began organising in two separate directions. As ever, this did no more than reflect the conditions of the differing strands of their work. In the voluntary hospitals the direction was towards professionalisation. Moreover, this was very much a top-down initiative. The RBNA, although it had set up a nurses' co-operative agency to protect nurses from being exploited by private agencies in 1896, was far more concerned with pursuing professionalisation and registration and had a membership comprising the more militant of the lady pupils. It openly declared itself to represent nursing's elite. The strength of the matron in determining union membership, even in the early days is clear:

> The moment the matron of a hospital is opposed to us (the RBNA) . . . no nurse from that hospital would join our Association; and then if a change takes place, and a matron comes in who is favourable to us, the nurses come in
>
> (Abel-Smith, 1960: pp. 65–6).

Typical of the early nursing organisations of the time (and many of them were springing up even if few of them survived beyond the mid twentieth century), the RBNA, this self-styled elite of nursing, had one third of its ruling body made up of medical staff.

The Institute of Midwives, which was to evolve into the Royal College of Midwives, shared women of a similar background and similar objectives and when the College of Nursing Ltd made its belated entry in 1916 it too was pursuing the twin goals of professionalisation and registration although directly challenging the dominance of the RBNA.

The most obvious exception was the asylums, predominantly staffed by men. It was not until 1910 that the National Asylum Workers' Union (NAWU) was formed and ironically, as well as their isolation, it was their conditions of work that hindered the progress of unionisation. But significantly, the growth of trade unionism occurred after a professionalising Association had broadly failed to meet the aspirations of the workforce. Initially, reform minded medical officers from the asylums, with senior nurses, tried to persuade the RBNA to accept nurses and asylum attendants, hoping that they could establish training, registration and professionalism as goals that would improve the status of the attendants and nurses whilst improving standards of care. The RBNA, under the leadership of Mrs Bedford Fenwick, were aghast at the idea. The next step for the reformers then became to form the Asylum Workers' Association (AWA), in 1895.

The AWA has been likened to a 'company union,' a union formed by the employer to negate true union rights and organise the workers in such a way that it benefits the company (Carpenter, 1988: p. 38). Whether this is correct or not, the AWA, led by doctors and senior nursing staff and with no real participation from lower grade asylum attendants or nurses, had very specific aims concerned with issues about quality of care and duplicating the agenda of the voluntary hospital organisations such as the RBNA. It was also clear about what it would not concern itself with, notably wages and the hours worked.

The Battle Comes to the Asylums

Training had already been instituted in some asylums and in 1899 was extended to two years. One of the AWA's objectives was to use training as a means to institute a promotional structure. However, the benefits of this for attendants were offset by three things. One was that there had been an influx of female general nurses, partly because of staff shortages, partly to care for women on the female 'side' (it was only in the latter part of this century that psychiatric hospitals began to integrate men and women on wards and, even in the 1980s, it was not uncommon to find single sex wards). Women would also work for less money. Although they had no experience or training in asylum nursing, the women often graduated quickly to the more senior positions. Women were also advantaged in being able to take over the nursing service for the whole asylum; the best the chief male nurse could hope for was to be in charge of the male side as he could not have responsibility for the female side at all.

Doctors had provided lectures for asylum nurses since the mid nineteenth century. They were the prime movers in seeking training for nurses in asylums and the process of reform, with the introduction of trained female nurses a lynchpin to their strategy. But therein was their downfall. The policy objective of achieving a trained workforce providing improving standards of care to the inmates, motivated by the same values and sense of vocational self-sacrifice as their voluntary hospital counterparts, content to accept low wages and work long hours in return for enhanced status and respectability, failed because of the lack of involvement of the staff actually working in the asylums who, in virtually every respect, kept the institutions running. Nor did it recognise the fear and disdain in which the asylums were held by the public or what was the essentially custodial nature of the work; inmates were not becoming 'well' and returning to the community. In most cases, that was not in any way the objective or nature of the asylums' punitive regimes. And, vitally, they were unable to offer material advance to the predominantly male staff who viewed themselves very differently to general nurses, often having a background of work experience elsewhere and to whom wages were of greater importance as they had families to support. In 1905, 172 staff, male and female, were caring for 1341 patients at Netherne Hospital in Surrey. Only 46 of the patients were regarded as possessing a fair chance of recovery. The matron was earning £140 a year while the head male attendant received £120. Male attendants earned £49 a year compared to the £37 annual salary paid to the female charge nurses. By 1912, all had seen their wages fall with the exception of the head male attendant, whose annual salary rose to £124. The medical superintendant earned £1000 (Netherne Hospital, 1924).

The AWA reached a peak of 5000 members, almost half the workforce in the asylums. Its legacy, at least in part, was the paradox of asylum nurses trained by doctors and largely dominated by general trained nurses. It had played a part in defeating strong attempts by radical asylum workers to unionise in the 1890s, particularly in London, but could not resist the momentum of the early twentieth century. Unemployment had fallen, the issue of wages was still central and the economic climate favoured the workforce. England was in industrial turmoil with massive strikes rocking Asquith's Liberal government. An apparently insignificant piece of legislation championed by the AWA to secure pension rights for all asylum workers badly backfired but, in reality, only served to symbolise widespread disenchantment with the organisation. One year after the Asylum Officers' Superannuation Act, in 1910, a group of charge attendants met in a Manchester pub, the Masons' Arms, and the National Asylum Workers' Union (NAWU), the first trade union to represent nurses and a forerunner of COHSE, was on the verge of being born (Carpenter, 1988: p. 47).

War Breaks Out

The world in which this new union found itself has to be placed in context, for it was one turned upside down. The years 1910–14 saw 'The workers of England, united neither in their politics nor in the grievances, with no single desire for solidarity, yet [who] contrived to project a movement which took a revolutionary course and might have reached a revolutionary conclusion' (Dangerfield, 1966: p. 196). Social and economic conditions had still not improved dramatically from the previous century. Faced with demands to accept reduced wages, longer hours and treatment at the hands of the employers that they felt were manifestly unfair, workers took action which even their unions could not always control. Strikes in the mines, railways, docks, all forms of transport and numerous industries and trades rocked the country. In 1912 over 38 million working days were lost with a total of 1 233 016 workers directly involved in 857 disputes (compared with 30 million days lost in 1979 and ½ million in 1992 from a much larger workforce). Some of those strikes were resolved peacefully, others only after bloody battles between trade unionists and the police or even the army.

By July 1914, the 'Triple Alliance' of railwaymen, miners and transport workers were preparing to lead the rest of the trade union movement against the employers in their demands for a satisfactory minimum wage. Industrial conflict 'before which that tired General Strike of 1926 pales into insignificance' was averted only because of bullets fired in far off Sarajevo (Dangerfield, 1966: p. 352).

In such a climate the activities of the NAWU seem timid. Lack of financial resources and a relatively small membership constrained the union's leadership and they concentrated their efforts, unsuccessfully, on reducing the working week to 60 hours. With the Asylum Workers' Association still a force, recognition of the new union was a problem and the cause of one of the first strikes in an asylum, in 1914. The importance of the working week for nurses, not just in the asylums, cannot be underestimated. In 1906, the suicide of two London nurses was linked to their long hours and hard work, while others were allegedly abusing drugs (White, 1978: p. 150). For the employers, any solution requiring extra nurses also meant more cash. They did not act.

World War One impacted on the asylums in several ways. Attendants and nurses, in common with many other trade unionists, enlisted in the army in large numbers, the industrial conflicts forgotten in a rush of patriotic fervour. Nonetheless, the sense of grievance piled up and when militancy broke out in the asylums it was women who were in the lead. As with the industrial trade unions before the war, the action arose from the 'rank and file' members, less concerned with following increasingly weighty and bureaucratic procedures; they wanted to secure specific gains by whatever means necessary. Strikes supporting demands for better wages and conditions were called from the Union's Lancastrian heartland, in some cases involving over 400 members, but also from places as far apart as Bodmin and Exeter. Recruitment spread and confidence grew.

By 1918, NAWU had a national programme that reflected much of its membership's aspirations and background. Equal pay was near the top of its list, which was headed by a demand for a 48 hour week with a minimum wage of £2 per week and 25 shilling war bonus per week. They also wanted joint bargaining machinery and state registration for all mental nurses. Although unsuccessful in their key demands, the success they did have was in the face of some of the most reactionary and authoritarian employment practices in the country allied to the strength and domination of the medical profession which, although not overcome, was sorely dented.

The Institutionalisation of the Unions

A factor soon emerged that was to pose serious questions to the trade union movement and health services alike as the twentieth century progressed. As NAWU grew into a strong national union, so did the need for centralised organisation and the resources to fund this. Offices, buildings, the salaries of union employees, all were necessary for the union to function properly. As with any organisation, a bureaucracy was establishing itself. If it did not quite meet the four principal characteristics of the classical system of bureaucratic control, it was very close. There was a hierarchy, continuity was quickly established and there was the establishment of a group of national experts who could rule on issues and worked to national rules. If impersonality was lacking in a small union, it would be true to say that the ordinary rank and file member would not have known the national officials and their day-to-day conduct would not have been subject to scrutiny. The hierarchy creates, at a stroke, a career path for the bureaucrats and a system of accountability. Within this comes a certain amount of stability for the organisation and job security for the individuals. Such a system should also produce efficient working and technical competence (Weber, 1947). That this was also a factor for the College of Nursing and, indeed, any other major organisation has to be recognised, as has the fact that a bureaucracy is a necessary consequence of any large organisation and should not be viewed as negative. Rather, it had specific consequences for the NAWU and the other unions and professional associations.

Recruitment became ever more important, not just to increase the bargaining power of its members but to support the union's infrastructure. The bureaucracy, the paid officials of the union, had vested interests and these would inevitably creep into their representation of the union's view and policy objectives. The financial management of the union became established as an imperative; its activities had to be cost effective as well as politically correct. Whatever the language and rhetoric of working-class solidarity, the unions were in competition for members, influence and power. This was as true of the NAWU as anyone else, particularly with general unions engaged in representing workers in local authorities, but these were held off as the NAWU excluded them from the bargaining machinery in asylums. Most importantly of all its greatest rival, the Asylum Workers' Association, was defeated, finally collapsing in 1920.

This move into a traditional trade union position by the asylum workers was strongly opposed from all quarters. Inevitably, the employers had resisted it wherever possible. Both the NAWU's first general secretary and assistant secretary were sacked almost as soon as it was discovered that the union had been formed (MHIWU, 1931). The medical profession, even through their own organisations – which had secured for them a position of power, status and income any trade union would have been proud of – condemned the thought of a shortened, regulated working week and overtime pay, which they claimed would be against all ethical consideration of the nursing profession.

Beyond the Barricades – Inmates and Nurses Fight Back

Perhaps the height of the Asylum Workers' radicalism came in April 1922, with the country's shortlived post-war boom over and unemployment rising in a recessionary climate. The Visiting Committee at the Notts County Mental Hospital, Radcliffe, decided to cut wages and reduce the days off from four to three per fortnight, thus putting up the hours of the working week. This went against the national agreements that the Visiting Committees were bound by. Strongly supported by the union's leaders, Radcliffe's asylum workers accepted the loss of wages but not the increase in hours. The dispute ebbed and flowed for a few weeks until all of the staff were told they had been sacked and would only be reinstated if they undertook to 'faithfully carry out all instructions of the Committee of Visitors, and to loyally obey the Officers of the Mental Hospital . . .'

Herbert Hough, a probationer nurse who had become branch secretary after his predecessor was sacked for 'sleeping out (of the hospital) without a pass', was faced with a group of male staff intimidated by this strategy, frightened of losing not only their jobs but their tied accommodation and pension rights. The women, alternatively, were steadfast. They followed through the union's strategy of a 'stay in', or occupation, refusing to leave the ward, and went on strike two weeks after receiving their notice. Supported by the patients, 17 men followed the 50 women already taking action, occupying three wards and evicting non-unionised staff. They were further supported by the local unemployed who urged people not to apply for jobs at the institution. The medical superintendent and clerk to the Visiting Committee, accompanied by strike breakers, 25 bailiffs and 63 police officers arrived on April 12th to remove the staff.

'There was no violence until the authorities . . . smashed down the doors', Herbert Hough has said. Helped by a patient, he turned a fire hose on them. The water was turned off. The story was in all of the following day's newspapers: bailiffs broke down each of the barricaded doors left by the retreating nurses and, 'After a fierce hand to hand struggle, the nurses on strike were overpowered and ejected . . . Insane inmates joined in the struggle on the side of the strikers. Many people were injured . . . and the furniture . . . was reduced to matchwood.' The *Nottingham Journal* described events as 'the most amazing proceedings in the history of trade unionism'. The women on the upstairs wards held out longer than the men and also used fire hoses to defend themselves. The battle lasted between three and four hours. The nurses were taken prisoner before being ejected from the hospital. Many of them, including Herbert Hough, were blacklisted, finding it difficult to get work for months, if not years (MHIWU, 1931 and Dopson, 1985a: pp. 18–19).

The importance of the Battle of Radcliffe was not simply that it was written into local folklore and was such a dramatic episode in history, nor that it was identified by the union as 'the worst case of victimisation and tyranny in the records of the service' (COHSE, 1960). It symbolised the deep sense of grievance experienced not only by the nurses but also the patients; this was a sense of grievance that had been built up by years of oppression and was shared by people throughout the asylums and far beyond. As with much larger disputes, when that grievance found a voice and sense of purpose it had, ultimately, been smashed by employers who proved they were prepared to use whatever force was necessary. The battle to preserve the shorter working week was lost. The union, nationally, lost 2000 members in that year and came perilously close to bankruptcy.

Perhaps this was not quite 'the most amazing proceedings in the history of trade unionism', but it was, and is, extraordinary to think of nurses barricading themselves onto wards and turning firehoses on police officers and bailiffs – but only when removed from its historical context. It was not just the episode itself – important as an all too rare example of an alliance between trade unionists and patients – and many others like it which were 'forgotten' or written out of the mainstream nursing history until relatively recently, when rescued by Mick Carpenter, COHSE's historian. The whole miserable story of the asylums and the way nurses were treated was proscribed. Battling nurses did not fit with the image so carefully nurtured and sold to nurses and policy makers. Nor did the conditions that drove them to it.

The Other Nurses and Their Trade Unions

COHSE's development has, in many respects, mirrored that of health care services. In so doing it reflects the primary concern of a membership seeking material improvements through pragmatic means. Thus the series of mergers between different health care unions has been arrived at through a policy adopted to ensure greater bargaining strength and organise health workers across the full range of the service. As we shall see, this is a policy that has reached its zenith with the merger with the National Union of Public Employees (NUPE), once an arch rival in the competition for members, and the National Association of Local Government Officers (NALGO). The first of these mergers was between the NAWU and the Hospitals and Welfare Services Union (HWSU), itself a hybrid of different unions and name changes that could be traced back to its origins as a Poor Law Workers' Union.

The National Asylum Workers' Union had forged for itself a position of some permanence but a further reduction in the working week was only won after 12 years hard bargaining. Nonetheless, other victories were achieved under somewhat less dramatic circumstances than the Battle of Radcliffe and gradually, during the 1920s and 1930s, union representation was established, both in terms of individual representation and through the process of collective bargaining. The NAWU even secured its members the right to marry without permission of the medical superintendent. But the balance of its membership had altered. Now it was predominantly male, as opposed to the almost equal split between men and women in 1922. The split was more than mathematical. The men opposed having female nurses on male wards and, with the almost total male domination of all senior posts within the union, women's reaction was to avoid joining it. It was also becoming more conservative as a result of its members' relative job security, something not enjoyed by most other workers. Both factors were to have consequences still felt even in the 1980s.

Before the merger with the HWSU, the Asylum Workers' Union became the Mental Hospital and Institutional Workers' Union, following the enacting of legislation by a Labour government that finally, in 1930, put an end to pauperism and redesignated 'lunatics' as patients. Asylums become hospitals at the same time but little else changed within them.

As difficult as trade union organisation had been in the asylums, in the Poor Law institutions it was even more complex and problematic. For one thing, the institutions and service were themselves subject to great change. As infirmaries and hospital wings were introduced into the workhouse the employment of pauper nurses was halted. Training schools had been introduced in some workhouses even before the end of the nineteenth century; this, with the requirement of trained nurses to take charge of hospitals and infirmaries, meant that, for the first time, a nursing hierarchy was being established here, too. Change was also affecting the client group of the Poor Law institutions, even though health care policy making remained largely piecemeal and unco-ordinated. Virtually one House of Commons select committee after another was sitting to consider health issues, prompted by a combination of influential individuals, medical and nursing organisations, official bodies of the hospitals and in response to wider social and political pressure. A plethora of legislation not only made changes to the running of hospitals and infirmaries, it also brought in social policies that enhanced the conditions of the working class, including introducing school meals, old age pensions and, in 1911, the National Insurance Act. One of the many effects of this, with the growing sophistication of medical science, was gradually to change the population of the Poor Law hospitals and infirmaries. The chronically sick, aged and infirm were being replaced by those with more acute illnesses. Although staffing levels had been extremely poor – only four nurses, paid £24–28 per year, cared for 400 patients in the Croydon Infirmary in 1866, for example – the argument that the productiveness of the working population was, in part, dependent on how quickly people could be treated and discharged from hospital was also being used to increase the number of Poor Law nurses (Mason, 1985: p. 9). Functionally, the hospitals of the poor were moving closer to the voluntary hospitals, no matter how strongly they were separated by issues of class and wealth.

The Liberals' 1911 Act had another important consequence for nursing and nursing trade unions. Prior to it, doctors working in different fields had been disunited and their disunity neatly exploited by such diverse groups as the friendly societies and government itself. However, as David Green persuasively argues, one of the chief results of the Act was to unite the medical profession at the expense of the consumer, particularly friendly society members. As a result of the BMA's agitation betwen 1910 and 1912 they freed themselves from lay control, insinuated themselves into the machinery of the state and nearly doubled their incomes. It was a position they were to consolidate again in 1948 and 1989, and nursing always suffered as a consequence (Green, 1985: pp. 107–15).

The progress of Poor Law trade unionism was impeded also by the fractured nature of the workforce. A variety of workers, porters, tradesmen and nurses were competing for improved conditions but, divided by their occupations and grading systems, often failed to do so collectively. Many were only a hair's breadth away from destitution themselves and the Guardians were able to exploit that by demanding loyalty and intimidating those who were more independent. But as nurses began to forge a distinct occupational identity they became less interested in advancing the cause of Poor Law workers as a whole and saw their loyalty as being to nursing itself.

This, again, reflected the views of nurses in the voluntary hospitals. Both the Poor Law nurses and their patients might have been viewed as inferior, but there was some commonality developing as nursing began to develop its own strong, distinct occupational and cultural identity, with clinical issues and changes in nursing practice and education assuming real importance and significance.

The Effects of Professionalisation

The College of Nursing and Royal British Nurses' Association were vying for prominence in the voluntary hospital sector but had members amongst nurses everywhere. As reform and change spread throughout nursing, the 'professional' issues dominated the agenda, both in the organisation of nursing and within the nurses' own organisations. Perversely, in formulating the professional agenda, the issues that would dominate trade union activity were also being shaped. The debate about the length of the working week was a good example of how 'professional' considerations were used to legitimise policy that was economically driven. The NAWU were clear on the issue. They wanted the working week shortened. The employers were equally clear. They did not. Although the overriding problem was one of a lack of money to employ extra nurses, the argument put forward by the employers was that the patient should not be subjected to 'unnecessarily frequent changes of nurses', whilst it was judged to be important to be able to pin responsibility for 'neglect' onto individual staff members, which would be more difficult if more nurses were employed as a result of working shorter shifts; prolonged absence from the ward caused by shorter hours would lead, they reasoned, to a loss of interest on the part of the nursing staff and increased administrative difficulties (White, 1978: p. 181). Yet this view was not just that of financially hard pressed administrators. The high number of hours nurses worked had been an essential plank in the process of reform, being seen as testimony to the dedicated young women's virtuous and vocational approach to their work, with the College of Nursing and RBNA arguing in its favour. It had become very much an integral part of the culture of nursing into which all new recruits were socialised.

Professionalisation had been central to the strategy of the RBNA, College of Nursing, Institute of Midwifery and a host of other, smaller, nurses' organisations, as it had been for the Asylum Workers' Association; for the NAWU it was of much less importance, although some of the aspirations contained within professionalisation's broad umbrella were shared and did assume greater importance as the union's membership plateaued and it settled into its period of conservatism in the late 1920s. Breaking down the constituent factors that made up the notion of the 'professional' nurse, it becomes apparent that, in fact, the more general trade unions would inevitably find themselves confronting them sooner or later. Many of the things believed necessary to attract young women of the correct background and calibre were alien to the material aspirations of the members of the early health service trade unions. The philosophical differences were compounded by the different backgrounds and membership of the organisations, with the lower middle-class and working-class members of the trade unions having different objectives from many of their counterparts working in the voluntary hospitals. Certainly, for those arguing on behalf of this latter group, status would not be achieved by a higher wage; their aspirations lay in being recognised and valued as skilled, trained nurses, professionals alongside their medical colleagues, of a similar status to teachers or other professional women. Additionally, those amongst their ranks who had early feminist views found satisfaction in forming themselves into a profession that could, if not directly challenge their medical colleagues, then at the very least achieve some level of independence as a professional group. Nurses could be described as an important part of the early feminist movement for that reason. Equally, the burgeoning feminist movement was also influential on the leading proponents of professionalisation emerging from the ranks of middle-class women looking for a role beyond that of the confines of the Victorian and Edwardian household, including Mrs Bedford Fenwick, as nursing moved firmly beyond the initial stages and boundaries of the Nightingale reforms (Carpenter, 1991). Within some quarters of the feminist movement there was a strong alliance with trade unions and, more particularly, the Labour party, but this was regarded by many as quite extreme and would never have included those of the temperament and outlook of Mrs Bedford Fenwick or most nurses (Dangerfield, 1966). Moreover, their culture was not one of collective action or a strong sense of communities working together in the face of adversity.

Professionalism versus Pragmatism – The Triumph of the College of Nursing

During the interwar years this polarisation crystallised. Moreover, competition between nurses' organisations was hotting up: the RBNA and College of Nursing had become locked in an inexorable battle to the death, the prize for the survivor being able to proclaim themselves 'the voice of nursing' and becoming the driving force in influencing policy making. Having gained the upper hand in the drive for registration, the College of Nursing made it clear that they would not relinquish their superiority easily. Formed after the RBNA, they did not have as easily recognisable a figurehead as Mrs Bedford Fenwick, but she had long been ousted by the time the College were to triumph through a mixture of principle and pragmatism.

Registration had in fact raised as many questions as it had answered, if not more. For instance, how could hospitals maintain a well-trained elite of registered nurses whilst still containing costs and, at the same time, sustain staffing at levels commensurate with the increasing demands being made on nurses by both patients and doctors as well as the increasing responsibilities which came with a more developed and sophisticated training?

As the nursing hierarchy had grown out of the Nightingale reforms, the role of the matron took on increasing significance once registration was attained. The need for cost constraint was constant and had been as early as the 1860s. Thus, in 1910, Tynemouth Union Infirmary's reasons for having nurse–patient ratios of 1:68 on night duty was cost (*Nursing Times*, 8.10.1910). By 1918, with the period of training extended, probationers were required to do more 'domestic' tasks such as cleaning and polishing at St Thomas' – to cut costs (Dingwall, Rafferty & Webster, 1988: p. 59). It was necessary for those trained nurses in the service to be spread as thinly as possible, for as long a period of time as possible, doing as many tasks as they could physically manage. All of which, it could be argued, was contrary to the professional ethic. Under such circumstances, the matron had to exercise such discipline and control to ensure that the rigid socialisation process was enforced and the contradictions kept from spilling over into overt discontent and conflict. Their success – or lack of it – could be measured by the high numbers of young women who left the service.

When registration was finally won in 1919 there had been a glut of practising nurses from all backgrounds able to become registered. This countered the fears that many politicians and those involved in the running of hospitals and workhouses had shared, that the shortage of nurses available would make registration a political and administrative albatross. Nonetheless, the period just after World War One was probably the only time that registration could have occurred and the underlying problems been masked. Shortages of trained and registered nurses quickly manifested. One problem was that the single portal of entry desired by nursing organisations had not materialised. Six separate categories of nurse training meant that nurses had to retrain if they wished to move from fever nursing to paediatrics or into general nursing, similarly with a move from mental nursing; but by 1920 the problem was focused firmly on a lack of trained nurses and probationers despite dramatic rises in the number of women claiming registered nurse status, with a doubling of the numbers in 30 years to 111 501 in 1931. The new register was closed to existing nurses in 1925; of course, all those allowed to claim registered nurse status had not trained to the standards required by the GNC, although at the same time, not all those eligible for registration actually bothered to do so. By 1931 only 12% were married, widowed or divorced, a major reduction from previous eras. The average age of nurses had also fallen, as had the minimum age of entry. Older women, particularly with families, were deterred from entering by the low wages, the requirement of living in and 'renunciation of bodily temptations' (Abel-Smith, 1960: p. 119). Indeed, it became common practice to advertise only for unmarried girls (sic) or widows. But even the younger, fitter nurses were unable to keep up with the demands being made upon them whilst registration and more uniform standards of training meant that hospitals could not lower local standards to increase the numbers of trained nurses available, either for entry into training or registration, nor could they suddenly recruit larger numbers of untrained women to carry out work that was meant for trained nurses. The problem was compounded by the high drop-out factor amongst probationers allied with high failure rates in the national examination introduced by the GNC in 1925.

The GNC was, nominally at least, in the position of deciding policy on nursing issues although in any number of matters the Minister of Health could overrule them, the withdrawal of training status from hospitals being an important example. Nonetheless, competition for places on the Council was fierce because of the amount of political influence it brought to any group whose members had a majority of seats on it. Of equal import were the patronage and financial support coming into the main two nursing organisations, the RBNA and College of Nursing, demonstrating how much their respective hierarchies were an established part of British society. The Bedford Fenwicks, having acrimoniously parted from the RBNA, received £100 000 in a single donation that enabled them to start a new organisation, the British College of Nurses, set up in opposition to the old rivals, the College of Nursing, as well as their old organisation. The significant thing about it was that it was the first to be run by nurses exclusively (with the exception of Dr Bedford Fenwick, who was its treasurer); however, one of its main preoccupations was to take its place in the internecine war between the professional associations, attacking the College of Nursing for its medical and lay leadership and opposing the College's attempts to get a Royal Charter.

The future of the smaller professional organisations, such as the RBNA and British College of Nurses, was severely limited, however, and their eventual demise was sealed by the crisis surrounding shortages of nurses. The RBNA had been weakened by the rifts that had led to the departure of the Bedford Fenwicks (although rows and disagreements never seemed far away when Mrs Bedford Fenwick was around) and the divisions between the organisations made growth a virtual impossibility for any but the most powerful. The College of Nursing had now established a majority on the GNC; it had as its major publishing organ the *Nursing Times* and its membership was much larger and broader in its base. But, most importantly, the College was pragmatic and politically astute. Despite its constant lobbying on issues of professional development, it also recognised the real problems facing those charged with managing and administering hospitals and health care. Equally, it recognised the government's wider predicament in formulating policy for a health care system that was being stretched to the limit; this tension resulted not least from the contradictions of a key body of nurses who were determined to see nursing develop, both educationally and professionally, despite the cost and wider implications for the service. So while Mrs Bedford Fenwick's position remained unaltered, leaving her further and further isolated politically, the prevailing voice of the College was able to whisper messages of compromise and to adapt to the material conditions restraining their professional objectives. This was not to say that there was no opposition within the College of Nursing. Their organisation's internal divisions mirrored those of nursing's wider membership and the conflict between its clinical, or professional, and managerial wings was particularly intense.

The Contradictions Catch Up – Nursing Shortages

The growing influence and membership of the trade unions could not be so easily undermined or ignored by the College, however. Moreover, the Labour party entered the fray by publishing a policy statement in 1926 calling for a 48 hour week, separation of nurse training schools from hospitals and student status for probationers with their own study time. These popular proposals were coupled with a claim that nurses needed to be organised along trade union lines to further their own cause and increase their bargaining power, a claim strongly resisted by the professional organisations. They quickly recognised they were increasingly vulnerable as these demands found some resonance within the ranks of nurses throughout the service. The debate became focused and sharpened as the shortage of nurses became more pronounced. The 1930 Bill unsuccessfully put forward by Labour MP Fenner Brockway called for a minimum wage and maximum number of hours to be worked in a week. It was opposed by the professional associations; its minimum wage was higher than staff nurses were getting, let alone probationers, and was higher than that recommended by the College of Nursing (Bell, 1987: p. 20).

A Commission of Inquiry was set up by the *Lancet*, reporting in 1932 that there was no overall shortage in England and Wales (they had received insufficient data on the state of hospitals in Scotland and Northern Ireland) but that in municipal hospitals in and around the London area particularly there were problems – as much as a 13.2% shortfall on establishments. It did not point out that many hospitals' establishments were regarded as minimal, at best, and that even the smallest shortage of nurses within their numbers would be acutely felt. Over 51% of hospitals were experiencing difficulty in recruiting suitable staff nurses. One third of probationers were not finishing their training and 78% of those were leaving within the first year. Interviews with 200 young women in different occupations showed that most of them had never thought of becoming nurses, their headmistresses or nurses' own tales of hardship having deterred them. The problem, concluded the Commission, was that 'An erroneous idea of overwork, underfeeding and underpay existed and exaggerated reports of treatment by seniors remained in the minds of possible candidates and their parents.' Their recommendations did encompass a shorter working week and fewer domestic chores, as well as improvements to accommodation and less intrusive control of nurses' lives in their off duty hours; however, in the main it concentrated on looking to the furtherance of the vocational appeal favoured by Ms Nightingale and recruiting better educated young women from the 'upper classes' (*Lancet* Commission, 1932). The College of Nurses and Hospital Matrons' Association largely concurred.

The bias of the Commission's report was to blame the nurse, particularly the ward sister, who took the brunt of their criticism for exerting overly harsh discipline. Liane Bell argues cogently that this was compromised by the Commission's determination to preserve medical superiority and continued subordination of nursing, having based its conclusions on wholly haphazard and inadequate research (Bell, 1987: pp. 16–20). The Commission had failed to recognise the importance of separating the educational needs of nurses from the managerial requirements of running the hospital, which meant that probationers had to attend lectures in their off duty hours and found no accommodation of their educational needs within their arduous and taxing working environment. This was a situation recognised five years later by Dr Balme, quoted in the *Nursing Times*: 'The root failure in the existing system of training nurses lies in its attempt to combine the education of young probationers with the necessity of utilising their labour in order to carry on the existing work of a busy hospital' (*Nursing Times*, 14.8.1937). The situation facing nurses in the 1930s was partly created by their own professional associations, in condoning and colluding with the medical profession's hospital based model of care and structuring the recruitment, training and work of nurses around it, shaping nursing culture to support that basic premise. It was, moreover, a premise accepted by government. Therein lay the contradictions that were at the heart of the crisis. Need had outstripped supply; there simply never had been, nor were going to be, enough 'suitable' women to meet it. Moreover, the war had opened up any number of occupations previously closed to women and nursing's relatively brief grip on the employment market was, in that sense, loosened. Conditions in hospitals were harsh. But it was not simply out of individual vindictiveness or flawed character that ward sisters and matrons exercised such severe and rigorous discipline.

Discipline had been a problem throughout nursing's history. In the pre-reforms period there had been few ways of imposing it, particularly for those nurses and midwives working independently, although it had been assumed necessary to keep the Gampish, untrained nurses in line in workhouses; it had also featured heavily in the asylums, where it was believed that the attendants would not want to carry out their duties unless bullied into doing so. But its imposition was an integral part of the reforms. In 1911 nurses late back from holidays were kept in by the matron to do 'punishment tasks' (*Nursing Times*, 21.1.1911) whilst the previous year newspapers reported that Glasgow nurses were having 'privileges' withheld if they committed any misdemeanours (*Nursing Times*, 8.10.1910). This latter development was criticised by the *Times*, although later denied by the hospital management, but often the nursing journals were supportive of the general thrust of discipline and conditions nurses found themselves in. In 1910 a matron *hoping* to give nurses one day off a fortnight was viewed as progressive, so some headway can be seen to have been made when nurses were working, on average, only 54 hours a week by 1937. But their sense of grievance was almost at breaking point. In fact, 1937 saw an eruption of militancy that dwarfed anything that had gone before, witnessing the formation of breakaway unions and intense political activity. As with the period prior to World War One, it is perhaps difficult to imagine where it might have ended had it not been so violently interrupted, but its importance in the development of nursing trade unionism cannot be underestimated. It was the first time since the National Asylum Workers' Union had taken on the Asylum Workers' Association that trade unions had seriously contested the professional organisations on issues of policy. Except now the conflict was being enacted in the professional associations' heartlands, the voluntary hospitals and local authority hospitals.

The cause of the 'crisis' (as it was labelled in the nursing press) lay clearly in the difficulties in recruiting and retaining both probationers and trained staff, which had worsened steadily since the 1920s, but the root of the problem lay in the contradictions between nursing's professionalisation and the practicalities of matching 'supply', or enough trained staff, to meet the demand. The *Lancet* Commission's report had not proposed solutions that could end the drought and serious shortages were being reported throughout the hospital service although, again, the larger voluntary hospitals were far less affected than their local authority and provincial counterparts. However, the voluntary hospitals were feeling the effects of financial hardship more severely as the cost of care and treatment soared, the nurses' wage bill being a significant part of the problem. Nor was the issue of pay being addressed. Ward sisters were being paid a starting salary of between £70 and £85 a year while staff nurses could earn £60–£80. Matrons were earning an average of £180. The salaries for staff nurses particularly did not compare favourably with average earnings in other, less demanding jobs, but it was probationers who were most disadvantaged financially. Hillingdon Hospital, typically seeking applications from 'single girls (sic) and widows aged 19–30' were only paying them £30 a year. Salaries for all grades of staff would have been lower in voluntary hospitals, as low as £20 in some cases for a probationer. The policy of the College of Nursing was that £18 was a suitable minimum wage for a nurse in training (*Nursing Times*, 14.8.1937).

Not just the nursing journals but the national newspapers were making much of the issue. Ironically, the nursing media were highly critical of the coverage given to their 'dirty linen' being washed in the dailies, as were some nurses themselves, but there was clearly a great deal of anxiety about what nurses might do. That anxiety was well founded.

Nurses were concerned with a wide range of issues. From letters sent in to them and other observations, the *Nursing Mirror* listed eight different factors and invited their readers to vote and place them in order of priority. The results, published on January 1st 1938, were as follows:

1. Hours of duty;
2. Rates of pay;
3. Petty restrictions;
4. Lectures in off duty hours;
5. Prospects for advancement;
6. Interchangeable pensions;
7. Compulsory living in;
8. The gap between the school and hospital (*Nursing Mirror*, 1.1.1938)

Letters were being published in each week's editions of the main nursing publications, the *Mirror* and the *Times*. Ms B.M.J.

Gamon was critical of the publication of articles relating tales of the scandalous treatment of nurses (*Nursing Times,* 27.11.1937), while three unnamed nurses – members of the College of Nursing – condemned the TUC's politicisation of nursing, arguing that the College must meet this new 'threat' and 'secure new members to fight a grave menace to the profession' (*Nursing Times,* 16.10.1937). On December 4th 1937, Mary A. MacAlister from Glasgow wrote in the *Nursing Times* that the 'washing of dirty linen in public is despicable' but, recognising that there were problems, hoped that 'we will shortly hear something constructive from progressive leaders of our profession'. The general tone of letters published in the *Times* was supportive of the status quo and the College of Nursing's strategy; however, from some letters on its pages and those in the *Mirror,* a different picture emerged. 'JM' (many nurses only had their initials printed or did not identify themselves when writing on this subject), explaining why she believed so many probationers were deserting their training, complained that when probationers had their 'privileges' taken away, staff nurses were also punished. She also criticised the way in which nurses were given 'menial tasks, often made to feel foolish and a nuisance' while being overwhelmed with lectures in their own time (*Nursing Times,* 13.11.1937). 'ITA' refuted any suggestion that the vocational spirit applied to most nurses, claiming that '99% of nurses work because they have to earn their livelihood'. Long hours, she wrote, last minute changes in off duty that the nurse had to comply with, plus low wages were responsible for probationers leaving (*Nursing Times,* 20.11.1937).

Which Trade Union?

The debate was not about whether or not nurses should join trade unions, as they were now joining in larger numbers than ever before. More, it was a question of what sort of trade union they should join. Should specific trade unions be formed for nurses or should they enlist in general unions like the National Union of County Officers (NUCO) or the MHIWU? Importantly, these generalist unions were not restricting their membership to registered female nurses; they were open to women and men, trained, training or even untrained, as well as those working in different areas such as fever hospitals and paediatrics, who were also excluded from College membership. The College might have many of the most influential nurses amongst its ranks but the NUCO and the MHIWU were growing in numbers and with a broader base. Moreover, the National Association of Local Government Officers (NALGO) had entered the fray and, as a non-TUC affiliate, was proving attractive to some matrons who then brought large numbers of their workforce with them into membership. At one stage, NALGO was describing itself as the largest nurses' union. Competition for nurse members was intensifying and even more general unions like the National Union of Public Employees and Transport and General Workers' Union started recruiting heavily.

The TUC view was that, to prevent the so-called snobbery affecting the College of Nursing isolating nurses from other workers, they should join general unions (*Nursing Mirror*, 23.10.1937). The TUC actually condemned the College of Nursing as unrepresentative of nurses as a whole and 'an organisation of Voluntary Hospital snobs', citing the matron, rather than trade unions, as the enemy of nurses. The TUC had also launched a strident attack on the College for opposing a private member's Bill in the House of Commons seeking the introduction of a 48 hour week. However, the TUC's view that nurses should join general unions was not widely supported by nurses.

The nursing press was inevitably drawn into the debate. Yet it was not just the established organisations who were involved as key participants. In the October 16th issue of the *Nursing Times*, Thora Silverthorne responded to attacks on the newly formed Association of Nurses (A of N), a nurses' organisation formed by a group of nurses from London. She argued that the thing 'real nurses do resent is unnecessary hardships due to inefficiency and tyranny', adding that the reform not only of pay and hours but also of the conditions of work was necessary to recruit adequate numbers of probationers. Despite its newness and small membership base, the Association could be seen as representative of a departure in terms of trade union membership and a change in the mood of a significant minority of nurses. Both the Association and its general secretary, Ms Silverthorne, were to become the focus of a lot of attention.

The Association of Nurses refuted accusations that a distinct nurses' and midwives' organisation would inevitably succumb to snobbishness. Also, they believed that any organisation bent on splitting 'nurses into separate and sometimes competing groups and classing them with workers who do not share their professional problems is doomed to failure'. In its first document, *The Association of Nurses, Why It was Formed and What It Hopes to Achieve*, it declared its primary objective 'to improve the status of our profession' (Association of Nurses, 1937), stating that this could only be done by establishing a national negotiating body, shortening the working week and improving pay and other conditions, thus solving the problem of the serious shortage of nurses. Whilst stating that it was not in opposition to other nurses' organisations and recognising the work of the College of Nursing particularly, it was unequivocal in its view that the College, committed to advancing nursing professionally, could not achieve the necessary material improvements. In other words, status might be advanced by professional development but was only achieved once material benefits were also gained, a philosophy which completely undermined the professional and vocational arguments so important to the nursing, medical and hospital establishments, the threads which bound together the fragmented bodies of nurses notionally described as the nursing profession. With committee members from institutions like Guy's, the London and University College Hospitals, they were at the heart of the service and were able to claim all of the staff at the Radium Institute in London as members. They sought a common bond with the MHIWU and allied themselves strongly to the proposals put forward by the TUC.

As mouthpiece for the College, the *Nursing Times* was not slow to pick up on this. Conscious that, in calling for the College to 'show more fight' (*Nursing Times*, 23.10.1937), its Glasgow branch was voicing a feeling shared by many nurses, the *Times* launched a determined and sustained, if subtle, attack on trade unions attempting to represent nurses' interests, written in a gentle, even prosaic style. In 'Trade Unions As We Understand Them,' it recognised that nurses might want to join a trade union but stated boldly that 'Nurses have the College of Nursing' (*Nursing Times*, 30.10.1937). Its attacks on the Association of Nurses had begun in September but reached a peak on November 27th 1937 in an article entitled, 'A Blow for Professional Unity?' Pointing out that the Association had adopted its 10 point programme from the TUC Nurses' Charter, it highlighted the similarity between their document and the goals of the College. It questioned whether or not Thora Silverthorne actually was a state registered nurse (which she was, as well they knew) and the Association's registration as a trade union. The College acknowledged that it was not surprising to hear the TUC demanding overtime payments for nurses but commented, 'surely it is (surprising) from a body of professional women', adding, 'This has little in common with the *ideals of service which must animate every nurse worthy of the name*' (emphasis added). 'Do we need the power of the TUC to make progress? We have already made much headway,' it concluded. By then, however, the disagreements could not be contained and were spilling out onto London's streets.

Behind the Mask – Chasing Change

Masked nurses walked through central London protesting at their conditions, calling for a 48 hour week and more pay, before holding a rally at St Pancras town hall attended by between 500 and 1000 nurses. It was unprecedented. The masks were worn out of legitimate fear of victimisation but captured the imagination – and headlines – of the popular press, who had already been highlighting the issue of nursing shortages and alleged ill treatment of staff. Yet no report of the march and meeting appeared in the *Nursing Mirror* at all, only an anodyne article concluding that nurses must learn to speak with one voice. However, removed from the context of such powerful contemporaneous events, this exhortation appeared incongruous. In the *Nursing Times* the march and meeting were only given limited space and reported in a somewhat derisory fashion. Nurses outside the capital would hardly have known what their colleagues had been doing if it was not for the efforts of the daily press, with banner headlines such as, 'They

Were Incognito', 'Masked Nurses March In City, "Demand Fair Play"', and 'Masked Nurses Protest'. Indeed, the introspective nature of the journals, with their bland stories about nurses on keep fit programmes and visiting stately homes, seemed a million miles from the crisis that featured most strongly in their letters pages.

Although they did partly acknowledge the strength of those radical protests and the feelings that fuelled them, the overall blandness of the nursing journals was no accident. They were doing no more than reflecting the values, ethos and tradition of those in senior nursing positions, which in turn were reflected by, and reflective of, the College itself. They sought to maintain the hegemony of those in power. Thus, it was inevitable they would not reflect the opinion and attitude of those nurses who were trying to break with tradition and undermine the value system that sustained mainstream nurses' organisations. The journals had played an integral part in normalising and propagating those same values. In a service where training was variable, hospitals independent of one another and community services even more so, the one constant was the nursing journal. And, as Laurence Dopson states (Dopson, 1985b: p. 11), 'The protagonists on both sides of the Registration argument, which was crucial to the development of the nursing profession, had no doubt of the need to have a platform from which to address the professional audience.' Indeed, Mrs Bedford Fenwick even went so far as to buy a nursing journal to propogate her views. The *Nursing Times* was the 'in house' organ of the College of Nursing and RCN until 1968 and throughout its history has espoused the same philosophy, from the same political standpoint. Even since the two formally parted company and the RCN founded its own weekly journal, the *Nursing Times* has charted a similar path, even when this has meant deviating from the purely professional agenda. Indeed, the *Nursing Times* was strongly opposed to the reduction of the working week in 1937 and pressed the vocational and professional argument at the time.

The *Nursing Mirror* demonstrated in its pages, with the use of sample rotas, that a 48 hour week was achievable, although any reduction in the working week would have to occur despite a major problem: the number of unqualified nurses working in hospitals had risen from 15 000 in 1933 to 21 000 by 1937. As the shortages worsened, the London County Council relaxed its policy on recruitment and advertised posts (albeit temporary ones) for married women, it was announced that the government was to appoint a committee, under the chairmanship of the Earl of Athlone, to examine the problem of recruitment and retention of nurses, including their training and registration, terms and conditions. The College of Nursing and the *Nursing Times* heaved a sigh of relief.

But who could lay claim to victory? It was clear that the Athlone Committee would have to recommend significant policy changes. But was the Committee the result of the gentle and noble persuasion combined with carefully orchestrated cross-party political lobbying, as practised by the professional organisations? Or had it been the militancy of groups like the Association of Nurses and the NUCO, who had organised the masked nurses' march through its nurses' wing, the Guild of Nurses? Both the College of Nursing and trade unions were cautious in developing their strategy; neither was prepared to go too far in denouncing the other and, if anything, there was a process of convergence. The College of Nursing was forced into developing an industrial relations arm to its organisation whilst the trade unions considered how to organise nurses as a discrete group.

The impetus for change had been building throughout the decade and nurses joining trade unions had been symptomatic of it, as well as then fuelling the process as different cultural attitudes, traditions and intellectual arguments filtered through. Most importantly, an alternative consciousness was developing, with different values and objectives. Significant numbers of nurses were now beginning to believe that things could be different, were not accepting the discipline and socialisation processes of their profession and were prepared to *organise* a platform to put forward alternatives. Moreover, they were also aware that, particularly with local authority hospitals and services, the means were there to pay them more; it was simply a case of political will. Fenner Brockway's attempt to introduce a Bill shortening the working week may have been shortlived and unsuccessful but it had brought disillusioned nurses together

under a common banner and provided a platform for further
organising; this had resulted in calling upon the TUC to take
action on behalf of nurses and although the TUC tended to
concentrate its attentions on the 'big battalions' of organised
workers rather than smaller or more dispersed groups, it obviously offered them the opportunity to recruit heavily in a
hitherto neglected – almost inaccessible – area. The NUCO,
recognising the strength of the arguments for nurses to have
their own organising platform, formed the Guild of Nurses,
designed to allow nurses to be part of a 'nurses' only' trade
union. The Guild scored several successes in establishing a 48
hour week in several parts of the country and drew in such rad-
icals as Iris Brook, Doris Westmacott and Thora Silverthorne
from the Association of Nurses. Ms Silverthorne could not have
been less the stereotypical registered nurse. Having served as a
hospital matron with the International Brigades fighting on
behalf of the Republican cause in the Spanish Civil War, her
strong political convictions took her into trade union activity as
a nurse and on behalf of nurses, standing for election to the
General Nursing Council with Norah Large in 1937 and, again,
in 1944 with Iris Brook. Advocating their support for a
National Health Service, they also pledged to do 'all in their
power to protect nursing interests' and 'raise the standard of
nurse education'. They claimed to be more representative and
younger than nursing's existing leadership.

As the Athlone Committee progressed its work, it became clear
that the current structure was breaking under the weight of contradictions it was supposed to contain. Florence Nightingale had
long ago pointed up the difficulty of adequately training staff in
sufficient numbers through a piecemeal system of private enterprise rather than planned government strategy. Now, both the
local authorities but more especially the voluntary hospitals were
finding it almost impossible to fund their services properly. This
was despite the fact that the voluntary hospitals had been driven
further and further into the market place, taking on higher numbers of fee-paying patients in an attempt to remain financially sol-
vent. State intervention on a strategic scale was becoming
unavoidable.

The Shortages Continue

1939 saw no end to the problems. Nor did the outbreak of war. The situation was certainly no better than it had been in 1937; if anything it was worse. The newspaper headlines told their story just as powerfully: 'Nurses Forced to Become Waitresses', 'Nurses Lose Jobs in Their Thousands', '"Persecutions" Drive Nurses to Revolt', 'Nurses to Demand Fair Deal'. The *Daily Mirror* on November 17th 1939 stated that:

> Trained nurses are in revolt. They are leaving their profession in hundreds rather than put up with petty persecutions, the hardships and injustices they are being made to suffer.
> Women whose skilled work is vital to the country in war are going as shop assistants and on to the land.

Low wages were also condemned in the same article, with a Nurse Askey complaining that untrained male first aiders were receiving the same pay as she was as a trained nurse.

Nurses in London were also losing their jobs in their hundreds. 'The latest example of muddle is in the nursing profession, and is causing suffering among thousands of London trained nurses,' reported the *News Chronicle* on November 16th 1939. 'It is estimated that 2,000 State Registered Nurses and assistant nurses employed in London hospitals were thrown out of work shortly after the war started.' The article continued:

> I have visited First Aid Posts and Casualty Clearing Stations ... In hundreds of posts I found auxiliary nurses, most of whom were at home or in offices three months ago and had never seen the inside of a hospital, taking the place of trained nurses.
>
> (Morgan, 1939)

The *Chronicle* described nurses thrown out of work with between five and 12 hours notice, destitute because, as professionals, they were not entitled to unemployment pay. The Guild of Nurses fought back, with highly publicised public meetings. Thora Silverthorne declared, 'The whole of the nursing services are in a chaotic state. The engaging of untrained nurses is a Government economy ramp' (Allan, M. *Daily Herald*, 13.12.1939). Iris Brook had also been willing to risk serious disciplinary action by revealing her name to the press, saying, 'I am determined at any cost to press for an inquiry and to put up the best fight I can for the trained nurses of this country' (*News Chronicle*, 16.11.1939).

The College of Nursing, recognising the changing mood of nurses, had already recommended to the Athlone Committee that national machinery should be set up to deal with issues of pay and conditions for nurses, with rights of representation being given to nurses' organisations. This was supported by other nurses' organisations and was one of the key recommendations of the Committee, published early in 1939. They actually took this a step further by recommending nurses' councils for every hospital, along the lines of the national Whitley Councils. It also recommended a 96 hour fortnight – something the London County Council had already reluctantly acceded to in more than half its hospitals as a result of pressure from the NUCO – and pay rises for trained staff. A second grade of nurse was endorsed, as was increased domestic staff to lessen the burden on nurses while a universal pension and increased holidays were another part of the incentive for trained staff. There was little to encourage the probationer but the most sticky issue, that of funding, was identified and a solution proposed. The government, the Committee stated boldly, should make grants available to the nation's voluntary hospitals to enable them to meet the proposed higher wage bills and associated costs. The system of grants, it said, should be further extended to teaching hospitals. A minority of the committee were even prepared to see national funding for local authority hospitals (Athlone Committee Report, 1939).

That the government shied away from the recommendations was no surprise, although a tremendous disappointment for the nursing organisations. Athlone's recommendations would have firmly laid the foundations for a nationalised service. If government money, however small at first, were coming into the voluntary hospitals it would irrevocably alter their status and they believed that the burden of funding would inevitably switch. They did agree to local authorities reviewing their arrangements in the light of the Athlone Report but without incurring extra expenditure. The Second World War meant that the work of the Committee, expected to continue as its report was only an interim one, was never completed. However, ignoring Athlone's recommendations did not mean that the fundamental problems would go away.

Chapter 3

A position of influence?
Nurses organise in the NHS

If the problems remained the same, the nurses' militancy of the late 1930s did dissipate. If it was never widespread, nor developed into overt and outright industrial conflict, it was certainly a radical departure for nurses in general hospitals and marked a turning point in how they viewed themselves regarding their work and their relationship with the employer. It also occurred at a time of trade union conservatism and moderation. In the period 1934–9 the number of working days lost as a result of disputes only once exceeded 2 million; in the years 1919–26 it never dropped below 7 million in any one year, averaging several times that figure (Pelling, 1971: p. 208). Changes in manufacturing, technology and spending patterns were influencing union membership. Of course, those figures were dramatically affected by the General Strike of 1926 when 'twice as many days' work were lost as in all the 25 years following World War Two, all to compel the miners to work longer for less pay' (Leeson, 1973: p. 86). Although the NAWU had supported the call for the General Strike by the TUC in May that year, its members were not directly involved in taking strike action. However, the union made several large donations to the miners and many branch officials and activists, particularly in the mining areas, were involved in giving their support even after the TUC had ended the General Strike and the miners were out for another six months on their own. Following the eventual defeat of 1926 and having suffered losses in the great depression of the 1930s, the older unions such as the Miners Federation and cotton workers' unions were still consolidating as war broke out, although those like the Amalgamated Engineering Union doubled in size as their industry evolved rapidly. The TUC was now aligned closely with the Labour party, with Ernest Bevin, the Transport and General Workers' Union (TGWU) leader, a key Party figure. The TGWU was another union experiencing growth as the depression faded, dwarfing all of the nursing organisations together with its 654 000 members. The NUCO had affiliated to the TUC in 1933 (the NAWU had already done so ten years earl-ier); its size can be put into propor-tion when it is seen that the Guild of Nurses was regarded as a great success when it increased its membership from less than 1000 in 1936 to 4000 within a year. Although the MHIWU had increased its membership to over 20 000, the Royal College of Nursing (having changed its name from the College of Nursing and been awarded a Royal Charter) – not affiliated to either the TUC or Labour party – had 29 000 members, all trained nurses.

The Unions Move to Centre Stage

Politics had changed to such an extent that the old Liberal–Conservative hegemony was shattered and the relation-ship between the TUC and the Labour party was now focusing on what would happen when Labour were elected as a majority gov-ernment. A programme for nationalisation was being drawn up, although sections of the trades unions movement were demanding that the plan go a step further, to have trade union official seats on the boards of the newly nationalised industries. The TUC and senior trade union officials were already recognised as serious participants in industrial relations strategies, not just within their own industries but also by government. This was in part a reflec-tion of the growing sophistication of the industries themselves, requiring more skilled workers whose labour was a more neces-sary and less easily replaceable commodity, and in part a recogni-tion that the unions had greatly increased their overall numbers and organisation. Activism and militancy was largely confined to unions with Communist leaders or large numbers of Communists amongst the rank and file workers, such as the London buses' sec-tion of the TGWU. There were Communist party members amongst key nursing activists of the period, some nurses having already been party members, others joining after they had gone to Spain as part of the International Brigades' effort to support the

Republican cause (Fyvel, 1992), Thora Silverthorne amongst them. Although relatively few in number, they exerted considerable influence.

The shortages of trained staff were further exposed by the Second World War, especially after the extraordinary steps taken in its early months to lay off trained nurses in favour of nursing auxiliaries. In London, the health services had to cope not only with being bombed along with the rest of the city but caring for war casualties in addition to all other work they might have undertaken. Croydon's Mayday Hospital, for instance, had allotted 500 of its 562 beds to casualties, although not more than 329 were eventually used, whilst treating over 1400 air raid victims in the war years (Mason, 1985). In such circumstances the demand for nurses, especially trained nurses, was greater than ever.

Those years saw the two sides of the class divide fighting a common, external enemy, although the truce was only temporary and often far more strained than the popular myth and propaganda of the time would ever suggest. A coalition government led by Churchill contained a large number of Labour Party figures, including Clement Attlee, with Ernest Bevin as Minister of Labour and National Service. Legislation was introduced at Bevin's behest to strengthen the negotiating machinery at national level; but it bound the unions procedurally as well as the employers. Skilled workers were required to register and could be directed into essential work. Again, however, there were compensatory factors in terms of minimum wages and conditions. Even the Communist Party was committed to increasing production in support of the war effort after the invasion of the Soviet Union. Nonetheless, industrial disputes did not become a mere historical curiosity. Arguments took place in the mining industry where the employers had taken advantage of the general mood to hold down already poor wages and the strike at Betteshanger, in Kent, in 1941 became a national issue, with the miners facing strong opposition and criticism for acting against the national interest as they challenged the Essential Works Order (Stevens, 1985). Nonetheless, the mood overall, particularly in the early war years, was one of co-operation and the trade unions took advantage of their tentative grasp on power. Days lost through strikes were at a low; membership, interestingly in view of the number of men taken into the armed services, rose dramatically, with NUPE more than doubling in size (Pelling, 1971: p. 218).

The work of the nurses' organisations during this period, mirroring that of the TUC in the preceding years, was about consolidation, with detailed negotiations to access power and try to change the structure in which they operated, both with employers and government. The clear intention was to attain a position where they were able to influence policy directly, at the formative stage, rather than endlessly reacting to it. In January 1941, despite strong opposition from the employers who feared that any negotiating body might prompt even more trade union organisation by nurses and give them an avenue to push up wages further, the Ministry of Health set up the Local Authorities Nursing Services Joint Committee. Its purpose was to deal with conditions of service for nurses throughout their hospitals and community services. Later that year the Rushcliffe Committee was formed with the aim of agreeing national pay scales for nurses. Both committees were an amalgam of representatives from, on one side, the employers and, on the other, trade unions and professional organisations. On the trade union side of the Local Authorities Committee half of the seats were held by the RCN. They also secured nearly half on the Rushcliffe Committee. These committees were only superseded in 1948 with the establishment of the NHS and the Whitley Councils that were an essential part of the national infrastructure established to maintain harmonised pay and conditions of services for nurses throughout the service. One of the early gains of the staff side was to extend the remit of the Rushcliffe Committee to look beyond salaries solely, examining issues such as pensions, and to apply their findings to all nurses.

Within two years nurses' organisations were in the position of being able to demand that Athlone's recommendations be rescued and acted upon. The government did so almost totally. Wages were increased – with government money contributing towards the new rates of pay – and, as a means of tackling the chronic problem of shortages of trained nurses, the enrolled nurse was recognised as a new entity. The Ministry's decision to push the recommendations through only hastened the day when they would become entirely responsible for setting nurses' pay and conditions. The RCN had been making demands for national negotiating machinery and now agreed with the findings of the Athlone Committee even though they had originally argued that the recommendations for nurses' pay were too high.

Similarly, the RCN underwent a major policy reversal in supporting the cause of enhancing the status of the assistant nurse. With shortages of trained nurses as bad as ever during the war, the College had recognised that the very structure of nurse training and registration was under threat. Faced with this problem they adopted a pragmatic and imaginative strategy. Having argued consistently for one entry route and elevated the position of the registered nurse, in the war years they commissioned a report and lobbied the Ministry in a way which opened the door for it to introduce a second tier of trained nurses, but who would require less training and be less well qualified academically, being admitted to a 'roll' rather than the register. The enrolled nurse would, of course, also be less costly to train and employ once qualified.

At the same time as all these changes, there were more that would prove far more fundamental and far reaching, these being the work led by Beveridge on the new welfare reforms, including the National Health Service.

An End to Hospital Flag Days

Much has been written about the way in which the NHS was designed and developed, but little from the perspective of the nursing trade unions and professional organisations. By the time it was born, in July 1948, the NUCO had changed its name to the Hospital and Welfare Services Union and merged with the MHIWU to form the Confederation of Health Service Employees (COHSE). For COHSE the NHS was seen as a tremendous achievement, claiming that they had paved the way for its formation by being one of the two key unions that had lobbied persistently to see a nationalised health care system.

In 1945, with bitter memories of the post-war period in the 1920s and 1930s, when the Liberals and Conservatives had promised them 'a land fit for heroes' but given them dole queues, mass poverty and a society still as divided on class lines as it had been 50 years previously, Britain's workforce had voted for change. The result was a landslide victory for the Labour party and its programme of nationalisation of the country's major industries. The Bank of England, the coal industry, transport, electricity and gas, and the iron and steel industry were all taken into public control. Another significant change was the way in which the leadership of the trade union movement was now inextricably bound into the process of power, working with a majority Labour government which included 124 trade union sponsored MPs – although, importantly, the larger objective of control, with trade unions having seats on the boards of the nationalised industries, did not materialise. Nonetheless, they had a 'direct corporate relationship with the government' that went far beyond industrial relations alone, encompassing 'manpower policy, regional planning, welfare and much else besides' (Morgan, 1992: p. 13).

The path to the NHS followed that of some of the other nationalised industries, but its place at the heart of the welfare state gave it greater meaning for many participants on both sides of the political divide and signalled the Labour movement's dominance of the social policy agenda. The notion of such a fundamental service available, free at the point of need, gave all working people something that they had never had before and the Conservative Party – which had failed to implement Beveridge's recommendations in 1943 – vehemently fought the passage of the National Health Service Bill in 1946, proposing amendments which would have effectively destroyed it in the form it was to take, particularly focusing on retaining the voluntary hospitals and voluntary contributions to the service. If the donnish Beveridge was the principal architect of the NHS and the struggles of the trade union movement had provided the foundations on which it would be built, Aneurin Bevan, a charismatic Labour MP from South Wales, was the stonemason. His characteristically blunt retort to Tory criticism was that, 'The only part of the hospital service destroyed by the Bill is the necessity to sell flags and to collect money' (Lister, 1988: pp. 22–3). The legislation ensured that the service was now funded directly through taxation, provided on a national basis, subdivided down and administered by regional boards, although the teaching hospitals still retained some elitist status, having their own boards of governors reporting directly to the Minister of Health. It was important not just to doctors but also the Royal College of Nursing that control of the service rested with hospital management committees rather than local authorities, as had originally been proposed. Gone were the local authority institutions and voluntary hospitals and with them local rates and voluntary subscriptions to fund them. It had been Bevan's declared aim to provide legislation for a service that would be there for all people in their time of need, regardless of their ability to pay. It was described by the author Alan Sillitoe as, 'Probably the greatest single factor in this century in creating a new pride in the English working class' (Childs, 1979: pp. 31–2).

Medical opposition, however, was less easy to sweep aside than that of a dispirited and poorly led Conservative party. As late as March 1948 doctors were voting almost 10–1 against the NHS Act, although Gallop polls showed 69% of the electorate favouring it, with only 13% against (Morgan, 1990: p. 38). Serious compromises were negotiated with Bevan, preventing doctors from becoming salaried employees of the state – as nurses would now be – and concessions about their employment rights were secured. But, as shall be explored later, the most lasting effect of the prolonged, often bitter confrontations that the doctors had with the Minister was that they effectively placed themselves at the heart of the system. In winning the support of the Royal Colleges, as opposed to the BMA, Bevan had been forced to open the door to consultation and negotiation on the most fundamental aspects of the service. It was never to be closed.

Nationally, the economic situation was depressingly familiar. The United States had abruptly terminated its lend-lease programme, leaving Britain, whose financial resources had been exhausted by war, in a position of virtual 'financial nudity' and although a loan was secured, the interest was enormous and restrictive strings were attached. Debts of £496 million in 1939 had mushroomed to £3500 million in 1945 (Childs, 1986: p. 23). The new NHS overshot its estimated budget of £180 million by a further £222 million, spending £402 million in its first year. Wage restraint was initiated for all health service employees and reluctantly accepted by both COHSE and the RCN, as the government were pressed into concentrating on increasing production for exports as a priority, closely followed by a massive investment programme in industry. The onset of the cold war also meant a large increase in defence expenditure and by the end of Labour's first period in office there had been tax increases and a major devaluation. The principle of a health service free at the point of need had been abandoned, with the introduction of charges for prescriptions, dentures and spectacles. Bevan had resigned from the Cabinet. Labour was on its way out of power.

Whitleyism Fails to Pay Its Way

The NHS had not just changed the way people's health care was organised and funded. The Athlone, Nurses' Salaries Committee, local authorities committees and Guthrie Committee in Scotland had all paved the way for a system of Whitley Councils, drawing on the precedents, amongst others, of the Civil Service, where such an arrangement had been adopted in 1919, shortly after J.H. Whitley's committee had recommended joint employer–employee machinery. The principal aim at that time was to achieve industrial harmony through the process of negotiation rather than campaigns and confrontation. It had had to do this in the face of a shop stewards' movement that had, in the words of a Ministry of Labour Industrial Relations Handbook of the day, established 'workers' control . . . on militant lines with the ultimate objective of securing control of industry generally' (Vulliamy & Moore, 1979: p. 9). Thus the centralisation of negotiations, pivoting on a relationship between national trade union officials and employer representatives, was seen as more easily controlled than leaving matters in the hands of local officials and the vicissitudes of local circumstances. Nurses' pay and conditions were moved now wholly within the ambit of government. The Whitley Councils were divided into management and staff sides, with the staff side being made up of representatives of different health service trade unions and professional associations. The Nurses and Midwives Whitley Council for Great Britain would now be the forum for all discussions relevant to nurses and their employers except those covered by the General Whitley Council, which spanned those conditions of service shared with all grades of staff.

The staff side of the Nurses and Midwives Council was not

necessarily a homogeneous group. Rivalry was intense; power and influence were not to be surrendered easily. Bitter arguments between the Royal College and the trade unions had peppered the work of the Rushcliffe Committee, particularly around the RCN's opposition to reductions in the working week and increases in nurses' salaries. But the professional associations, having secured control by virtue of the majority of staff side seats on earlier committees, ensured they retained their majority on the new Whitley Council. The RCN claimed 12 seats out of 41 and, while they had the support of a number of other professional nursing organisations such as the Association of Hospital Matrons, were pleased that the RBNA and British College of Nurses, their old rivals, were excluded. COHSE had four seats. 'Management' was now identified as representatives of the local authorities – later lost – and personnel from regional health boards and hospital management committees. Essential to the changed nature of the employer/employee relationship, there were also five representatives of government departments.

Thus the focus for nurses shifted to the national stage, with a pattern becoming established that was to last until the reforms outlined in the Thatcher government's White Paper, *Working for Patients* were implemented in the early 1990s. Policy could, potentially at least, be influenced through the new relationships within the Whitley Council, with other, less formalised avenues for influencing policy rapidly forming as a byproduct of this centralised negotiating forum, with nurses' representatives now in regular contact with Ministry officials. But the expected windfall did not arrive. The costs of the NHS soared. This occurred against the expectation of the Labour government, which had actually based their financial projections on the belief that demand, and thus costs, would fall as people's health improved once they had immediate access to the comprehensive health care facilities provided by the NHS, combined with improved housing and social services (Klein, 1989). The control of wages, as ever, was essential as a key means of containing expenditure, albeit on a national scale. Pay rises could not be regarded as automatic and were not awarded on regular occasions in the early years of the NHS (Cowie, 1982: p. 229). If the Treasury did not have a seat on the Whitley Council their spirit sat on the shoulder of the government officials who did. Although the government would very rarely oppose union calls for arbitration if there was no agreement about wage settlements, nor frequently tamper with the results of the arbitration process, the cycle settled into one of long periods of erosion, due to inflation and wages being held down, followed by short bursts of anger and militancy leading to a brief catching up with national wage levels before slipping further back again. Even in 1948 there were problems, with London nurses demonstrating in Hyde Park at the delay in revised pay for student nurses (COHSE, 1960).

Whitleyism proved a heavy burden, both administratively and technically (Klein, 1989). The various councils had to deal with everything to do with conditions of service and pay as well as numerous other factors to do with the delivery of the service and apply national uniformity (although they only had the power to make recommendations on pay and conditions to the government (Lister, 1988)). They were soon being criticised by both management and unions. By the late 1950s, with 26 out of 53 major pay settlements having had to go to arbitration, Whitleyism's credibility was severely undermined with management's attitudes being branded as unresponsive and out of touch, although representatives of management would often decry the problems of dealing with 55 different unions, many of which had different objectives and few of whom consistently agreed with one another (Klein, 1989). The only reason for its survival was that no agreement could be reached on alternatives. The McArthy Report identified the need for local bargaining, regional Whitley Councils and decentralisation to remove inflexible and inappropriate national agreements, also recommending multilevel negotiations on a variety of issues and a reduction in the number of unions participating to increase the effectiveness of those remaining (DHSS, 1976). Indeed, government had used Whitleyism's 'cumbersome, arms length machinery ... as a means of containing costs by depressing health workers' salaries. [Whitleyism] had failed abysmally' (Sethi & Dimmock, 1982).

The medical profession, however, set about securing for themselves a special place. They complained that, comparatively, their salaries were far below those of other professionals and that their pay had been eroded by inflation. As has often been the case, and despite the fact that they were a far from homogeneous group, they used the power of their profession plus a solid 'trade union' tactic (they threatened mass resignations) and led the way in forcing a confrontation with the government which, in 1956, led to the setting up of a Royal Commission which ultimately recommended the independent Doctors' and Dentists' Review Body – although it stated that it did not think doctors were comparatively worse off than other professionals (Sethi & Dimmock, 1982). With the implementation of the review body the medical profession wriggled free of any incomes policies and the politico-economic stringencies holding back nurses and other health-workers, reinforcing their position of superiority. Such stringencies, in the form of an incomes policy in 1962, stirred latent passions and forced a confrontation between the then Health Minister, Enoch Powell, and nurses. But without the doctors' ruthlessness it ended in neither victory for the nurses nor an increase in trade union membership or activity, which remained fairly static.

In 1966 the National Board for Prices and Incomes (NBPI) issued a report on pay among local government and NHS ancillary workers which many had hoped would recommend substantial increases in basic pay; instead its report concentrated on 'low labour productivity', recommending the rapid introduction of incentive bonus schemes for the NHS. Although there were no direct implications for nurses, a series of events that would transform health service trade unions and industrial relations was set in motion.

The Thread of Consensus Snaps

The system of national negotiation had had important consequences for the development of industrial relations. Unlike the situation in private industry, where local shop stewards and convenors would negotiate everything, including levels of pay, the role of local trade unionists in the health service was very limited, restricted to consultation on local policies and interpretation of policies set out at national level. Managers saw industrial relations at a local level as unimportant for the same reason and this was reflected in low trade union membership throughout the NHS. At a national level, the management side were perfectly happy with this and consistently restrained the use of local or regional autonomy. Clegg and Chester reported in 1957 that the management side were not afraid of the unions, whose choices were limited to acquiescence or, at worst, arbitration in the event of disagreement. The most they were able to do was mount a rather abstract campaign about matters affecting nurses throughout the country in very different ways (Bosanquet, 1979). Moreover, whilst they might be campaigns important to those involved in national negotiations, they did not always mirror the main concerns of those nurses working away on the wards, something that was to emerge with some clarity during clinical grading.

The introduction of incentive bonus schemes (IBSs) for ancillary workers changed all that. Trade unionists at a local level now had something to negotiate on which could be seen to materially affect the lives of their members. What followed was the beginning of a period of significant growth in membership and organisation for COHSE and other general trade unions, particularly NUPE. A series of disputes affected particular sections of the workforce, with nurses becoming involved in a pay dispute in 1970 from which some gains were made. Suddenly industrial relations was an issue but there were now two sides of the table involved: the period of deference on the part of the workforce was over. Several factors had brought this about. There was the growing disillusionment with Whitleyism and the holding down of health workers' pay. Stewards in the general unions were gaining experience and confidence from the effects on local organisation of IBSs while a 'new managerialism', modelled on that of private industry, demanded of the workforce a change from previous attitudes and practices. This coincided with the development of 'health factories', large, district hospitals where management was centralised, impersonal and functional (Carpenter, 1988).

Thus, management's position changed: for the first time they were officially encouraging staff to join organisations and unions. The unions themselves, basically conservative and aware of the need to respond to charges of having failed to confront satisfactorily the low pay and poor conditions of their members, were beginning to see the need for organisational restructuring that would reflect greater democratic participation at local level, an exercise led by NUPE. Of course, a further benefit for the unions in this exercise was that it was beneficial to recruitment and, with the increased membership, greater bargaining power with management. Thus 'new unionism' and 'new managerialism' were in place for the first major conflict of the 1970s, which was primarily economic in nature at the outset but which took the unions considerably further – to challenge management on the issue of control.

By 1972 nurses were beginning to lose the gains made two years previously. That success had prompted more local activity amongst their ranks and the competition between the Royal College of Nursing and unions like COHSE was especially fierce. But for COHSE there were other groups of workers to consider and for the next decade the ancillaries in both that union and NUPE dominated, in terms of recruitment, campaigning and industrial action.

With an expanded workforce and improved local organisation in their union branches, over 100 000 ancillaries followed a call for a one day strike in 1972 and eventually 750 hospitals were affected by industrial action as the ancillaries campaigned for more money, a shorter working week and longer holidays. That, eventually, they did not win many concessions from the government is undoubtedly less important than the wider consequences of the action. Suddenly ancillary workers were 'important': management also had to come to their shop stewards to negotiate about emergency cover and rotas and the longer that process went on, the more confident the staff and their stewards became. They had also, for the first time in the NHS, decided that they would confront the notion that patient care was sacrosanct. Dunlop's 'web of rules' that guaranteed industrial stability demanded a shared ideology between the actors but, as Lister observes, 'the pretence of consensus was broken' (Lister, 1988: p. 96). This was not to be lost on nurses, where those who had broken from the ideal of vocation and sacrifice (if they had ever held to it in the first place) could now join a trade union that was able to articulate their voice with real authority, speaking to government directly, a part of the TUC and Labour party, with all of the connotations of power that went with that. There were real divisions amongst nurses as their differing views and objectives found expression.

That breakdown of consensus went further still and, again, the issue was about control rather than pay as a bitter three way dispute between consultants, the government and trade unions developed over pay beds in the NHS. NUPE prompted a strike at the Charing Cross Hospital at a crucial point in the renegotiation of NHS contracts for senior medical staff. The confrontation, involving a work to rule by the consultants, that ensued between ministers and the medical profession was 'more bitter than any in the history of the NHS' (Klein, 1989: p. 117). A compromise was eventually worked out but by then there was plenty to take its place. Industrial relations was not seen as an issue in the NHS prior to 1972 but within eight years that had changed so dramatically that it was identified by some as '*The* problem for the health service,' with nurses just one of a wide number of competing groups (Haywood & Alazewski, 1980: p. 28).

1974 saw Bosanquet's observation of a four year cycle of discontent within the nursing profession reach a new peak (Bosanquet, 1979: p. 4) (Plate XIV). Successive incomes policies had pushed nurses' salaries further and further back. The management side were unable to mitigate this process in the imaginitive ways their counterparts in private industry could and nurses' anger broke. Although the RCN were the first to meet Barbara Castle, presenting her with their report *The State of Nursing* (RCN, 1974) and threatening mass resignations as part of their 'Raise the Roof Campaign', it was COHSE, under intense rank and file pressure, that led the way with a comprehensive campaign of industrial action. The issue was defused with the announcement of a special committee of inquiry under Lord Halsbury and both the RCN and COHSE claimed success for the eventual gains of the Halsbury Report. But it was COHSE that benefited most, enjoying unprecedented success in recruiting nurses over the next 12 months outside its heartlands in the large psychiatric institutions. Indeed, contrasted with the response to Powell's 'pay pause' and the lack of success COHSE had with their campaign then, a consistent pattern of membership flow can be seen to have begun to form, although antecedents for this could be dated all the way back to the Bodmin Asylum strike in 1918. Intense activity and campaigning, raising a positive profile for the union, led to nurses joining COHSE. But the numbers would remain high only if the outcome of the campaign or dispute was perceived to be a success, otherwise they would eventually drift away again, with the RCN picking them up in later years.

Freefall

Aside from all the drama, other important developments were occurring. Increased local activity from stewards was now being matched by managers and personnel staff – a relatively new development in themselves – who were busy negotiating local agreements, particularly on disciplinary matters and facilities agreements and, in some cases, setting up consultative committees. But industrial relations were in a state of freefall by 1976. Virtually every profession or discipline had been involved in industrial action of one sort or another and trade union membership had soared. Nationally, there was continued tension about government economic policies in the areas of pay and public spending on the welfare state, whilst within Britain's hospitals there was enormous tension between different grades of staff and professions/disciplines, with an awareness of great inequalities in pay, conditions and status developing between different occupational groups.

Different unions, often working to different policies and agendas, were not above trying to adopt apparently contradictory stances for different audiences, in order to prosecute their wider objectives while aiming to recruit doubtful members of rival organisations. Nursing organisations might already be working in opposite directions whilst trade unions with no nursing membership might be heading off at yet another tangent. This was obviously focused in the Whitley Councils where there was often no clear line of agreement from the different unions: this problem was magnified between the different Councils and they would very often be bargaining in isolation from one another (Bosanquet, 1979). The Councils, all meeting regularly, were accorded enormous importance by the trade union side but with the national structure of Whitleyism was manifestly failing to deliver, the concept of the vocational nature of working in the health service was gradually being replaced by a pragmatic, 'industrialised' consciousness in the workforce. This was matched by management practice and objectives which were increasingly industrialised and ruthless. New technological developments with increasingly complex occupational demands had changed the nature of the work and there had been significant shifts in the power relations between managers and managed and staff and the government.

The National Health Service, basically a backward and reactionary employer, had been unable to adapt to the cumulative changes affecting it and had been severely damaged, in industrial relations terms, by the reorganisation of 1974. This occurred following several years of debate, initiated by the previous Labour government. But Sir Keith Joseph was at the helm for the Conservatives, as Minister of Health, when plans for 90 new area health authorities were drawn up (subdivided into district health authorities in the larger areas), administrative and managerial tiers extended and the basis on which the service was managed at a local level altered. With the actual policy implemented by the incoming Labour party, management by consensus was introduced at a local level, with doctors and nurses now having seats on the new authorities. The matron was dead but nurses had a serious voice for influencing policy. However, the right of veto was given to representatives of local consultants and GPs, an 'acknowledgement of the reality of medical syndicalism' (Klein, 1989: pp. 92–6). The balance of professional power had barely shifted.

Significantly, the reorganisation failed most seriously because it did not resolve the problem of a lack of a coherent, workable local system for resolving difficulties, despite the widespread recognition of a need for one. Overly bureaucratic and complex in structure, expensive to set up, it did not even allow central government to control the application of policy, something less important in 1974 but to be of dramatic importance as financial strictures reimposed themselves in the years immediately after it took effect.

Managers trying to deal with these increasingly sophisticated problems faced several problems. They were encumbered with the Whitley system still, with all its failings, but also had to take responsibility for government policy and the uneven application of incomes policies which worked to the detriment of health workers. Not only did the unions not have a coherent pay policy: far worse, government did not and there was not one clear pay structure that everyone could work within. In introducing new industrial management practices both Labour and Conservative governments had irrevocably altered what were already delicate workplace relationships without having the intricate joint consultative mechanisms and local negotiating bodies to deal with the problems in their early stages. Moreover, managers did not always have the skill themselves to apply solutions to these problems: their attempts to manage the changes, albeit changes enforced upon them, were often remarkably crude – for instance, a committee of inquiry into the causes of industrial action in Liverpool in the late 1970s found that different managements had, at one time or another, threatened two thirds of the hospitals in the city with closure.

Into this industrial relations maelstrom another factor dropped. It was no stranger to the scene, but in 1976 was key to policy direction again. Faced with an economic crisis, the Labour government guaranteed to cut public spending as the price for securing a loan from the International Monetary Fund. This was coupled with a 'social contract' that was in operation, with the unions nationally agreeing to wage restraint. As ever, it was public sector workers who bore the brunt of it. Having inherited a package of £1.2 billion in public spending cuts from the Heath government, Chancellor Healey added a further £1 billion in April 1975, £3 billion in March 1976, with another £1 billion four months later (Lister, 1988: p. 98).

The Labour movement had been exerting its relatively new-found strength but was still not necessarily pulling in one direction. NUPE and COHSE were under immense pressure from their members to resist any closures of hospitals and reductions in expenditure yet wanted to support the Labour government. Behind the scenes attempts at persuasion were rendered meaningless when 70 000 people marched in London against the cuts. Nurses were, to a large extent, on the margins, with ancillary workers leading the protests. While there were some unions unprepared to oppose the government publicly there were still others, particularly from the engineering sector, who went a stage further, picking up on the arguments that the NHS had contributed to an accumulation crisis, whereby spending on the welfare state had impeded economic growth and undermined the government's 'wealth creation' programme (Taylor Gooby & Papadakis, 1987: p. 22 and Sethi & Dimmock, 1982: pp. 84–5).

Six thousand beds closed in 1976, mostly without dispute (Bosanquet, 1979: p. 11). However, hospital occupations and long drawn out fights to save small, local hospitals threatened with closure became an increasingly frequent and bitter occurrence. The large district hospitals, teaching hospitals and so-called centres of excellence, meanwhile, were quietly protected by an alliance of forces, notably the consultants, supported by the 'professional wings' of various nurses' organisations and trade unions. Inexorably, industrial relations between all the actors involved deteriorated to the point when, in 1978, Jim Callaghan's government's attempts to impose a further 5% limit on pay increases prompted action throughout the country in both the private and public sectors. However, the dispute was fiercest in the public sector, where the vast majority of workers were low paid. In what came to be termed 'the winter of discontent', health workers were accused of turning away cancer patients from outpatients' departments, denying food deliveries to wards and a wide range of other illgotten tactics to advance their cause. Although the unions were usually able to prove the allegations false, the reality was a lot less important than the perception of events and their efforts to win public understanding and support were, largely, wasted. A return to work was negotiated with the formation of the Clegg Commission (which was subsequently to award a 9% pay increase – ironically honoured by the new Conservative administration, despite their criticism of the public sector unions' dispute) and the winter of discontent became part of a new mythology about trade unions, featuring high in the Tories' anti-union propaganda for years to come.

The Unions on the Defensive

The Callaghan government fell in 1979, paving the way for the Thatcher years. This was to be an era when control of the unions was established as an early priority, with the Tories' 'winter of discontent' demonology articulating a newfound public sentiment: the unions were too powerful, too undemocratic, they had to be tamed. Now, legislation assumed a new significance because of its objective of controlling the trade unions. Although industrial relations legislation had no more specific effect on the NHS than any other sector, the health service trade unions were subject to both the confusion and constraints caused by the new measures. Trade unions had not become accustomed to having things all their own way but had resisted much in the way of restrictive legislation; having previously benefited from a series of Acts, this was a new experience. Acts such as the Employment Protection Act 1975, the Trade Union and Labour Relations Acts of 1974 and 1976, the Health and Safety at Work Act 1974 and legislation against sex and race discrimination gave new rights to staff and their representatives, with the latter having an increasingly active role to play, particularly with health and safety legislation, where representatives could initiate action that had a basis in specific legislation.

But none of this affected health workers uniquely: these were changes happening throughout the Labour movement. Similarly, despite the massive campaign from the trade union movement against Ted Heath's Industrial Relations Act 1970, perhaps the most significant thing for health service unions was COHSE's expulsion from the TUC after it complied with the legislation and registered as a trade union. Although later readmitted, much short term damage was done, both in terms of its reputation within the movement and internal divisions. Nonetheless, none of this compared with the legislative onslaught the unions faced under Thatcher; ballots, picketing, secondary industrial action, political funds, closed shops, all of these and much more came under the scrutiny of successive ministers. As the unions adjusted to one set of changes, another proceeded hot on their heels. For professional organisations such as the RCN, almost all were insignificant, leaving them free to develop organisationally.

One of the clear changes to emerge in the Thatcher years was the refusal to implement any official incomes policy – anathema to a government determined to see the workings of the market dominate – although it consistently attempted to hold down health workers' pay below the level of inflation. However, an independent pay review body for nurses and midwives as well as professional and technical staff was set up following the 1982 pay dispute (Plate XIV). Until 1988 it was to be the longest and most bitter pay dispute nurses had been involved in in the NHS, although it was more comprehensive, involving nurses from all parts of the country coming together in co-ordinated national campaigns.

It ran for eight months and highlighted the great strength of the health service unions but also their weakness. It also represented the deep resentment of many at what was being done to the trade union movement and the injustices being meted out to trade unionists and employees under the new administration. No one could represent that sense of outrage more than the country's nurses and health workers; thousands rallied to their cause as it became a fight not only for those seeking an improved pay offer but also those who saw nothing good in the new repressive and divisive trade union legislation. A march through London's streets in September, when the campaign reached its height, attracted over 120 000. The editorial from the *Nursing Mirror*, whose journalists stopped work for two hours in support of the nurses, demonstrated the excitement and expectancy – but also the anxieties – of the period:

> The wave of sympathy from the TUC at this time, when trade union leaders risk jail sentences under the 1980 Employment Act, which outlaws solidarity action, cannot fail to warm any nurse's heart.
>
> These are stirring times. Who said the nurses have no industrial muscle? The RCN leadership – traditionally arch moderates – must view the developments with mixed feelings. It has conjured up a genie it would dearly like to send back into the bottle. (*Nursing Mirror*, 8.9.1982).

Despite all of this, the unions had been unable to decide with any ease on a coherent strategy. Some NHS unions were unwilling to take part in the action at all and a major problem was that unions representing very few NHS staff had an equal say with those with the vast majority of members. Again, the leaders' tactics and demands were more conservative than those wanted by large sections of their members (Lister, 1988 and Carpenter, 1988). After a period of unity there developed a clear and marked disagreement between the TUC affiliated trade unions and the professional associations, notably the RCN, which had voted not to join the TUC itself only three years earlier. Trevor Clay, the College's general secretary, was in favour of negotiating with the government, an option rejected outright by the TUC affiliates (*Nursing Mirror*, 22.9.1982) and after RCN members had rejected the government's offer in two separate postal ballots (*Nursing Mirror*, 14.7.1982 and 1.9.1982).

The RCN, however, held the balance of power on the Nurses' and Midwives' Whitley Council, which the government exploited to great effect and eventually split off the College. It made it inevitable that the nurses would then have to settle, with the promise of the review body and a two year deal. The dispute eventually came to a messy end with a revised offer from the government, greater than that originally put forward but short of the unions' demand of 12% (Salvage, 1985).

This could be seen as a failure for COHSE, which stuck out for its original demand right up to the point when it had to reluctantly recommend acceptance of something less. Although 1982 saw nurses in hospitals and branches able to organise action for themselves and a level of activity that was sustained for several months before it started to flag, many COHSE activists argued that defeat came only because of a lack of a clear national strategy. The more flexible approach of the RCN, their willingness to be seen to negotiate and pave the way to a settlement that many nurses wanted, made it easier for them to portray themselves as being in control of events, the architects of victory, particularly claiming the pay review body as their achievement, a claim supported by the Tories and Margaret Thatcher herself.

The militancy of the ancillaries in the 1970s had not been forgotten and a determined government was imposing change on the NHS on a number of fronts. Ancillary workers particularly felt the brunt of policy changes as their services were commercialised and sold off to private contractors. The unions' vain attempts to fight back only emphasised their lack of power and failed to carry the support of the majority of nurses. By October 1984 two thirds of domestic, catering and laundry contracts put out to tender had been awarded to private firms (Lyall, 1986) and by 1988 it was estimated that the NHS ancillary workforce had been reduced by

40 000, most of whom had been trade union members. Only the RCN's membership was consistently climbing amidst generalised accusations that trade unions were oldfashioned and out of step with their membership being echoed by those in the health service.

The RCN's steady increase was all the more remarkable a phenomenon because of the decline of the TUC affiliated unions' membership, COHSE included. Looking at the respective nurse membership for the two organisations from the vantage point of the 1990s it might seem hard to believe that COHSE had more nurse members in the early 1970s than the RCN. However, it reached its peak in the early 1980s as a result of the 1982 dispute and was battling constantly to arrest the decline after that, struggling to keep its numbers over the 200 000 level. The College, meanwhile, could play up its relationship with a government that was so openly and overtly hostile to the unions, claiming that it was in a position to protect nursing by maintaining a positive dialogue with ministers and the Department. Indeed, they were able, annually, to invite a Conservative Health Minister to their conference as proof of their influence, something COHSE could not do even if it wanted to. Moreover, the RCN's centrist stance suited the mood of the 1980s after the confrontations of 1978–9 and 1982. Membership was undemanding; at a time when consumerism and the ability to offer a service were being touted as basic necessities in any organisation, they were actually able to make great play of the range of services they offered, from professional indemnity to one of the best nursing libraries in the country, as well as a range of professional groups that were open to the career-minded nurse.

The overall shift to the right in Britain's politics necessarily included nurses and after 1982 calls for action against government policy were largely to fall on deaf ears for a further six years. The position of political acquiescence to, even if not the wholehearted support of, the Tories was the position of the majority of nurses who followed the drift away from trade unions seen in other occupational groups. In 1983 42% of nurses were estimated as having voted Conservative, with 36% polling in favour of Labour and 20% for the Alliance. This was slightly more for Labour than the overall electorate, less for the Tories, but was still a marked trend away from any radicalism. In 1986, polls showed a swing back to Labour amongst nurses, rising to 40%, with the Conservatives dropping to 27%, the same result as for the Alliance. These changes were more extreme variations than were expressed generally, although there was actually a Conservative majority amongst nurses in the central England regions. The NHS featured as the most prominent factor in determining voting patterns. There was also a massive majority against strike action – 75% to 17% – although a slim majority said they would support other forms of industrial action, 45% to 40% (*Nursing Times*, 8.10.1986).

The RCN also had a popular leader in Trevor Clay, who took over in 1982. He firmly stamped his own personality on the organisation, leading in the most visible manner possible, and rarely was any other full-time officer of the College directly quoted in articles or features. He was adept at putting a positive spin on the fact that the College would not take industrial action on any issue, while using his tactical skills to develop a political lobby that brought the RCN even more access to the corridors of power in Westminster and Whitehall (*Nursing Times*, 13.7.1988). Continuing to present the College as the voice of nursing, he also had a platform for almost anything he wanted to say on the subject, but knew how to exploit it and use it to its greatest effect. More than anything else, Clay was able to articulate the mood of the majority of nurses at a time when there were no high profile alternatives and when the health service unions were putting forward unsuccessful policies and were visibly in retreat.

The Pay Review Body

Trevor Clay had taken a lot of personal credit for what was trumpeted as the RCN's greatest achievement of the period, a pay review body for nurses, midwives and health visitors – the same mechanism as determined pay for doctors. This was the reward for their efforts at negotiation and persuasion as opposed to confrontation and extremism, a claim backed by the government, which initially sought to exclude from the PRB's recommendations any unions which took industrial action (Salvage, 1985: pp. 142–3). Submitting evidence to the PRB was a major change for the unions. No longer were their national officers engaged in face-to-face negotiations with DHSS officials, able to consult with their National Executive Committees or, in extreme cases, wider membership; they were bound to a system where they had to pre-pare an evidential submission to the independent review body, usually seeking a specific percentage increase, knowing that the DHSS would be doing the same – except their arguments would be based on holding nurses' salaries down. This would be fol-lowed up by providing oral evidence, then awaiting the decision of the PRB, although the government made it clear they would not be bound by its recommendations and frequently refused to implement them in full or fund the awards in their entirety, leav-ing many nurses feeling embittered and disempowered by the pro-cess (Samuels, 1984 and Ganz, 1985). Although the RCN's members were apparently satisfied with the process, if not always happy with the results, regular calls were made at COHSE confer-ences for withdrawal from the PRB, albeit always heavily defeat-ed. Both David Williams, COHSE's general secretary, and his successor, Hector MacKenzie, argued in favour of the review body, pointing out that it had given nurses better pay rises than could have been negotiated through the Whitley system (*Nursing Times*, 29.1.1986 and Vousden, 1986).

One defeat for the RCN with the PRB had been their attempts to exclude untrained nurses from its remit. The purpose of keep-ing nursing auxilaries out was twofold; firstly, it promoted the notion of improving the status of trained nurses by separating them from their untrained colleagues. Secondly, it raised the pos-sibility that the PRB, looking at the case for a smaller staff group, would be encouraged to recommend higher awards. Nonetheless, in the teeth of strong opposition from the TUC affiliates, the gov-ernment kept the two groups together although it was agreed that the PRB could make separate recommendations, something that was never popular with the lower paid, untrained workforce. Nonetheless, in terms of its profile within nursing, the workings of the PRB were not of particular interest and the RCN's original position and failure to secure it did not damage them.

For COHSE, as with so many other TUC affiliates, struggles often waged outside its direct sphere of influence had inevitable repercussions as particular unions either confronted the government directly or became embroiled in issues that symbolised the struggle between the labour force and hostile employers. It was a characteristic of such confrontations in the early 1980s that the government would often be lending barely visible support to the employer or the latter would be using one of the pieces of recent trade union legislation. On occasions it was a mixture of both. Bitter disputes at Warrington and Wapping saw Eddie Shah, firstly, use the government's legislation against the print unions as he introduced new technology and non-unionised labour, followed by Rupert Murdoch's News International, which used it to effectively break the power of the two main print unions, SOGAT and the NGA, some of whose members in the Fleet Street end of the newspaper industry enjoyed, perhaps, the most favourable terms and conditions of almost any group of workers in the country. Other unions, including that of the once all-powerful dockers, staggered in their resistance against further legislative changes in their already weakened industries; those such as the steel workers and shipbuilders appealed vainly for government assistance as they saw their industries almost disappear with the loss of hundreds of thousands of jobs.

Having inherited an unemployment level of little over 1 million in 1979, the Conservatives presided over record rises, hitting 2.5 million in 1981, rising to 3.6 million jobless within a further four years, with approximately 20% of manufacturing industry lost. 1984 saw Britain's balance of payments record go into the red, with imports exceeding exports for the first time since the Industrial Revolution. But one event dominated the political and industrial landscape of the mid 1980s more than anything. It was the miners' strike. A year long, it brought Britain as close to 'open class war' as it ever had been since 1926. It split the nation, ebbed and flowed as the government came close to economic and political disaster before a steady return to work gradually undermined a union that did not command enough support from either the TUC or Labour party, despite the efforts of thousands of rank and file workers, many nurses included, across the country.

The defeat of the National Union of Mineworkers (NUM) had many implications for the trade unions. First and foremost, it had exploded the myth of trade union solidarity; the spectre of sequestration raised its terrifying head when the NUM's funds were frozen by the courts after the union defied its rulings; in fact, almost every aspect of the Thatcher government's trade union legislation had been used on them, with thousands of its members arrested for breaking the new laws on picketing; the radical tactics and political arguments of the miners' leaders, notably Arthur Scargill, had become increasingly out of tune with the miners returning to work and, more than anything, the vanguard of Britain's trade unions had been worn down, almost starved into submission. They had taken on the might of the British political establishment and lost (Morgan, 1992: pp. 473–4). The message was clear for many in the trade union movement: if the miners could not win, nobody could. Certainly, this became the coded message from the leadership of the health service unions. Survival, rather than pushing forward, became a key concern, waiting for the election of a Labour government that would restore their lost fortunes and influence, removing much of the legislation that was smothering any attempts they believed they could make to resist.

There were further parallels and points of interest for the health service with the miners' strike, however. For it was not in any way a straightforward industrial relations issue; it was deeply political. Its backdrop was not only an argument about the role of trade unions and their relationship to politics but also about more nebulous notions such as the value of communities, whether or not government was powerless in the face of market forces and about the right to work. Should every industry only operate according to how much profit it could achieve shorn of government investment and a long term, strategic view? It raised questions on the long term cost effectiveness of deciding, as a matter of policy, to withdraw investment in an industry, recognising that this would lead to unemployment and then having a shrinking workforce trying to support an expanding number of people requiring welfare benefits. Much was lost with the defeat of the miners. It appeared that market forces were to reign supreme and that society was shifting fundamentally, with the individual – the consumer – taking precedence over the collective. These were all issues that were to assume great significance for those in the health service in the late 1980s as the consumer oriented reforms of the White Paper, *Working for Patients* were put forward. Moreover, the disorienting effect on the NUM of the arrival of the Union of Democratic

Mineworkers–non–TUC affiliated, opposed to strike action and seeking a concilliatory relationship with government and clearly being favoured by Mrs Thatcher and her Cabinet – mirrored, to an extent, the problems faced by COHSE in relation to the RCN.

Who's in Charge?

Ironically, earlier governments' fears about how strongly they might become associated with 'the employers' if they became directly involved in policy making for the NHS, particularly around the issue of nurses' pay, could be said to have been borne out by events in the NHS, despite the presence of local administrators and then managers. For nurses, the matron may have been seen as the person in total control, even if enormous power was vested in medical staff and the administrators had the responsibility of overseeing the running of the service as a whole. But the jealously guarded authority and control of the matron was dissipated by reorganisation and modernisation, which created buffers in the hierarchy between the most senior nurses and ward sisters. The decision making process on any number of policies was not readily identifiable and the sense of ownership was not held at a localised level. On issues to do with the terms and conditions of nursing staff and other health workers, managers were seen to be powerless, particularly regarding pay. Even when management side representatives from the Whitley Councils made statements they were quickly rejoined by Health Ministers while it became commonplace for union officials and staff representatives to consistently attack the government, blaming them on issues of industrial relations that many would have thought were – or should have been – far more the province of managers. The question of who was actually in charge was one that vexed more than Sir Roy Griffiths when he was asked to investigate NHS management in 1983.

Safe in Their Hands?

The Thatcher government was consistently vulnerable on its policy towards the NHS, resulting in the Prime Minister being forced into making the now famous assertion that 'The NHS is safe in our hands' at the Conservatives' 1982 party conference. The public perception, fuelled particularly by clinicians and the unions, was that the service was being starved of cash and the public made clear their willingness to pay increased taxes to ensure that the NHS was improved in poll after poll except, arguably, the poll that really counted – the general election – although welfare provision is rarely the single most important voting issue for the electorate (Taylor Gooby, 1986: p. 229). The public saw the NHS as a 'good' service and concern expressed was more often about resource levels than standards of care or lack of consumer participation. But the Conservatives had taken power at a time when spending on health had reached its peak, 6.1% of gross national product. The annual budget for 1980 was £11.875 billion. The largest proportion of this was being spent on staffing costs, estimated at 70%, with nurses making up 36% of the workforce, having risen in numbers from 137 000 in 1948 to 350 000. The number of hospital consultants had trebled and, with them, NHS spending on hospitals had risen from 54.9% to 62.7% of the total health service budget, despite consistent government priorities to shift it towards the community and, in particular, the 'Cinderella' services of learning difficulties, mental health and elderly care (Lister, 1988). The birth rate had fallen; life expectancy had increased. But could these be attributed to the success of the NHS? Hundreds of thousands of people were now being treated each year and medical advances were allowing ever more sophisticated techniques to be used to extend patients' lives. But to what effect? And was it the best use of a country's limited resources? Whatever its abstract popularity with people generally, intellectual criticism of the NHS was not new, particularly from radical left wing thinkers who accused it of failing to fulfil its promise as a socialist health care system. Criticism did not stop at the kind of service being provided and how that service was organised and run. It extended to those providing it, both in terms of the allegedly self-interested professionals and trade unionists placing material reward for themselves before the interests of the patient. Those voices from the Left had been joined in the latter part of the 1970s by other, harsher critics. Here, however, was a government prepared not only to listen but also to act. Nurses were not to escape its attention.

Chapter 4

All for one?
The RCN and COHSE. A study in contrast

Table 4.1   Relevant Dates

Royal College of Nursing	Confederation of Health Service Employees
1834	*Poor Law (Amendment) Act*
1902	*Midwives Act (England and Wales)*
1907	*Notification of Births Act*
1910	National Asylum Workers' Union formed (NAWU)
1911	*National Insurance Act*
1914	NAWU affiliates to the Labour Party
1915	*Midwives Act (Scotland)*
1916 The College of Nursing Ltd founded and began trading	
1918	Poor Law Workers' Trade Union formed (PLWTU)
1919	*Nurses' Registration Acts*
1919	Joint Conciliation Committee established between NAWU and employers
1920 Free legal service started	

Table 4.1 *continued*

Royal College of Nursing	Confederation of Health Service Employees
1920	*First General Nursing Council (GNC) elected*
1922	PLWTU becomes Poor Law Officers' Union (PLOU)
1923 College's library opens	NAWU affiliates to TUC
1925 The College is approved as a training centre by the Minister of Health	
1928 Royal Charter incorporated	Poor Law system ends: PLOU changes name to National Union of County Employees (NUCO)
1929	*Local Government Act*
1930	*Mental Treatment Act*
1931	Mental Treatment Act ends Insane Asylums: NAWU renamed Mental Hospitals and Institutional Workers' Union (MHIWU)
1933	NUCO affiliates to TUC
1937	*Athlone Committee set up*
1937	Guild of Nurses formed within NUCO
1939 The title 'Royal' bestowed on the College by King George VI	NUCO becomes the Hospitals and Welfare Services Union (HWSU)
1943	*Nurses' Act – heralds arrival of enrolled nurse*
1946	*National Health Service Act*
1946 RCN granted its own coat of arms	MHIWU and HWSU merge to form Confederation of Health Service Employees (COHSE)

Table 4.1   *continued*

Royal College of Nursing	Confederation of Health Service Employees
1948	*Inception of National Health Sevice*
1959	*Mental Health Act*
1960 All registered nurses allowed to become members, including men	
1968 Membership opened to students	
1970 Admits enrolled nurses and pupils	
1971	*Heath government's Industrial Relations Act*
1971 Beginning of steward scheme	
1972	*The Briggs Report*
1972	Expelled from TUC after complying with 1971 Industrial Relations Act
1973	*NHS Reorganisation Act*
1974	*Trade Union and Labour Relations Act*
1974	*Health & Service Act*
1974	*Halsbury Report*
1974	Rejoins TUC
1977 Registers as a certified, independent trade union	
1978 Health and safety reps appointed for the first time	
1979	*Nurses, Midwives and Health Visitors Act*

Table 4.1 *continued*

Royal College of Nursing	Confederation of Health Service Employees
1979 AGM votes against affiliating to TUC	
1980	*The Clegg Commission*
1983	*Pay review body established*
1983	*The Griffiths Report*
1984 Regional structure introduced	
1985	Members vote overwhelmingly to retain Union's political fund
1988	*New clinical grading structure introduced*
1989	*Working for Patients*
1989 Bid to introduce elections for post of general secretary defeated at Congress	Conference vote to explore merger with sympathetic unions
1990 RCN's Students' Association links up with National Union of Students with the arrival of Project 2000	
1992 BBC TV begins showing 'RCN Nursing Update' as part of educational package on nursing	Membership votes to merge with NALGO and NUPE to form UNISON
1993	COHSE ends as UNISON is formed

NB: In addition to those Nurses Registration Acts and Trade Union Acts listed, there have been numerous amendments and new Acts, some of which are referred to in the wider text.

A Tale of Two Cities

20 Cavendish Square, formerly the London home of Prime Minister Herbert Asquith, is a rather grand looking building, tucked into one of the many central London squares leading away from the Oxford Circus area. It was part of a £500 000 'gift' for the purchase of that and adjacent properties and building work to create the current headquarters of the RCN, from Lady Cowdray, an early supporter of the College, who was literally persuaded to part with her money during a taxi journey to Victoria Station (Bowman, 1967: p. 72). Although the square is now, in part, dominated by the hustle and bustle of big West End shops and cafes, in its Edwardian heyday it would have been imposing, almost regal, more than a suitable home for a Royal College.

Entering the building, obvious concessions have been made to the modern era, with security cameras, pass systems and polite but firm receptionists who control a busy area with great efficiency as visitors of all sorts file through on a frequent basis. The walls are adorned with classical murals and photographs of visiting royalty. With its small conference facilities, in almost constant use for educational courses,, dining rooms and one of the most comprehensive nursing libraries anywhere in the country, it is more than a headquarters for an organisation employing relatively few people; it is more than a centre for a nursing organisation with over 3 000 000 members. It is somewhere that the 'ordinary' member, in no way active within the College, can visit and identify with (although in reality most of its daily visitors would be from London hospitals, mostly the teaching hospitals). It carries an eclectic air of academic centre, functional business premises and ancestral home, at once anachronistic and modern. Perhaps the only people looking slightly out of place are its smartly suited officials – mostly men.

Contrast this with the Surrey head office of COHSE, suburban, neat, with only a small plaque outside on a wall by the door to separate it from the other anonymous small business offices surrounding it. There is a visitors book in the reception area, mostly signed by full-time officials from COHSE or other trade unions. It is not the sort of place most members would even be able to find, let alone visit. The single receptionist-cum-switchboard operator is friendly and on first name terms with most people going in and out. Security is clearly not a major problem. The only references to the organisation's tradition are two plaques citing the union's presidents and general secretaries. At first glance it could be home to almost any small British company, selling any one of a variety of commodities. There are no services of immediate benefit or availability to members located in the building and from anywhere but the local area, it is not easily accessible. With little available space, its staff work hard in small offices but its main business, in terms of meetings for its lay bodies such as the National Executive Committee and its subcommittees, is conducted in anonymous central London hotel conference rooms.

If it is hard to project an image for nurses collectively, it is all the more difficult to do so for a wider group of health workers. How can a union project an image of an ancillary worker in relation to a nurse? With members in virtually every occupational group in the health services, highlighting the image of one group of workers would almost always be at the expense of another. The possibility of developing a clear, homogeneous image easily communicated to both health workers and public alike was to be one of continuing difficulty. Publicity and recruitment material became 'group focused', seeking new members from a particular discipline, with photographs and text aimed at the particular concerns of the target group as well as more general material about pay and conditions or cuts in services. Perhaps, also, the difficulty projecting a homogeneous image reflected a wider lack of a clear identity for COHSE. Was it a combination of a professional nurses' organisation and industrial type trade union? In which direction did its best interests lie? In the mid 1980s, as more and more health care started to be hived off into non-NHS services, whether back to local authorities or into the private or voluntary sectors, it started calling itself the health *care* union, losing its identification with the health service solely. But the consistent problem was how to be all things to all members, especially when nurses' aspirations might not be the same as those of the laboratory technician or the porter.

Nurses themselves seem to be reasonably consistent in identifying reasons for joining each organisation: the RCN is 'for nurses', and stands for professional issues while those joining COHSE perceive it as an 'act of solidarity' with their colleagues – although these are usually nursing colleagues. In areas outside general hospitals, that solidarity will run 'through the ranks', from untrained nurse to charge nurse – often including nurse managers. Membership of unions changes from grade to grade far more in general nursing. (Bellaby & Oribor, 1980: pp. 152–68). The RCN is also seen as an organisation for *senior* nurses (Smith, 1982 and Mackay, 1989). This undoubtedly does influence the way junior nurses make decisions about membership of a nurses' organisation, particularly when those in senior positions wear their RCN membership on their sleeve and display varying degrees of antipathy towards trade unions – it can be a good incentive to joining a professional association (Bellaby & Oribor, 1980: p. 158). Some nurses will join a trade union because it is affiliated to the Labour party and TUC or because of previously held commitments to a trade union, but these are relatively few.

A study of why nurses join different organisations, reported on in October 1991, revealed much the same but also highlighted the importance of nurse tutors and teaching staff in shaping the decisions about trade union membership of students, particularly those who joined the RCN. Notably, it also confirmed that a significant number of nurses changed from either NUPE or COHSE to the RCN when they became tutors, with the RCN gaining by as much as 20%, taking their membership of the sample group to over 75% (COHSE, 1991). The age-old pull of the matron or senior figure as a role model or dominant figure in trade union recruitment has already been noted. A nurses' organisation that dominates the senior echelons in a service that places so much stress on loyalty and obedience can thus be seen as being in a prime position to continually reproduce itself.

The image of the RCN as an organisation 'for nurses' perhaps sums up nursing's problem, then. The inevitable question is whether this means all nurses or not. In some ways, their problem is a more refined, discrete one than that faced by COHSE: one group of nurses can only be favoured at the expense of another. Certainly, the RCN *is* for hospital nurses, especially those working in acute settings, even more so in the larger teaching hospitals. And this dominance would run from top to bottom, with senior nurse managers, as well as most nurses in even more senior positions, leading the membership, followed by the large majority of ward based trained staff and students. But if that part of the membership dominates the structures and decision making of the College, this only reflects the wider divisions and conflicts between differing nursing groups. To some extent, the College can surmount this by having specific specialist groups, of which there are 67, with conferences, seminars and courses focusing on special interests. Its educational wing even takes in advanced nursing practice. It also has what, in these organisationally focused times, might have been called a 'mission statement', that outlines its core values, aims and objectives. These are contained in documents like the Royal Charter, very much concentrating on promoting the 'science and art of nursing', the 'advance of nursing as a profession' and the 'professional standing and interests and interests of members of the nursing profession'.

Remember Your Roots

Of course, each organisation's image is, at least, partly bound up with its origins. That the RCN came out of the voluntary hospitals, as an initiative from those in the most senior positions, is a legacy that has not been lost. The original thrust of those involved, to win the battle for registration and get nursing established on a fully professionalised footing, again is not only reflected in the Royal Charter but also in how the organisation projects itself today. So intimately does it tie itself in with the professional voice of nursing that some outsiders could easily confuse the College with nursing's actual professional bodies.

As has been described earlier, the provision and, particularly, the organisation of nursing services during the early stages of World War One were chaotic, at a time when nurses were needed on an unprecedented scale and large numbers of untrained nurses were being drafted into voluntary aid detachments (VADs). Many of these were from wealthy backgrounds, although some were previously trained nurses who were returning to work as a consequence of the war and demand for carers. Jealously protective of their relatively newfound trained status, the existing workforce were suspicious of their new colleagues, suspicions deliberately fuelled by Bedford Fenwick's RBNA. The problem was that, on many occasions, with litle training they were working alongside trained nurses and not being distinguished as different, either by the public or doctors (Abel-Smith, 1960: pp. 85–92). The British Red Cross Society (BRCS), responsible for managing the VADs, sought order from the chaos. The order they sought was in the shape of a new nursing organisation.

The new organisation had three principal founder: Sir Cooper Perry, Medical Superintendent of Guy's Hospital, Dame Sarah Swift, Chief Matron of the BRCS, formerly of Guys, and the Honourable Arthur Stanley. Not only was he chairman of the Joint War Committee of the BRCS and Order of St John, he was seen as being relatively removed from the bitter wrangles there had been around the issue of registration. Stanley wrote to all of the major nurse training schools, proposing the formation of the College of Nursing Ltd and it was founded in April 1916. Its principal objects were promoting better education and training for nurses and uniformity of curriculum; the key parts were, however, setting it up as a body for recognising approved training schools, maintaining a register of trained nurses and promoting bills in Parliament for 'any object connected with the interests of the nursing profession' (Cowie, 1982: pp. 218–20). Based on these principles and with such pre-eminent leaders, both of which offered nurses real status, and the fact that it promised control of the organisation to nurses themselves – albeit nurses of a very senior grade and already in positions of relative power within the training schools – the proposals were accepted and the College born. Moreover, as an added attraction for those being courted and involved in its inception, it had articles which specifically forbade it becoming a trade union. Any idea of amalgamation with the BNA, canvassed at one stage, was virtually doomed from the outset precisely because both organisations harboured similar ambitions, not only for the 'advancement and betterment' of nursing but also to control it. Prolonged conflict was to follow and the feud between the two organisations wrecked any chance there ever was that nursing would ultimately control its own destiny as their respective bills and proposals foundered in the wake of their mutual opposition – a condition perhaps perpetuated by their relative powerlessness.

The College expected to be the registering body and was both disappointed and surprised when the Nurses' Registration Act 1919 made provision for the General Nursing Council of England and Wales. It meant an immediate redefinition of its role and it set off on the path of campaigning for the betterment and advancement of nursing, particularly around issues of training and registration in its early days, rather than being in charge of them.

One of the areas that the College was not interested in expanding into (although it was claiming 13 000 members recruited in the three years from its inception to the Nurses' Registration Act) was the asylums. Moreover, men and asylum workers were excluded from potential membership. The National Asylum Workers' Union was thus allowed unfettered growth amongst part of its potential membership once the Asylum Workers' Association had disappeared. The organisation that came out of the NAWU's early history, with its strong trade union tradition, strongly dominated all of the mergers that were to lead to COHSE's formation in 1946, with the depth of organisation and branch structure being strongest and most unified within the asylums and then mental hospitals. With an instinct for survival shaped by the harshest and most repressive regimes in the early asylums, unequalled anywhere else in the health care services, the NAWU's strength was forged through the long slog of trying to set up structures where they could negotiate with the employers, as did their future colleagues from the Poor Law institutions. Contrast this with an organisation whose leading members did not just have a framework for discussion, but were an integral part of the management of the institution in which they worked. For one of the most profound formative factors for COHSE was its oppositionalist roots, just as the managerialist tradition within the RCN can be directly traced back to its earliest days and founding figures.

It is perhaps ironic that the NAWU was formed by a group of charge nurses in 1910, for its membership was mostly amongst the lowest grade workers, as with all of COHSE's predecessors. Many of its leading figures held relatively junior positions in the health service, at charge nurse level and below. Its oppositionalist culture, common to most trade unions, can thus be more readily understood. Not only did its representatives have to fight to get their voice heard by the employer, they would also be relatively powerless when in the workplace as low paid employees. Their position as 'outsiders' in the decision making process was firmly implanted into the structure, their sense of identification with their fellow members strengthened by this. The demand for democratic participation, equality, opportunities for members and lay officials to have their voice heard were reflections of this, all enshrined in the rule book. This could be interpreted as overly prescriptive, rigid, stultifying and favouring those who know how to manipulate bureaucratic procedures, but its origins were in trying to ensure that the union's internal mechanisms would not favour any particular individual and that those who held positions of seniority were elected through a scrupulous and pristine process as representatives of the majority and would only act on a delegated basis, making their own decisions when clearly mandated to do so, otherwise being bound by policy and procedure or a specific mandate from their branch.

The experience of senior members in the College of Nursing would have been completely different. Within the parameters and constraints of a system that they broadly supported, they were decision makers and held positions of responsibility and relative power. When they wanted change, they had ready access to those with influence. If they did not get what they wanted it was rarely visible as a public defeat and there were almost always consolations from employers who would recognise the value not only of working with the College but also of pacifying senior nursing staff within their own hospital. A managerialist culture meant that there was less emphasis on the democratic structures stipulated by the trade unions and necessary for their development, as is shown by the late adoption of a branch structure and introduction of stewards. In such a tradition, it is more readily accepted that relatively low level decisions can be made by those with the necessary information to hand when they need to be made. Discipline and hierarchy are an integral part of the culture and the identification with the employer and the employer's needs/situation would be much stronger with the senior nursing staff who were often the local representatives or held positions of power within the College. The Salmon Report, in 1966, had introduced a managerial structure into nursing (Bellaby & Oribor, 1980: pp. 168–9). The RCN had been closely involved in lobbying for it, which had had a dual effect: it created a career structure and seduced those nurses interested in management, many of whom were already RCN members or went on to join the College. In increasing substantially the number of nurses involved in managing, it also reinforced that whole aspect of nursing culture, both in the NHS and the RCN. It widened the divisions, however, between clinical and managerialist nurses. So while the mechanisms of control initiated by the grade system were emphasised and strengthened, the tensions and potential for conflict increased.

Differences in the aims and objectives of the RCN and COHSE in their early days also marked out the territory they would occupy, both politically and within the nursing world. With pay and conditions a negative issue for the College, they were tied to certain positions from the outset. It would be impossible to be arguing that status and professional development were more important than improving working conditions and pay and still retain the unquestioning loyalty and membership of those most disadvantaged by that approach. Equally, placing pay and conditions before all else for most of the time would inevitably alienate those nurses loyal to the vocational ideal.

Mirror Image?

For many nurses, attitudes to industrial action could be described as best symbolising the professional organisations and nurses' trade unions. However, there are many paradoxes in a relationship that is, in some respects, symbiotic. Thus the RCN and COHSE were closer than is popularly imagined (and many in their respective organisation would wish to publicly acknowledge) whilst, conversely, the differences run a lot deeper than that one issue.

The popular, stereotypical images of the Confederation and the College were largely representative of the different wings of nurses' organisations. Although NUPE came to be identified most explicitly as the public sector workers' union, with the old 'cloth cap' image and reputation for defending poor and outmoded practices such as overmanning on behalf of low paid, working-class members, COHSE were not that far behind. Male domination was part of the legacy of the late 1920s and 1930s when the union became increasingly conservative within the asylums. A membership that had been largely evenly divided began losing women for a variety of reasons, including inroads into the ranks of female asylum nurses being made by the College. Additionally, as well as bringing previous experience of trade unionism from earlier jobs, any men interested in trade unionism were also precluded by the College of Nursing's decision to exclude men. All of the NAWU's London branch secretaries in 1918 were men; of over 130 COHSE branch secretaries in 1949, only four were women (Walker, 1992). Similarly, at a national level, the union was dominated by men. Only one woman has ever stood as President (and was not elected), there has never been a female general secretary and only two female regional secretaries in COHSE's history. This particular phenomenon in a union that had approximately 80% female membership by the 1970s has undoubtedly affected the way in which it was perceived by its members. It was 1990 before the National Executive Committee achieved a balance of 50% women. Another paradox is that whilst it is a union of largely low paid workers with a significant minority of non-nurses (estimated at approximately 40% in 1985), its leaders were more often from a nursing background, albeit mental health, and often at charge nurse grade and above.

Sherry sipping, middle-class women from the Home Counties complete with twin set and pearls would probably be most COHSE members' caricature of the leaders of the RCN until Trevor Clay's arrival. Although it had doctors in positions of prominence in its early days, as did all of the professional organisations, and was established to mirror the Royal Colleges of the medical profession, it is now perceived as being totally nurse dominated, 'run by nurses for nurses'. Its links with the heart of the establishment could not be more pronounced with the Queen and several other members of the Royal Family as its patrons while its vice presidents contain a duke, several ladys, dames and a countess. The people who have RCN fellowships read like a *Who's Who* of nursing.

Having remained with its completely female membership until

1960, it is less dominated by men, with the majority of its Council members being women and a fairly even split amongst its officers. Yet, while COHSE and other trade unions are moving towards a recognition of the needs of their large female majorities, the RCN remains open to criticisms that it has failed to pay adequate attention to women's issues and the needs of their membership, while more men are gaining positions of seniority in the organisation (Salvage, 1985).

To Affiliate or Not to Affiliate?

The RCN has remained in 'splendid isolation' throughout its history, rejecting any proposals to affiliate with a political party or the TUC. With no readily identifiable political camp in which it would remain and representing more than a quarter of a million nurses, it is not simply a case of an organisation out on its own; rather, it has been wooed with varying degrees of intensity over the years, especially as its membership has exploded since the mid 1970s. From the time when a possible merger with the RBNA was explored there have been obvious links with other professional associations. Proposals that it affiliate to the TUC have always been defeated overwhelmingly. Similarly, the RCN has never sought links with the Labour party and proudly boasts of its cross-party lobbying as one of the means it has of ensuring *greater* political influence than its rivals, something that has been especially pointed during a period when the political landscape has been painted a deeper and deeper blue. The only hiccup came in the mid 1980s when the Conservatives feared that Trevor Clay was close to publicly endorsing the Labour party. Indeed, Labour have consistently encouraged links with the RCN. In one telling moment of apparent insignificance, it demonstrated the importance it attached to this when its NEC, under intense pressure from Neil Kinnock, reversed an earlier decision resulting from a COHSE resolution banning the College from having a stall at the annual Labour party conference because it was not affiliated to the party.

The image of political conservatism that the College carries as – unwelcome for many of their number – baggage is partially accurate, but it is clear that its two parliamentary officers, as well as senior national officials, are able to have greater access to ministers and hold the attention of backbench Tory MPs far more easily than COHSE could ever hope to, even if it had wished to cultivate such avenues. COHSE's parliamentary liaison officer's role was much more straightforward, with responsibility for briefing the MPs COHSE sponsored (each such MP has a small amount of money provided towards their constituency costs and campaigning) and seeking their assistance on issues relevant either to the health service or trade unions, as well as lobbying other Labour Party MPs, particularly those with a health responsibility. This role is not dissimilar to that fulfilled by the RCN officers, but is obviously restricted and lacks the ability to become involved with actual policy shapers. During the Thatcher/Major years the value of COHSE liaising with politicians from a weakened opposition left them with little realistic hope of influencing the policy making process, thus weakening its own position. But this reflects the loyalty and deeply binding ties that hold the Labour movement together, born out of their origins and traditions and an assumption that, ultimately, achieving power is dependent upon a degree of mutuality that has to be preserved. For many in COHSE, expulsion from the TUC after the union complied with Ted Heath's industrial relations legislation when all other trade unions had voted to defy it was close to its nadir. Bernard Morgan, one of the activists leading the struggle to get the union reinstated, struggled out of his sick bed to speak at the 1972 annual conference, but to no avail. It was another year before he was successful in leading the return to the fold, having stated that, 'We have suffered the greatest ignominy and disgrace known to a trade union' (Walker, 1992).

Carrying Nightingale's Lamp in a Hall of Mirrors

The RCN did not just inherit a certain tradition. With its vital role in the development of nursing, particularly in the debates around registration and training, and membership of nurses in key posts such as the matrons from the major teaching hospitals, it was instrumental in forging and promulgating the vocational ideal for the trained, registered nurse. Its historical support of lower wages for students, long hours based around tedious tasks and domestic chores, harsh discipline and mandatory lectures conducted in the nurses' own time was part of a wider philosophy. So was its contribution to the vocational myths that legitimised the harsh regimes, giving nurses a sense of pride in their work and profession, a unity of purpose and continuing with the objective of developing a homogenised workforce, subservient to the medical profession yet loyal to their own hierarchical mistresses. Although Nightingale was already dead when the College of Nursing was established in 1916, the College appropriated the myths and the image built around her, many of which persist to this day. Scutari Publications, named after the site of the field hospital in the Crimea, and Lampada, the stewards' newsletter, are just two tangible examples.

However, internally there were differences of opinion about strategy and direction. These became manifestly clear as the contradictions of the vocational, professional ideal were exposed and insufficient numbers of suitable women and 'good nurses' were able to meet the growing demand for nursing care. Having struggled to get nurse training and registration established as regulatory controls on entry and practice for nurses, the College then had to consider how to deal with the problems this posed, politically, once it was clear that nursing would never survive on the path ploughed for it by the professional organisations and nursing reformers. Mrs Bedford Fenwick finally lacked the political acumen to recognise a way out of the conundrum, despite – or perhaps because of – her aggressive pursuit of the betterment of nursing on behalf of her self-styled elite. But the leaders of the College saw that the uncompromising development of professional standards and commitment to a highly skilled, trained workforce would have to be sacrificed for the 'common good' of the profession. This notion of the 'common good' came from the then Ministry of Health, far more concerned, fundamentally, with ensuring there were enough people available to carry out the necessary nursing tasks and duties as cheaply and efficiently as possibly. In identifying what was necessary they would have taken professional advice, but their relationship with the medical profession was always stronger than with senior nurses and the nurses they had regular contact with were of a particular back-ground and professional outlook, which was largely managerial.

The 'common good' encompassed the Ministry's methods, objectives and political reality; however, as well as being shaped by the politicians, civil servants and doctors involved in making health policy, its prevailing political reality had, in part, been influenced by sections of the College working with it, notably the matrons and generalists. They had, in turn, been locked in debate about standards of care, training and general nursing duties with nurses representing other views and ideas about the future of nurs-ing, particularly the specialists and educationalists and, almost inevitably, those outside a general hospital environment. In align-ing themselves with the Ministry and recognising the real needs of the service and the practical constraints on supplying that service, it was not so much a victory for the RCN but for a significant fac-tion within the RCN. The 'common good', putting the needs of the *service* first, became the accepted political reality of the College and nursing as a whole. That it could be absorbed into the process of myth and the vocational ideal subtly altered to encom-pass this shift was all the more testimony to the political manage-ment skills of the College (White, 1985: pp. 27–33).

The RCN's 'no-strike ruling', Rule 12, can be viewed in this context. The question of industrial action being harmful to patients is, for many nurses, an immediately recognisable notion strongly supported by many, but it can also be seen as being against the 'common good', the good of the service. For any man-ager, even one able to identify serious problems within the service, would not sanction anything that interrupted that service. Problems have to be worked out from within, through discussion or even negotiation, but the needs of the service must prevail and, above all, nurses must remain obedient. Within the RCN it is never expressed thus. Dr June Clark, explaining how her attitudes to limited industrial action changed over a period of time, particu-larly after witnessing action taken by members of other unions, says that, 'What matters is the policy, the attitude, the stance towards industrial action which Rule 12 represents. We need the rule as a means of defining our behaviour but its real importance is symbolic. Rule 12 tells us, and the world, what we stand for' (Clark, 1988). Trevor Clay, the RCN's then general secretary, put it slightly differently: 'We are the Royal College of Nursing, not of nurses' (*Nursing Times* 9.3.1988). The next year, Mr Clay identified one of the problems of any form of industrial action thus:

> We have to be honest and admit that last year many of the protests about funding and about clinical grading made the health service look unmanageable.
>   I warned at the time that such tactics in the long run would be used as an excuse, as they have been, for major reorganisation in the NHS.

Clearly, hidden within the prevailing philosophy was the expectation that disobedience would always be followed by punishment.

Behind the Mask, Behind the Smile

Different traditions and origins, policies and politics mark out the areas of separateness for the RCN and COHSE, for professional organisation and trade union. But there are also, clearly, enormous internal differences if not divisions experienced by the respective members of both organisations. How each of them has dealt with these has, again, been affected by their traditions, with the RCN having a polite system of acknowledging disagreements and debating them whilst COHSE's have, on occasions, exploded into quite ferocious rows at its annual conference. One way that individual nurses resolve their difficulties with the organisation is to leave and join one of its rivals and there is no doubt that there is a regular flow of members back and forth between the two, particularly at times of conflict. A study from Glasgow University in 1988, conducted for COHSE, showed that nurses switched from the RCN to COHSE where the former was seen as remote, with stewards weak or overstretched, and COHSE was seen as a campaigning union or had a strong workplace presence, with effective stewards (COHSE, 1991). Conversely, the issue of industrial action or a perceived militancy in a branch will be factors pushing some nurses from COHSE towards the RCN.

For those who stay within their chosen organisation, however, the road to change is long and arduous. Policy making processes tend to be limited to annual conferences but even getting a resolution passed does not necessarily mean that attitudes and behaviour from the union's membership, or even the organisation itself, will necessarily follow (see below). Each organisation's 'dissidents' are difficult to categorise. Within the RCN they tend to be more concerned with professional issues and how nursing is developing, while COHSE's have been distinctly political. Those with differing professional concerns and the political views that might accompany them are, in part, accommodated by the College's different specialist groups, which break down into representative forums for nurses from almost all clinical, managerial and educational backgrounds. They do not change the way in which the RCN operates or its overall prevailing philosophy or politics, but they offer a voice to those who are principally concerned either with services away from the general hospital or with facets of them.

Apart from the very small minority who are in particular political groupings such as the various Marxist groups, those deviating from the main policy and political thrust of either organisation – if, indeed, they do not compartmentalise their membership in the 'silent majority' cupboard – are usually disorganised. Those with a radical inclination often have a dislike of bureaucratic, hierarchical structures, this being one of the factors inhibiting any attempts at formal alternative organisation. In 1988 this meant that some of the initial, spontaneous protests from COHSE and RCN nurses were rather chaotic, unco-ordinated and, most worrying for the officials of the organisations, impossible to predict or control. Under quieter circumstances, nurses have come together within such loose organisations as the Radical Nurses Group, conducting themselves in non-hierarchical, informal structures. But, inevitably, the weakness that is implied in such a method of coming together has meant that they have been able to have little impact. Nonetheless, the fact that there have been groups of Radical Nurses, Radical Midwives and even Radical Health Visitors all imply that there has long been something lacking for nurses who want something out of the mainstream. For the RCN may carry the label of being 'arch-moderates' (*Nursing Mirror* 8.9.1982) but COHSE has been criticised from a different perspective for being equally conservative within its own parameters and terms of reference. In the early and mid 1980s, however, its leadership adopted a rather unusual approach to lay activists in the internal pressure group, Group 81. This was a broad Left grouping drawn together from across the country, functioning

Plate I The search for the suitable woman: Nurses receive their certificates from Princess Alexandra, Buckingham Palace, 22 July 1904. (Mary Evans Picture Library)

Plate II Refuge for the destitute: The female ward at the Playhouse Yard, London, 1856. (Mary

Plate III A nurse, angelic expression to the fore, collecting money for her hospital: an essential part of the late 19th century nurse's duties. (Mary Evans Picture Library)

Plate IV A critical view of the Poor Law. (Mary Evans Picture Library)

THE WORKHOUSE MRS. GAMP.

Pauper Nurse:—"SORRY TO DISTURB YOU, MUM, BUT THAT CHILD—"
Superintendent:—"OH, BOTHER THE CHILD! IT'S NO USE ITS BEING ILL WHEN I HAVE A FEW FRIENDS TO TEA!"

Plate V　A different view of the early nurses. (Mary Evans Picture Library)

Plate VI   Not the usual image of early nurses, or nursing. Two early district nurses in London, 1877. (Mary Evans Picture Library)

Plate VII   The Poor Law Act was deeply unpopular and often the cause of serious civil unrest. Here, local people attack the Stockport Workhouse in 1842. (Mary Evans Picture Library)

Plate VIII Larbert Asylum, Scotland, 1899. (Mary Evans Picture Library)

Plate IX Nurses in the rest room at Prince of Wales Hospital, London, c.1920. (Mary Evans Picture Library)

Plate X   Mary Seacole, a forgotten heroine. (National Library of Jamaica)

Plate XI The myth lives on: nurses arriving for the funeral of Florence Nightingale at St Paul's Cathedral, 1910. (Mary Evans Picture Library)

Plate XII Where it all started? Florence Nightingale at St Thomas' Hospital, shortly before her death. (Mary Evans Picture Library)

Plate XIII Out from behind the mask – a new image for nurses. A striking nurse from the North Manchester General Hospital, January 1988. (Don McPhee, *The Guardian*)

Plate XIV The thread of consensus snaps. Nurses demonstrating in the 1982 pay dispute. (Gerry Weaser, *The Guardian*)

Plate XV   Nurses united in a common cause and enrolling the support of Bentley Todd on February 3rd 1988 at King's College Hospital. (Gerry Weaser, *The Guardian*)

Plate XVI Breaking free of the vocational myth: Angela Hughes leads the nurses at the Maudsley Hospital, February 2nd, 1988. (E. Hamilton West, *The Guardian*)

Plate XVII   Waiting for change. A nurse campaigning for more pay in 1974 maintains a vigil by the statue of Florence Nightingale. (Hulton Deutsch Collection)

Plate XVIIa The light still shines: nurses at a commemorative service for Florence Nightingale at Westminster Abbey. (Kenneth Saunders)

Plate XVIII Nurses and their work. Staff Nurse Norris from the London Hospital 1953. (Hulton Deutsch Collection)

Plate XIX Carrying a new torch: Staff Nurses Mandy Sharp (L) and Melanie Barlow carry the protest to Downing Street, February 1988. (David Osborn, *The Guardian*)

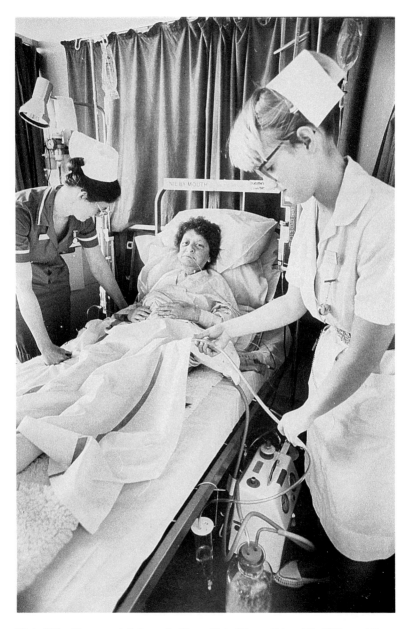

Plate XX Nurses and their work: Sister Clair Gibson (L) and Staff Nurse Alison Brown caring for Mrs Dorothy Coultas at St James Hospital, Leeds. (Don McPhee, *The Guardian*)

Plate XXI Back to the future? Nurses in Trafalgar Square in 1940, ready to raise money for their hospital. Is this where nursing is heading in the 1990s? (Hulton Deutsch Collection)

Plate XXII A challenging image for nurses everywhere, created by artist Mick Ridge and used by COHSE in 1988, shows a nurse leading the struggle to raise the banner of the NHS. Is this an alternative to the recent years of despair?

mainly at the union's delegate conference, aiming to co-ordinate support for what were regarded as 'Left leaning' motions for debate. Some of its early key members, such as Jim Devine from Scotland and Pete Marshall from the West Midlands, went on to be appointed as full-time officers. Others went on to be elected to positions within the union's official structures, including the National Executive Committee (Walker, 1992).

The absorption of malcontents willing to 'work for change from the inside' is a time honoured way of diffusing possible internal conflict. In many respects this is one of the primary functions of any trade union or professional organisation as the bureaucracy's agenda and the organisation's needs – however the organisation's needs are defined, and by whom – take precedence over all else. Some Marxist analysts argue that trade unions work only as an adjunct of the capitalist system, performing a key role of social control by seeking constant political and social reform which softens the harshest excesses of the system, making them tolerable if not acceptable but, in the process, undermining any effective mobilisation and organisation of the working class in the real struggle against capital. As such, whether consciously or not, they are effectively colluding with the employers who seek to use them to keep order in the process of, and diffuse the pressure for, change while acting as a buffer between the harsh demands of the working class and their masters.

Whatever the merits or rights and wrongs of such an analysis, there is little doubt, as shall be seen later, that both the professional organisations and trade unions do act as a buffer to an extent and do diffuse the pressure for change. A key part of that is, naturally enough, achieving enough to keep the majority content and doing enough to keep the malcontents busy, partially satisfied or marginalised.

Internal Policy Making

One of the biggest differences in the internal policy making of the RCN and COHSE is the role of their respective annual conferences. COHSE's was always made up of delegates elected from individual branches, hearing and voting on motions put forward from branches. Its NEC could also place motions before conference. This was relatively rare, apart from amendments to the rule-book, until recent years when the NEC took to placing one or two key policy proposals before the delegates. Conference is regarded as the supreme policy maker of the union, with resolutions passed to be acted on by the NEC and/or the union's officers.

Congress, the RCN's equivalent to COHSE's conference, takes a back seat to the Council as the principal policy maker in the College. The voting membership of the Congress comes from branches and other membership groups. Recommendations as well as motions can be submitted by branches, national membership groups, the Council and its standing committees, the national boards, the UK Stewards' Committee and the general secretary. However, even if passed, these have then to be referred to the Council for further consideration. The Council is also concerned with laying down the broad lines of RCN policy which the general secretary, as the chief executive for the College, is responsible for implementing (RCN Handbook, 1993). Similar policy making processes exist at regional level for both organisations; again, the composition of the regional committees of the RCN is made up from a variety of sources, including professional groups and branches, while COHSE's are delegates sent from branches.

The development of any member led organisation can only occur if there is a structure in which its members can operate, meeting, making decisions and with mechanisms to express themselves collectively. Furthermore, a means of progressing the decisions made by the collective, in such a way that they can influence the organisation as a whole, has to be available. It is this collective process and its expression that is vitally contained in the workings of a local branch of a trade union or professional association. That branches are relatively new to the RCN is a reflection of the changing nature of industrial relations in the NHS. They were introduced as a recognition that, even for a professional association, it was going to be necessary to strengthen itself organisationally at a local level, particularly in the light of the massive increases in membership sustained by their rival trade unions in the 1970s. The College had already recognised that holding a now discredited line on low pay and conditions of service was untenable. They were necessarily moving towards putting improvements in pay and conditions higher up the policy agenda and using them as the focus for campaigns.

The steward system most easily recognisable to nurses today was pioneered by NUPE in the 1960s, quickly followed by other trade unions, including COHSE. It meant that there was a network of recognised branch representatives who could have devolved responsibility, bringing greater trade union accountability and participation to a level much closer to the members. Training programmes were set up for them and they were accorded particular roles, depending on the needs of the branch and workplace. The RCN copied this development in a further strengthening of their industrial relations arm. But whereas COHSE branches were most often based on the workplace, the RCN's were more diffuse, often being based on a geographical area or health authority boundary, encompassing several workplaces. This inevitably led to difficulties of access and, consequentially, participation. Coupled with the nature of the College and its dual role of seeking to advance nursing professionally while concerning itself with industrial relations matters, the type of involvement of its members at branch level was still different to that within an industrial type union like COHSE. With that relationship so different at branch level it then followed that the member's relationship with the organisation as a whole kept a different quality. However, it needs to be remembered that often nurses join different organisations for specific reasons in the first place and are not looking for the same things from them both.

Although the branch structure and steward network now form the hub of the RCN's local organisation, another point where the RCN diverts from the path of the trade unions is the way in which it can make direct approach to the Council, something that is not technically possible within the bureaucratic procedures of a union like COHSE.

Indeed, the RCN Council may be the constitutional governing body, only subservient to the Royal Charter, but one senior official is able to say, 'Council gives the direction but has to be responsive to the needs of the members, as do officers. The power within the RCN comes from the support of the silent majority who let you know if you put one foot out of line'. The implication is that the 'common good' will prevail, that any and every situation will be managed in such a way that the contented majority will not be troubled. But is silence always acquiescence? Is it, in itself, a positive affirmation that members are content? It is a clear message to any vocal minority. The same officer believes that full-time officials have 'a stronger relationship with the members than the (elected) Council has with the members,' and understands where the members want the organisation to go. Other officers in senior positions within the College would acknowledge that they manage it to a large extent, but do so with the best interests of the membership and the RCN itself, guided by its broad principles and the specifics of the Charter, pointing to the difficulties of meeting the needs of the College on a day-to-day basis, particularly in such a rapidly changing political climate, with new service proposals coming out of the Department of Health and NHS Management Executive more frequently than ever. There are those who would decry such an approach to the running of a trade union or professional association, but similar accusations have been levelled at trade unions by activists frustrated at what they see as the union's inability or refusal to accommodate more radical policies, putting the blame squarely on the shoulders of the union's full-time officials and 'leadership'. Perhaps the RCN are simply more honest about how they operate, in the knowledge that their members are more likely to accept such an explanation than trade unionists with more democratic and participatory traditions.

These are, of course, serious issues about how an organisation 1/4 million strong can and should respond to rapid policy shifts on the part of government or the employers, particularly when the supreme policy making body of the union – its delegate conference – meets annually and the NEC only come together every three months. As shall be seen in the case studies, on clinical grading particularly, COHSE paid dearly for the resulting policy and decision making vacuum that was a direct result of such structures.

Moving with the Times

To a large extent, the College has enjoyed organisational stability throughout its history. There have been small scale mergers, more akin to takeovers, with groups such as the National Council of

Nurses (Bowman, 1967: p. 156). But they have plotted a steady course throughout their history, even while developing new parts to the organisation.

Conversely, COHSE has a history that, in many respects, mirrors the development of health care services, with mergers occurring at times of significant reorganisations of services. Thus the NAWU rechristened itself (albeit after its conference had once voted to retain the title of asylum workers following an Act of Parliament which renamed the asylums as mental illness hospitals!); it then went on to merge with the Poor Law Officers Union when the existence of the miserable Poor Law system was finally brought to an end. COHSE itself, bringing together health care workers from voluntary hospitals and local authority services, preceded the NHS only by two years. Ironically, as health care services have been broken up again, with local authorities taking on community care responsibilities and the voluntary/independent sector assuming a greater and greater role, 1993 saw COHSE join in a merger with one of its fiercest competitor unions, NUPE, as well as the other union with the largest share of local government membership, NALGO. This was not done solely out of any great sense of comradeship or desire to unite the workers of the world. More, for COHSE with its gradually shrinking membership taking it down the trade union league table into the small union section, it came from a recognition that, alone, they faced the threat of going the way that many others have – into extinction. This is as true as it has ever been in a period as hostile to the fortunes of trade unions as the 1990s.

The three partner unions were all struggling to stem the steady haemorrhage of members, either through job losses in their respective services, competition with other unions or people lost to the union movement altogether. Of these three causes, job losses are by far the most significant. 172 177 whole time equivalent (WTE) ancillary workers in 1979 were reduced to 107 619 by 1988. These NHS losses were echoed in local government for NUPE and NALGO as privatisation of services took people not only out of public sector employment but also trade union membership. The natural consequence of loss of membership is loss of income, even more difficult to sustain at a time when each union's infrastructure was more complex and costly than ever, with members being given the expectation of receiving more and better services than ever before as each of the unions were brought, helter skelter, into responding to the demands of what was, ironically, the Thatcherite inspired age of consumerism.

COHSE had had much to do during the 1980s to modernise itself. The period since its inception had seen it enjoy mixed fortunes, with its early success being followed by a fallow period during the late 1950s and 1960s. The explosion of radicalism experienced by almost all of the public sector unions in the 1970s had turned sour in 1979 and COHSE was facing a government whose hostility was unprecedented. This was not simply because COHSE was a trade union; it stemmed from a political philosophy that was opposed to the principle and practice of publicly provided welfare provision and deep suspicion of professions busy, as the government interpreted it, protecting vested interests expressed under the smokescreen of 'professional concern.'

Within nursing, COHSE also had other problems. Its base in psychiatric hospitals had begun to erode as the larger institutions emptied out as a result of the changes brought about by the 1959 Mental Health Act and effects of widespread use of phenothiazine medication on patients with psychotic type disorders. More and more people were being discharged into the community who would otherwise have occupied a bed in hospital for years at a time. Imagewise it had also been damaged by its involvement in representing nursing staff on the wrong side of a number of high profile scandals.

Between 1968 and 1981 there were 24 major public inquiries into allegations of abuse and/or ill treatment of patients at mental illness and mental handicap hospitals throughout the country. The allegations ranged from petty pilfering to systematic misuse and stealing of money from patients, from minor acts of intimidation to gross acts of ill treatment and cruelty. Incidents investigated included a series of deaths by suicide of patients at Warlingham Park and the deaths of individual patients at other hospitals (Beardshaw, 1981: pp. 84–9). Inevitably, at times like those, individual nurses facing potentially damaging allegations would turn to their union and, in many cases, that was COHSE. It was not only COHSE's duty to represent its members in such situations. Their individual predicament reflected a wider reality of a union, a large number of whose members were working in an outmoded service where the staff were still defending nursing practices that were clearly not only better left behind but also were often damaging to the patients. In part at least, Albert Spanswick's vigorous defence of nurses facing allegations of cruelty towards patients following the publication of *Sans Everything* (Robb, 1967) in 1967 won him the close run election for the post of assistant general secretary (Carpenter, 1988: p. 332)

Of course, it was not simply a case of bad nurses; far more it was a sorry tale of badly administered services, with *laissez faire* management at best or, at worst, a system that condoned if not actively encouraged harsh regimes at ward level. Too often, nurses were working on overcrowded, understaffed wards where no money had been spent on improving poor environments that still bore all the hallmarks of their Victorian origins. Psychiatric nurses were still being trained very much in the medical model, with little experience of developing therapeutic interventions specifically of a nursing nature. Most nursing care being initiated was unplanned and unco-ordinated. As it had been for decades, the large part of the nurses' role was custodial, with the most significant change being their responsibility for administering an increasing number of prescribed medicines.

An important part of COHSE's defence was about the environmental factors and poor working conditions the nurses faced, but critics pointed to better standards in other hospitals where external factors were apparently no different. Criticism was also made of the lack of support given to the nurses making the allegations, who were often COHSE members themselves. It was not rare for complainants and staff supporting their allegations to face intimidation, veiled threats and, on occasions, actual violence from their colleagues. The climate was such in a number of hospitals that nurses would stay silent rather than risk the consequences of making formal complaints (Beardshaw, 1981). Olleste Weston and Brian Ankers, for instance, only made public allegations about conditions at St Augustine's Hospital after being ridiculed and victimised by their own management. However, in the ensuing inquiry many of the nurses offering supportive evidence were intimidated. The situation at St Augustine's was not dissimilar from a number of other inquiries in that some of the nurses being investigated were either COHSE branch officials or ex officials, an added complication for the union. Equally, COHSE branches, and individuals such as Vic Palma, branch secretary at Brookwood Hospital, may have been vindicated by a UKCC report that found they had little alternative but to take industrial action as and when they did, but this was often away from the glare of the earlier publicity when they were being condemned.

COHSE were also right to point up the injustice of scapegoating individual nurses rather than acknowledging the structural deficiencies of anachronistic, underfunded, understaffed mental health services. But the spate of inquiries were, as much as anything, about the outside world finally getting a peek into the asylums. Many nurses, seeing their own image refracted through a different light, did not like what they saw. It was the end of an era.

The process of reform was recognised by COHSE and the Mallinson Report (COHSE, 1983) attempted to articulate this. However it is read today, and it is judged quite harshly by some COHSE insiders, the Mallinson Report into mental health services was quite influential in its time. Put together by full-time officials, senior lay activists and members working in the field, it looked at community care provision, offering a critique of government policy and, importantly, what it considered as policy options for the future. As such it was to be the starting point for similar projects over the next decade. It may have borne, in its final version, more of the stamp of the full-time officers and been too medically oriented and institution led than many would have wished but it was an important development away from the difficulties of the previous decade.

From this it was, then, a remarkable transformation for Bob Abberley, COHSE national officer, to be quoted saying, 'We should be seen as an organisation that fights for the rights of people who use our services, as well as for members' (Vousden, 1989: p. 18). Publications such as *Future Services for People with Learning Difficulties* embraced normalisation, and included a number of radical proposals, inluding an end to the RMNH. Links were established with user groups like MIND, MENCAP, Survivors Speak Out and others, which have culminated in publications such as *User Empowerment in Mental Health Services,* which in Hector MacKenzie's introduction, acknowledges the less than creditable aspects of COHSE's past.

COHSE set up a professional officer's post, with the responsibility of developing both professional services and giving the union a profile on clinical and professional issues. One post soon grew into two and eventually saw the launch of COHSE's own specialist advisory groups (Simon, 1992: p. 18), but in reality it was never going to be able to compete with the RCN on their home ground and the College continued to dominate on almost all professional issues. Nonetheless, this shift in emphasis, almost as an investment for the future, was significant as the number of nurse members grew as a proportion of the union. General Secretary Hector MacKenzie understood the necessity of recruiting nursing members for COHSE's continuing viability, and it was a bold move that was greeted with some suspicion by some COHSE traditionalists, particularly as the professional development began to make its presence felt within the union.

The RCN were, paradoxically, moving in the opposite direction, developing more industrial relations officers' posts, branch and regional structures that would enable them to compete in the workplace and expanding their specialist groups, seeking inroads into professional areas where they were not traditionally strong. It was partly their setting up of an association for psychiatric nurses, with a specialist full-time officer, that prompted COHSE's change in policy.

Alastair Graham, of the Industrial Society and a former trade union general secretary, quoted the College as one of the success stories of the 1980s. At a time when trade union membership generally was falling from a peak of 12.2 million in 1979 to well below 10 million, the RCN's membership almost trebled, rising from 101 000 in 1978 to just 300 000. A large part of this new membership is part-time workers, mostly women, often working in the private sector, that TUC affiliated unions have failed to attract, be it in health care, industry or the service sector (Graham, 1987: p. 29).

Perhaps the one overriding reason behind this success is the ability of the RCN to renew itself at key moments in its history, almost reinventing itself when necessary. Thus it moved away from its opposition to a second level trained nurse; admitted men and then enrolled nurses into its own ranks, followed shortly after by students (even if they did not have full voting rights) and reversed unpopular positions on pay and conditions to the point where it now submits evidence to the pay review body broadly in line with that of the trade unions in terms of its demands and is prepared to campaign on them. Quick to recognise consumerism as a selling point, it set up a range of services including insurance, travel and personal finance, branched out into publishing (setting up Scutari Publications as a separate company, publishing the *Nursing Standard* as well as a number of highly regarded clinical works – raising serious financial concerns as they accumulated a £1 million plus deficit as they did so (Pownall, 1988b: p. 19)) and established a free counselling service for members. Its indemnity insurance was always believed to be a strong recruiting point and COHSE had to follow suit, as did other nursing organisations, all of which set up a range of secondary member services of their own. The RCN also developed direct mailing for members, which meant that its silent majority were regularly receiving information about what was happening within their organisation in a way that only activists attending all branch meetings in COHSE would do. Again, COHSE followed suit but the RCN were the proven innovator.

Although the HVA, with its radical history, had a long history of close involvement with other organisations, especially user and community groups, on campaigning issues, the RCN began to develop alliances with consumer and user organisations, projecting a radical image through Council members such as Sally Gooch, in London, who regularly comment on pushing back the boundaries of care rather than nurses aligning themselves with a medical model that can be seen as increasingly irrelevant to the chronically sick. In all public statements the RCN is able to capitalise on the authority of its professional voice, often supported by its own research. This results in its domination of the media on nursing issues, making it immediately identifiable to virtually every nurse, whatever her/his background and field of nursing. With so many well-known nurses on its Council, such as Steve Wright, involved in radical and innovative practice, the RCN can not only be seen to be moving with the times but breaking the mould and moving ahead of its time.

Equal Opportunities?

'What's wrong with them all,' wrote Jane Salvage in 1985, referring to the lack of representation for women and people from ethnic minorities in all of the trade unions and professional
organisations (Salvage, 1985: pp. 124–7). In an organisation with
consistently 70% plus of its membership made up of women it
took COHSE until 1990 to have women making up 50% of its
NEC. Helen Weatherley, the woman elected to achieve that par-
ity, was also the NEC's first ever student nurse. Gradually, more
women have been appointed to national officer and regional officer posts although, as it went into UNISON, COHSE only had
one female national officer, leading on nursing issues. Salvage was
equally critical of the College, although it now has a female general secretary, a fact it advertises in its members' diary. Yet the
RCN remains stubbornly middle class and, thus, still not particularly women friendly to the large numbers of its members who
come from poorer backgrounds. Its officers are fairly evenly balanced between men and women but women dominate on the
Council, perhaps not surprisingly since they are elected by postal
ballot. As soon as postal ballots were introduced for COHSE's
NEC elections – arguably allowing women to have their say,
directly, through the ballot paper, unhindered by any male presence – women started defeating male candidates far more than
they ever had under the old system, when members were elected
at regional council meetings dominated by male delegates.

The lack of proportionality for women in the nursing organisations does no more, however, than reflect the failings of the health
service in this area. As in so much, the organisations, particularly
COHSE, are almost a mirror image of the host service. Women's
employment is less likely to be continuous than a man's. A
woman might move to further her own career if she is single but
it is unlikely that she will do so if she is married, where the
husband's work takes precedence. It would be more likely she
would have to move to accommodate him and damage her own
employment prospects. Part-time working and maternity breaks
all damage the possibility for promotion and the age group
between 25 and 34 is the hardest hit, with fewer working than
any other age group between 18 and 55. 'The cumulative result of

these biases means that one man in two aged 25–34 has a full-time job and belongs to a union – compared with *one woman in twenty* in the same age range' (emphasis in original) (Coote & Campbell, 1982: pp. 156–7).

The ratio of men to women in senior positions in the health service far outweighs their total numbers in the overall workforce. For example, equal opportunities monitoring in the East Yorkshire Health Authority revealed that 25% of its workforce were male, but 67% of all senior management positions were occupied by men; 7% of male staff were senior managers as opposed to 1.1% of their female colleagues (Siefert, 1992: p. 331).

It is nonetheless strange that women should be so underrepresented in positions of influence on both sides of the negotiating table, particularly when the dominance of the early matrons is considered. It throws a new emphasis on how the division of labour within the NHS both reflects and reinforces the existing class and sexual divisions within society (Doyal, 1979: pp. 200–1). With nursing traditionally defined as women's work, taking on the caring and nurturing role as well as the management of anxiety of both medical staff and patient (see Chapter 5), its more 'scientific' aspects, decision making and rational, hardheaded management are thus taken over by men. The suppression of the historical role of the matron is simply another example of how myth can very quickly overtake reality in nursing. The blossoming of men into senior nursing positions in general hospitals and overall health care provision – for their relative domination is no less true in community services and they have long had traditional control of mental health services, at least on the male side – as well as nurse education is a relatively new phenomenom. Although there is no qualitative research to support the fact, it does coincide, approximately at least, with the admittance of male nurses into the Royal College of Nursing.

The experience of the RCN seems to suggest, however, that it is not as simple as a straight female/male divide. Women have long held the senior positions, with Trevor Clay being a break with the norm in his appointment as general secretary. Among its founders were women who held positions of power, Dame Sarah Swift being among the key triumvirate at its very beginning. Its general secretaries enjoyed long reigns in which to nurture internal policy programmes that could have both empowered women within the College and, as a consequence, improved their position in the workplace. It then becomes more difficult to believe that class was not and still is a serious factor in preventing certain groups of women from moving into positions of influence.

Women from poorer backgrounds, especially those with family commitments and children, would be most disadvantaged, especially when trying to cope with the shift system that anchors them to work at unconvenient times. As well as economic stressors and possible resentment from within the family – husbands especially – the demands of a stressful job and running the home are well documented obstacles to prevent women then committing themselves to a 'third career' as a trade union representative. Even for younger women without home responsibilities there are factors that hinder involvement and progress in the movement. Male domination in the unions has, in the past, been frequently associated with sexism or, at the least, a strongly male and hierarchical culture where the bureaucratic rules and methods of operating have traditionally made it difficult for women to participate. The professional associations, meanwhile, are seen as being dominated by middle-class nurses from a managerial background with little or no sympathy for women from lower grades, poorer and with possibly conflicting interests and needs and to whom little encouragement to participate is offered (Lister, 1988: p. 97; Mackay, 1989: p. 126, Salvage, 1985: pp. 123–7).

It is NUPE, perhaps perversely as they were regarded as one of the most blue collar unions of all and therefore most susceptible to the cloth cap, beer swilling male dominated image, that has moved the farthest in trying to provide equality of opportunity for women. It was the first to appoint a national women's officer as well as a women's working party to identify obstacles, and solutions to them, to greater participation in the trade union. It was also the first to identify seats on committees, including the NEC, for the low paid and women, a policy adopted by neither COHSE nor the RCN, although COHSE did set up an equal opportunities subcommittee of its NEC and both organisations began to address it as a serious issue as the 1980s wore on. NUPE's policy of paying its branch secretaries a small percentage of their branch members' subscriptions has no doubt also assisted the low paid, including women, to participate more fully in the union.

None of these steps has solved the problem of underrepresentation from members from black and ethnic minorities, however, where the lack of representation at all levels is still notable.

Originally, people came for jobs with better pay than they could earn in their own countries to a Britain whose indigenous population could not meet the demands of its expanding economy. Most of the jobs offered were manual, low paid and poorly regarded – the NHS was, as such, a typical employer. The problems of equality of opportunity were started then and compounded by the character and inflexibility of that and the other institutions they found themselves in (Brown, 1984: p. 316). Although the majority of black workers coming into the NHS, both male and female, were pushed into ancillary jobs, in 1975, 20.5% of all student and pupil nurses were from overseas, an all-time high. But many had been encouraged to come to Britain and train as enrolled nurses, whatever their previous skills, experience and academic record. Of course, this denied them promotion and career development opportunities. They were also overrepresented in mental health, learning difficulties and care of the elderly, all services which were undervalued. Few were to be found training in the prestigious teaching hospitals (Doyal, 1979: pp. 205–6). Again, these early disadvantages have been difficult to recover from. Moreover, the job flexibility of people from black and ethnic minorities waxes and wanes with the vicissitudes of the labour market far more than it does for white workers and their perception of their prospects has steadily diminished, whether it be in the health service or elswhere, continuing to experience discrimination at every stage of the employment process, at interview stage as well as when applying for promotion or a change of position. In the NHS there is also some evidence to suggest that they are more likely to be disciplined in their workplace than white colleagues (Brown, 1984; Ollearnshaw, 1983; Carlisle, 1990: pp. 25–32).

With union positions less frequently going to low paid, low status workers, black people were already facing a disadvantage if they wanted to become involved as a representative. They also had the economic pressures resulting from their low pay as well as issues of wider social dislocation and isolation with which to contend. There has also been racism within the trade union movement. In the 1950s and 1960s this was shown by trade union branches in some cases going so far as to pass resolutions that they were opposed to any black recruits being brought into the workplace; the dockers marched in support of Enoch Powell after his 'Rivers of Blood' speech in 1968 (Morgan, 1990: pp. 285–6).

Changes have followed the introduction of the Race Relations Act 1976, with the establishment of the Commission for Racial Equality to succeed the old Race Relations Board and Community Relations Commission, which was designed to 'work towards the elimination of discrimination and promote equality of opportunity and good relations between persons of different racial groups' (Nixon, 1982: p. 367). In some areas the change in attitudes has been led by the trade unions lobbying on racial and equal opportunities issues, as well as Left wing pressure groups. Advances have been made for black employees in the NHS and in health service trade unions and professional associations. Progress has also been made by women. In COHSE this was, in part, due to the determination of its last general secretary, Hector MacKenzie, to increase the presence of women in the union at a higher level as an encouragement to the membership to become involved. But the distance still to be travelled can easily be worked out when looking at the senior positions, whether amongst lay committees or full-time officials in both COHSE and the RCN as well as their health service competitors. The HVA and RCM are very much the exceptions, probably largely due to their even larger, proportionately, female membership.

More positive measures are now taken in promoting the involvement of women, with greater emphasis on childcare and creche facilities, thought being given to the timing of meetings as well as getting women to and from the venue. But critics point to the need for more to be done in terms of making training available to women stewards and securing time off arrangements with employers. More controversially, some have called for reserved seats and positive discrimination to get women and people from black and ethnic minorities into senior positions: UNISON has set itself a timetable for achieving proportionality over the next decade. It is perhaps surprising that, historically, none of the organisations seems to have taken a rational policy making approach to the problem but, particularly for the trade unions, they are bound by the democratic voting process, weighted very much in favour of the majority participants – white males.

There also seems to be confusion about the differences between positive discrimination and affirmative action. This has plagued policy formation in other areas and the resulting ambiguity and vagueness that results from this has damaged both causes. Positive discrimination is a policy of setting quotas or targets for recruitment which must be met and advancing people into those positions from particular groups, be they women or ethnic minorities. It was widely advocated and used in the United States, assisting the emerging black middle class while failing to assist poorer blacks and proved counterproductive in terms of white resentment (Kirp & Halsey, 1982; Edwards, 1987: p. 31). This experience has then tainted opinions on affirmative action, which places an emphasis on advancement of minorities through indirect pressure, selected training programmes, carrot and stick policies to change attitudes and legislative support aimed at changing attitudes (Ollearnshaw, 1983: pp. 151–4; Edwards, 1987).

Different Sides of the Same Coin?

Although there is so much that marks out the differences between COHSE and the RCN, between a traditional trade union and professional association, there are many aspects where those divisions became increasingly blurred. This has been especially so over the last decade, with COHSE developing its professional services and aligning itself to user groups and the RCN extending its labour relations services and trade union services. But more than that, there is a mutuality on nursing issues that is not overtly expressed or acknowledged. It shows that, in many respects, the two are interdependent.

The College supplies the professional input into policy making that, on occasions, some COHSE insiders acknowledge has helped nursing develop (although often it has argued that the RCN's conservative, professional positions on specific issues were detrimental to nurses' interests) and that the trade union neither had the resources nor the opportunity to do. Although this clearly benefits the RCN and allows them to retain their authority as the 'voice of nursing', the argument that the representation of nursing interests in policy making is invaluable and absolutely necessary in a service so strongly dominated historically by the medical profession is difficult to counter. Obviously, as has been explored earlier, there are questions about what that nursing voice is saying and on whose behalf it speaks. But it is, nevertheless, there and the RCN point to serious victories gained by the use of their lobbying and involvement in the policy making process throughout the history of the NHS and, indeed, at its inception (Bowman, 1967).

COHSE would argue the issue slightly differently. One national officer says that the College are able to get the best of both worlds, pushing a hard line in negotiations at a national level, knowing that if things break down the trade unions can take some form of industrial action to put real pressure on the government. This allows the RCN to await the outcome, choose the best public front to put on matters and then claim that any victory won was because it negotiated firmly but sensibly. Victory is its reward for its loyalty to the service and the recognition from the employer or government that the nurses have a case – a 'new realist' approach with a dash of real flair (Graham, 1987: p. 29; Clay, 1987).

Perhaps the truth lies somwhere in between. As partners on the Nurses' and Midwives' Whitley Council, the two organisations long ago carved out their roles, with the RCN holding secretary's position while the chairperson has been from COHSE. Their dominance of nursing has led them to take predatory and territorial positions in relation to other nursing organisations. Both wooed the Health Visitors' Association when it was clear that serious financial and organisational difficulties were likely to force them to merge with a larger trade union. It was partly because of this predatory outlook that the HVA went with a broader union, MSF, who offered greater autonomy and independence within the merger that eventually took place (Snell, 1989: p. 19 and Jerrome, 1993). The RCN has also had its eye on the RCM for many years, although the Midwives' organisation has always enjoyed sufficient financial stability as well as strong representation within its own sphere and a voice that resonates as profoundly on midwifery issues as the RCN's does for nursing. COHSE could never have seriously dented NUPE's nurse membership which, though relatively small, amounts to a significant minority. But the merger that takes them both into UNISON undoubtedly strengthens the old COHSE position far more than the simple adding together of the figures. Now the union has just one front to face in the competition for members and has an opportunity to build on its professional services base. Competition for alliances with other organisations that represent nurses is obviously limited by the absence of any other notable contenders; between them UNISON and the RCN have the vast majority of nurses, with minority stakeholdings in midwifery and health visiting.

Where would COHSE have been without the RCN and vice versa? It does seem like questioning the viability of Steptoe without Son or Tom without Jerry. The Odd Couple, with their different traditions and policies, philosophies and practices, are not accidents of history. They have shaped today's health service as much as they have been shaped by what has gone before. To that extent, at least, for good or bad, they are different sides of the same coin.

That nurses join the respective organisations for different reasons is clear. However, one thing any nurse enrolling in a trade union or professional association wants to be confident about is that it will be successful in achieving its stated goals. As such, which of the two is the more effective in influencing policy? Each, obviously, claims its successes and argues that its own distinctive methods influence the government. But when measured in terms of each organisation's own policy objectives, the question is not an easy one to answer. Which is more successful, the tough negotiating stance of the traditional type trade union, using whatever industrial muscle it has at its disposal? Or a professional association using more sophisticated lobbying techniques, trading on its reputation for moderation and aligning itself with the needs of the patient and service? It is all the more complicated by the fact that it may actually be a combination of the two. This, however, will be more fully explored in Chapter 7.

Table 4.2 Membership figures, COHSE and the RCN

	COHSE	RCN
1947	40 000	N/A
1950	N/A	44 239
1967	66 240	47 366
1973	113 401	92 773
1977	200 455	95 668
1979	212 930	158 640
1980	216 482	177 399
1981	230 709	192 392
1982	231 504	219,137
1983	222 869	231 256
1984	214 321	240 792
1985	212 987	247 121
1986	212 312	258,859
1987	207 731	265 641
1988	218 321	279 957
1989	209 344	283 713
1991	207 831	
1992	197 518	

The growth in membership for COHSE during the 1970s reflects its successful radicalism during this period, although it also coincides with the longest period in power the Labour party has enjoyed. It rose to become the TUC's twelfth largest union, all the more creditable when it was considered that it was up against a number of competing unions and with a limited workforce. However, the achievement of the RCN to grow so comprehensively throughout the 1980s, a period of dramatic decline for the TUC affiliates – although gamely COHSE held its position above the 200 000 mark – is quite remarkable. It is testimony to their ability to manage their position as the 'voice of nursing' with great flair and imagination whilst always understanding and reacting to the need for pragmatic politicking during a period when such a fiercely market oriented government has done all it can to hold down expenditure, and therefore staffing, in the public sector. It also needs to be remembered that because of the high turnover of nurses, both those leaving the NHS altogether and changing workplaces, the RCN and COHSE would have to recruit at a steady pace just to stand still in overall terms. For example, COHSE would recruit over 1000 nurses a month but might still show a negative balance because of more nurses leaving membership. This is less of a problem for the RCN, many of whose members pay by direct debit from their bank rather than having their subscriptions deducted from their salary. Part of the changing membership numbers, not always reflected in once yearly figures, is the flow between the two organisations, perhaps the clearest statement of all about which of the two nurses see as most effective. In 1988, amid COHSE claims that RCN nurses were defecting in droves, the RCN claimed 8000 recruits in a six week period, 2500 more than would have been the normal (*Nursing Times,* 9.3.1988: p. 19).

Chapter 5

Pity The Poor Nurse.
Nurses and their work

The Division of Labour

The origins of nursing in domestic service have been a determining factor in much that has happened in the service ever since. Without a doubt, the most influential aspect of this has been its identification as women's work. That nursing was identified as women's work is perhaps unremarkable in itself. What it did, however, was accord it a certain status and it is that status, with the accompanying power relationship with the medical profession and the way that nurses were subsequently treated, that is at issue.

The work of the woman/nurse was subordinated to that of the man/doctor, reflecting the wider social divisions in the deeply patriarchal Victorian society; class, gender and race were key determinants and nursing was further divided itself along those lines. 'Medical men defined femininity in terms of patriarchal feminine subordination . . . to safeguard their own dominance' (Gamarnikow, 1991: p. 111). But as the medical role became more complex and demanding, accompanied by the growth in the provision of service, it was necessary for nursing to evolve and expand. This began the search for a 'better' type of woman, one able to give nursing a degree of respectability believed lacking and respond to the training and disciplinary demands being placed upon the workforce by the changes to the service and required by the doctor. Nursing values and culture were thus appropriated by women of a higher social status and greater wealth than those largely working-class women who had formed the bulk of the earliest nurses. Calls for registration and training were used as much to limit those who could come into the service as to improve the quality of care they would be able to provide.

As nursing became more sophisticated, a hierarchy developed, partly based on one of the other strands of nursing's origins, i.e. military service, and nurses began to receive their orders from more senior nurses rather than directly from doctors. But, as in any military service, obedience was essential. The burgeoning women's movement was interpreted in nursing in a middle-class way; the position of nurses would be improved through achieving a higher status in relation to other occupations. Terms and conditions were not seen as important to that goal and the early professionalisers continued to stress the vocational dedication and discipline required of nurses. The question of the nurse's role being subordinate to that of the doctor was not directly challenged, with the curative role remaining superior to that of caring, which was seen as a necessary support for the more scientific, invasive procedures performed by the medical or surgical staff.

The status of doctors grew steadily as science assumed an increasingly important position in industrialised society. Nurses providing the care and support remained in the shadows, carrying out sufficient tasks for the patient to be well enough to receive the doctor's treatment, administering prescribed medication, recording observations, washing the patient and taking care of all other hygiene functions s/he was unable to do for themselves or the doctor thought it unwise for them to do. In between, a variety of domestic chores were completed. Any learning necessary for the nurse had to be conducted in her own time.

Cracks in this perfect world began to appear almost from the outset. As techniques developed for medicine it was necessary for nurses to know enough about them to assist. Similarly, they had to know enough anatomy and physiology to understand certain things about a patient's condition. Although the knowledge passed onto them was framed within the medical model many doctors rightly suspected that it could be a subversive process. Nurses also had to interpret their observations and filter out what they believed unimportant before making their reports to the doctor. Increasingly, they were using their powers of discretion in a number of important areas of their work. Most importantly, the arrival of the nursing hierarchy and the discipline and control exercised within it bred a loyalty to nursing itself rather than anything else. And then, of course, there were never enough 'suitable' women. Shortages of trained nurses became a long running sore for all health care policy makers.

As the power of the medical profession grew they took more and more under their aegis, medicalising various behaviours, complaints and conditions, gathering authority as they went, until they had extended their domain too far (Darbyshire, 1987: pp. 32–4). Inevitably, more discretionary power fell to the nurse, especially outside the hospital setting. Other disciplines became involved too. Health visitors, midwives (a group who had originally enjoyed far greater freedom than nurses before being emasculated by the medical profession), occupational therapists, psychologists, social workers, all gradually became essential adjuncts to the work of the doctor or, in some cases, alternatives. However, the hospital remained the domain of the medical profession, its stronghold and powerbase, and it was here that the vast majority of nurses were employed. Within the hospital setting, nurses inevitably became more involved with the technical care provided to patients, particularly in intensive care units, theatres and accident and emergency departments. But as those nurses in favour of specialising and developing the role of the nurse were arguing for greater autonomy and a merging of the roles of nurse and doctor, the work of caring, the expressive, purposeful task of feminine nurturing began to be devalued by nurses themselves, further perpetuating one of the most potent myths of all – the superiority and healing powers of the curative role and its greater importance to the sick than that of caring. This was, of course, reinforced at every stage by the policy makers: services where care took precedence because cure had failed – in mental health, care of the elderly, the chronically sick – were underfunded and marginalised. The work of the nurses was 'unproductive'; both they and the patients were stigmatised and punished for being unable to respond to the curative model.

Of course, men had made their entry, gradually, into nursing but were still largely confined to the asylums until after the Second World War. If nursing was classed as women's work, looking after the male insane in the latter part of the nineteenth century, where strength was one of the key requirements, was regarded as the work of men. There was never any question of seeking 'suitable gentlemen' for the asylums. As has been noted earlier, the work was often that of the last resort, so poorly paid that it would attract men who could not work elsewhere. Women who did come into the service from general hospitals experienced preferential treatment when it came to promotion, as doctors and superintendents sought to bring the asylums some of the credibility nursing was establishing in the voluntary hospitals (Carpenter, 1980: p. 136). This was the root of a constant tension in the early asylums, with women of a higher social class being brought in and advocating the vocational values of the voluntary hosptials, failing to support the men as they were drawn towards the new trade unionism. Although the number of women representing this view was only a small proportion of the workforce in the asylums – the majority of them coming from the working class, who might otherwise have been drawn into domestic service – other factors that have always been found in women's work influenced the attitudes of their male colleagues: they were less likely to be unionised because they stayed in the job for shorter periods of time and, as with all women in late Victorian and Edwardian times, were inculcated with the need for their sex to adopt a subservient and submissive role. Nonetheless, as a wave of strikes and industrial action peppered the asylums in the first years of the NAWU it was often women who led the way, most notably during the Battle of Radcliffe.

Even if men had wanted to take on the particular form of women's work that nursing had become, it was very difficult to do so. No London hospital would accept a man for training in the late nineteenth century and in 1937 there were only 120 men in training (Pyne, 1982: p. 36), with 315 male registered nurses, excluding those working in mental health, out of a total of 84 000 (White, 1985b: p. 11). Male dominance in the asylums had also been set back by the 1914–18 war; not only did it rob the service of many potential recruits amongst its millions of casualties, but it also lost a great many attendants who volunteered to fight but did not return. Registered male nurses formed their own society to advance their position in the local authority and voluntary hospitals, allying themselves with the professional associations, especially the College of Nursing, and the RCN provided the umbrella for them to obtain a seat of the Nurses' Whitley Council in the new NHS. One of the Society's early campaigns was for male nurses to care for male patients, a long argued case put forward even more strongly by the NAWU, who wanted female nurses excluded from the male side altogether and cleverly had its most senior female activist, Maud Weisse, leading on the issue (MHIWU, 1931). This was not one-sided discrimination, however. Women in senior positions in nursing had actively tried to keep men out of 'proper' nursing, i.e. non-asylums, altogether (Owens & Glennerster, 1989: p. 40) and were largely successful for a long time. It was only the chronic shortages and the post-war social climate that undermined their strategy.

Senior nurses were almost certainly reluctant to have male nurses because of the fear that they would bring with them traditions of trade unionism and be unwilling to accept the vocational ideals, autocratic discipline and unquestioning obedience, as was the case in the asylums and then mental hospitals. Undoubtedly, the Society for Registered Male Nurses went some of the way to allaying the fears of the matrons that men might be a threat to nursing's discipline and hierarchy; still they did not make major numerical inroads into nursing, which largely remained women's work but, after 1960, once they gained a foothold in the RCN, they did start to climb the hiearchical ladder outside the mental hospitals. This advance was consolidated by the Salmon Report of the mid 1960s, which created far more managerial positions and, by creating a more structured approach, broke the stranglehold the women had enjoyed. The increasingly male oriented managerial culture of that and subsequent periods were major factors in men's eventual dominance in senior positions compared to their small numbers in the workforce overall.

Task Allocation – Industrialised Nursing

Task allocation's origins were in the growing mechanisation of nursing as a means of supporting medical staff in the most efficient, least expensive way, with hospitals becoming something akin to health factories. It also grew out of the mainly domestic duties that the earliest nurses undertook on the wards. As a system of care for nurses it lasted decades, embodying the discipline and hierarchical nature of the workforce in the tasks that were allocated to specific grades. Thus the ward sister and no one else would accompany the consultant on his ward round, assisted by a junior nurse trailing behind to carry anything required, such as instruments to be used by the doctor; reports were written by certain grades, beds made by untrained nurses and/or students and all tasks for the ward, such as the temperature, pulse and respiration round or 'bottle/bedpan' round, were listed out for completion by the nurses, with each of the ward's patients being 'done' one after the other (Owens, 1992: pp. 48–50) (Plate XVIII).

It also had its roots in the building of an occupational loyalty to nursing away from a particular doctor or ward. With task allocation organising the work into blocks based on a certain but predetermined skill level, anonymous individuals could theoretically be slotted into any particular task, especially students who would be temporarily based on the ward, but also any nurse who was shifted from one work area to another (Dingwell, Rafferty & Webster, 1988: p. 216). This style of nursing was endorsed by the RCN's Horder Committee in the 1940s but criticised by the Ministry of Health's Wood Committee in 1947. It persisted nonetheless. Task allocation also employed a degree of collectivity. Each patient knew what was happening at a set time and was participating in the process of being nursed, not just as individuals but as part of the group. For the nurse involved, there was a degree of 'factory care', moving from one patient to the other rather than spending time with an individual, of moving up and down the ward as if it were a production line, but they could enjoy a 'public' relationship with every patient on the ward based on the shared experience of their colleagues and the patients themselves. This occurred in a context where each task involved relatively anonymous exchanges based around the clinical nature of the nurse's work at that given moment rather than allowing for more intimate discussion or observation from either party.

The importance of this form of social construction was not simply about the way that the uniformity of tasks performed by nurses of different grades and experience reinforced the hierarchy – something also embodied by the actual uniforms, with hats, belts and even the actual colours of the dresses used to physically differentiate between nurses of different grade and status. There was another, far more esoteric reason for the way in which nurses at all levels focused on the hierarchy, petty rules and the codes and traditions of nursing. By doing this it became a major defence system for nurses against the anxieties experienced as a result of the nature of their work, notably the close physical and emotional contact with sick, and possibly dying, patients (Menzies, 1970). These unconscious anxieties were almost too great, too painful to get in touch with and articulate verbally. They were thus projected into the structures of the way in which the service and the hospital were organised. Nurses were not given the opportunity to resolve their feelings about how and why patients died, the suffering they witnessed and, ultimately, the powerlessness of the doctors and themselves in the face of it. Nor could they overcome the generalised anxiety they experienced by being, literally, close enough to touch – and be touched – throughout their working day.

In a groundbreaking piece of research, Isabel Menzies (1970) examined the techniques nurses in hospitals use – unconsciously – to defend themselves against this anxiety. The problem was that all of the techniques Menzies discovered were being used were actually not helping. These included: the splitting up of the nurse–patient relationship; minimising the number of decisions to be made through the task system; diffusing responsibility through needless checking and counterchecking; depersonalising the workforce by the use of the term 'nurse' rather than someone's name; the delegation of responsibility upwards; avoidance of change and, most damagingly, the denial of feelings. The service was maintained but in an inefficient and costly way. The defence system did not work. The wider, unconscious anxieties persisted in a vague and debilitating fashion, contributing to the high 'wastage' levels of nurses leaving the service.

Close Enough to Touch: the Nurse–Patient Relationship

The revolt against task allocation was spearheaded by nurses influenced by practices developing in the United States. The nursing process made its way across the water in the 1960s, but did not fully impact on this country until the next decade, pioneered by nurses mainly from an educational background, interested in professionalising nursing.

It was dissatisfaction with the public and anonymous nature of the nurse–patient relationship that was at the heart of the change they were seeking, wanting to replace it with a more intimate, private relationship that sought to communicate with the patient and treat him/her as a whole person rather than a series of symptoms to be addressed through the carrying out of a variety of tasks by different nurses. This holistic approach was no historical accident but mirrored wider social concerns about relationships, the individual and society and changing socioeconomic patterns. It also gave the professionalisers the opportunity to enhance the status of nurses by modelling practice on that of other professions, basing it on a private relationship. Moreover, it put the nurse directly next to the patient; no one, not a doctor, a manager or even a nurse manager, would be an obstacle or intermediary.

Whether or not the nursing process was directly to do with curing problems experienced by patients or nurses has been the subject of some dispute but it was a development unwelcomed by many nurses who saw it as overly bureaucratic and woolly, while working-class patients in particular were discovered to prefer to deal with doctors on a technical level, wanting to be 'fixed up rather than subjected to what they regarded as intrusive personal inquiries' (Dingwall, Rafferty & Webster, 1988: pp. 217–19). It was in areas where patients were least equipped to resist its advance that the greatest early gains were made, such as the care of the elderly. It was also an extension of the analysis of seeing ill health as the individual's responsibility, with its roots in 'disordered life choices' that could be remedied by the correct educative intervention on the part of the nurse.

Whatever the rationale and its background, the introduction of the nursing process would inevitably have an impact on nurses almost everywhere. Suddenly, the protection of task orientation was gone. Nurses were intimately involved with the same patient for a long period of time, washing them and helping them get changed, perhaps applying a dressing, providing catheter care, assisting with physiotherapy, taking observations of TPR and blood pressure, encouraging dietary and fluid intake, making their bed and liaising with the doctor about their treatment. Not only was the distraction of having 30 beds to make no longer available, the nurse now had responsibility for writing care plans that other nurses would have to follow, having negotiated this process with the patient. She would be individually accountable for the care she was 'prescribing'. The doctor and other health professionals might come to her for information about the patient's condition and seek her advice. She had a lot more responsibility as well as a lot more paperwork to complete. More than this, she had intense contact with the patient for prolonged periods when it would be far more difficult to avoid talking about the patient's family, background and home or work life. And, of course, their concerns about the condition they were suffering from. It is far harder for a nurse to avoid discussing someone's pain and fear if she is with them for a prolonged period than if she is passing by offering a bedpan or urinal.

It was concern to care for the whole person, their psyche especially, that apparently prompted pressure for the development of the nursing process; it is thus ironic that so little was done to help nurses with their own distress and stress as a result of the change to their working practice and the extra responsibilities they faced as a consequence. No psychosocial training was prepared for nurses involved in the nursing process, no education about how to talk with patients and their families – for they, too, came to know that their relative would now have a particular nurse or group of nurses caring for them – or about how to deal with their own feelings and anxieties. In fact the issue was largely ignored, despite the publication of the work of Isabel Menzies and others about the subject. Nurses were still expected to be uncomplaining and able to cope, the legacy of the discipline and vocational ethos imposed upon nurses from the middle-class mistresses who needed to show the administrators and doctors that they were really in control of their 'girls'. Most nurses would be completely unsurprised that dealing with bereavement or violent patients was seen to be one of the most stressful aspects of their work (*Nursing Times*, 13.1.1988: p. 8), but it was the less dramatic aspects of the one to one relationship, where the stress is less identifiable, like the complaining patient or the feeling of being unable to provide all of the care necessary to a particular patient and verbalise those limitations that took their toll. Teaching a nurse to say 'no' or 'cannot cope' was not put on the curriculum.

In mental health it was no better. Difficulties in introducing the nursing process and individualised care were compounded where the multidisciplinary team were confined in their clinical approach by the work of the consultant psychiatrist and, in many cases, a strict adherence to the medical model. The limitations on the role of the nursing staff were covered over by an unstructured, often haphazard approach to patient care, perhaps more benignly custo-dial but one in which admission lengths were kept to a minimum on acute wards, neuroleptic medication and/or antidepressants and minor tranquillisers were widely administered and nurses would attempt little in the way of therapeutic input.

Where the old 'two shift' system existed – whereby two groups of nurses worked as separate teams, alternating weekly on early and late shifts – patients might be nursed in completely contradictory ways depending on the time of day and which team was on duty.

To expose nurses was potentially damaging, especially those with limited mental health experience (and most of the whole-hearted advocates of the nursing process tended to be relatively inexperienced staff nurses and students in the early days of its implementation). In an individualised care system they would have prolonged contact with individual patients suffering from acute psychosocial distress and/or disturbance without adequate super-vision or staff support systems, where getting in close to the patient would inevitably mean being close enough to be touched by their distress and disturbance. Yet, again, this was expected in settings where the nursing process was introduced, apparently without the understanding that changes in the structure of the nursing service would be necessary if the new practices were to work successfully (Hart, 1991: p. 142). Inevitably, stress, sickness levels and absence from the wards were part of the response from nurses (Salvage, 1985; Bond, 1982; Tschudin, 1985).

The Quiet Revolution – the Nursing Process Arrives

In part this was because of the splits in nursing. The nursing process was pioneered largely by educationalists seeking to professionalise nursing. But it had to be implemented by managers who were less supportive of the 'new nursing'. As stated above, this new nursing, the nursing process and then primary nursing, were both individualised systems of care that arrived in Britain from across the Atlantic, where they had been pioneered. It was greeted with considerable interest by those professionalisers seeking change.

There is evidence of growing discontent with the system of task allocation in *some* nursing circles since the 1950s, with team nursing the favoured option, separating out technical tasks and basic nursing care from 'non-nursing' duties. However, immediate problems were identified, notably a lack of trained nurses. The RCN stated that it would 'be neither numerically possible nor economically justifiable' to increase the numbers of qualified nurses in line with the recommendations of the Goddard Report, commissioned and published in 1953 (Ersser & Tutton, 1991: p. 16), which would seem to have been a major setback for any new initiative. Nevertheless, concerns remained and the desire for change was pursued, focusing on a perceived lack of job satisfaction for nurses.

Pilot studies demonstrated that nurse satisfaction increased with the new system but Dingwall has questioned whether or not this was the 'Hawthorne effect', i.e. a feeling of satisfaction derived from the apparent importance attached to the workers as they themselves are studied rather than the effects of whatever work changes are being implemented (this was discovered in pre-war Germany where production increased so long as studies went on, regardless of the nature or effectiveness of the changes being introduced) (Dingwall, Rafferty & Webster: p. 216).

The nursing process was introduced into the training curriculum in the late 1970s but, in its implementation, it failed to make the impact that the professionalisers were seeking. Patient care was not individualised and nurses were not gaining in status from the new system. Moreover, a lot of the more generalist nurses were resentful of the changes imposed upon them, particularly the increased paperwork and writing of care plans, which often only reflected the medical instructions given to the nurse or the patient's medical needs. There was also the suspicion that they were at greater risk of criticism if the care they were having to prescribe was viewed as inadequate, whether by peers, patients or, more importantly, senior nurses. The system had been sold heavily through the schools of nursing but they had no control over its implementation. Many health authorities or hospitals convened working parties, set deadlines, wrote and circulated policies and even introduced new stationery; but in most cases its implementation was haphazard partly because of the differing natures of the wards and units but also because of a lack of widespread enthusiasm from nurse managers, who had long been accused of neglecting the development of nursing practice (Salvage, 1990: pp. 84–5 and White, 1985a). A lot of discretion was devolved down and it was at these lower levels, on the proverbial shopfloor, that nurses gave their verdict about whether or not they thought it was a system worth pursuing because, inevitably, it posed difficulties and not simply because it was a matter of introducing change. There were some challenges to the medical model inherent in it, as well as a challenge to the managerial and hierarchical relationships within nursing. It did ask more of the patient as well as the nurse and put the nurse firmly in the spotlight; when there were inevitable shortcomings in the system, she was the one who had to explain them to her patient and the stress levels inexorably rose in the face of the new way of working.

By the time it found its way onto wards in Britain it had lost some of the essential components developed in the United States, most particularly the individualised care, negotiated with the patient, that was at its heart. Also 'missing' were the accountability of the nurse and the intellectual components that gave it its status. The lack of value placed on nursing care by most hospitals was evidenced by the fact that all of the new, elaborate documentation, including nursing information sheets and care plans, was thrown away when the patient was discharged (de la Cuesta, 1983). In many cases the nursing process was simply a more complicated way of delivering task allocated care or, more usually, became team nursing.

It also resurrected the debate about whether nursing was an art form or a science. This was really the debate about the degree of education required to enter nurse training and the amount of theoretical knowledge needed to underpin practical work on the wards as well as the revisiting of the old conundrum about whether good nurses were born or made. In many respects, this meant that individual nurses were being judged as good or bad, depending on how they practised and their professional aspirations. This ignored the organisational and structural systems in which they found themselves practising, the financial constraints of the health service, the availability of trained nurses and any number of strategic and policy making issues that were a long way out of the reach of the individual nurse. In many respects, hoping to achieve a smooth change from task orientation to the individualised care promised by the nursing process was rather like wanting to forgo the industrial production line in order to produce even more goods through a process of rural handicraft.

New Nursing – Models of Care and the Pressure for Change

The appetite for change was, nevertheless, whetted. American influences continued to permeate nursing debate. Because of the lack of managerial motivation behind the implementation of the nursing process, in those places where it did take root it was largely a 'bottom-up' initiative, i.e. it was championed by nurses on wards or in units where their commitment to its principles and practice were what made it succeed.

It had not even been written about in the UK until 1975, but the nursing media were quickly to join its ranks of supporters as well as prove the power of the nursing journals as vehicles for ideas and change. 'A series of articles starting in *Nursing Times* in 1977 was the first detailed explanation available to the nursing profession at large in Great Britain' and the NT was later able to report that, 'The nursing process is all the rage in nursing circles' (Dopson, 1985b: p. 19). Just which circles, the NT failed to define. But despite its faltering start, the nursing process had established a foothold. The American influence continued and nursing models of care emerged on both sides of the Atlantic, broadly falling into three categories:

1. Those emphasising a balance between physiological and social systems, such as Orem's self-care model, with selected actions on the part of the nurse to 'assist individuals or groups to maintain self-care';

2. Interactionist models. These used an interaction process between patient and nurse during the period when goals are first percieved, set and acted upon. The models looked at how transactions occur and/or how the individual perceives the world and relates to others;

3. Peplau's interpersonal model, focusing on the nurse involving herself in 'a goal directed interpersonal process to promote the patient's forward movement of their personality and personal living' and the 'growth and development of the nurse/patient realtionship' (Royle & Walsh, 1992: pp. 2–11).

Regardless of the difficulties with the nursing process, advocates of the new nursing still saw in it advantages in providing continuity of care, with all nurses following carefully constructed care plans, written by a registered nurse, with the assistance of the patient wherever possible. The holistic approach would mean that all of the patient's needs would be met in a system that recognised the individual's own hierarchy of needs. They also believed that the increased responsibility for nurses was constructive and would build towards them assuming a full degree of accountability for their individual practice. The pressures that came with this would be more than offset by the increased satisfaction the nurse derived from her work. The debate went still further and yet another new system of nursing was reported from the United States, one that was designed to ensure that individualised patient care would become a reality: primary nursing.

The New Nurses and Their Work

The new nurse, as identified by the *Nursing Times* in November 1987, was 28, female, had 4–5 'O' levels and one CSE, drove a car and was either married or cohabiting (Plate XX). She read the *Daily Mail*, *TV Times*, *Woman's Own* and *Cosmopolitan* – although the most popular newspaper for nurse teachers by a long way was the *Guardian*. She had moved away from her predecessors in a number of other ways, as well as the material changes such as homeowning and being able to get married when she wanted (Lathlean, 1987). A larger number were working part-time and:

She is much more vocal in her criticisms of nursing's long established traditions. She almost certainly belongs to one of the staff
associations or unions agitating to improve her lot. Pay and conditions dominate her life and not state regulation and the 'vote'.

(Maggs, 1987: pp. 25–9).

The traditions persist, nonetheless, as do the myths. Only one
thing is certain and that is that the profile of the nursing workforce has been one that has constantly changed. The number of
whole time equivalent (WTEs) nurses working in the NHS *did*
rise under the Thatcher Government, despite trade union and
Labour party rhetoric, increasing from just over 350 000 in 1979
to 400 000 a decade later – although the reduction in the nurses'
working week from 40 to $37^{1}/_{2}$ hours in 1980–1 meant that there
had to be an increase in nurses of approximately 20 000 to com-
pensate for that particular change.

Nurses formed 51% of the NHS workforce in 1989 but
accounted for 45.4% of the total pay budget. Significantly, with
all of the emphasis on priority services such as mental health,
learning difficulties and care of the elderly, as well as an apparent
commitment to community care, no real shifts in nursing staff
ratios between the areas of service occurred, with 85% engaged in
hospital nursing and less than 10% working as midwives or as
primary health care staff. The numbers of midwives practising fell
by 20% between 1981 and 1989. Most other areas enjoyed
increases, with education and paediatrics having their numbers
boosted by 30% in the same period. In 1989 the preponderance
of male staff remained in mental health and learning difficulties,
the latter being the only area where more men were working than
women. The next highest after those two was education.

As was noted in the previous chapter, the ratio of male to female
senior nurses and managers far outweighs their representation as a
percentage of any one group of staff as a whole. Of all 'G' grade
nurses, the largest percentage from their own occupational group
were health visitors at 85%, followed by ward sisters/charge nurses
and district nurses at 67% and 65% respectively. The largest clus-
ter of nurses, 30% across all groups, were graded at scale 'E', with
those at scale 'G' next on 24%. Fairly minimal changes in the age
profile of nurses occurred between the years 1970 and 1989, but
the under-25s fell significantly from 29% of the workforce to

20.6% at the same time as the number of learner nurses fell to 16% of the workforce (from 28% in 1974). The age group 25–29 formed the smallest part of the workforce by age, in line with national statistics for female workers.

Of most significance, however, was the growth in hospital activity. Although there was a small increase in the numbers of nurses, activity or the work undertaken by them rose steadily since 1979. This was most dramatic in the number of day cases treated – increased by approximately 90% by 1990 – while the number of inpatient cases had risen by approximately 40% in the same period (Appleby & Brewins, 1992: pp. 24–9).

The Politics of Primary Nursing

The workforce that primary nursing was now being sold to was, then, a major national resource as well as a major cost to the nation – 3% of all government expenditure was being spent on nurses. With more registered nurses than ever before and a long awaited training curriculum on the way, which made student nurses supernumerary and with a sound academic base, the professionalising arguments seemed to be in the ascendancy. The apparent omnipotence of the medical profession was being challenged and its limitations recognised. No longer was it widely believed that medicine was capable of curing all ills; in many cases it could, at best, only temporarily arrest the progress of a condition. Many people, despite the best attentions of their doctors, would remain in a chronic phase until death (Mitchell, 1984: pp. 119–41).

Primary nursing was in place as advocates of a developed form of nursing practice could point to the need of the chronically sick to be better cared for, as criticism about the provision of hi-tech, medically oriented health care was mounting and public expectation about the services it should receive increased. As well as being an organisational system for nurses it was said to have a philosophy of care, a significant advance on the nursing process (Hegyvary, 1982). The four key concepts within the new system were responsibility, authority, autonomy and accountability, with one nurse responsible and (usually) accountable for all decisions about the nursing care provided, on a 24 hour basis, for a group of named patients – their primary patients – to whom they would normally remain allocated throughout the patient's stay. It was from this responsibility, enshrined in written care plans that had to be signed by the primary nurse in a semi-contractual form, that the authority and autonomy was derived. This 24 hour responsibility was obviously about the strategy and direction for care rather than 'hands on nursing' but meant that the primary nurse should be involved in any serious change of care, even if not on duty. In theory this would mean waiting until the primary nurse returned to the workplace or calling her up at home, a policy adopted in some units (Ersser & Tutton, 1991: p. 7). However, a support to the primary nurse was available in the form of associate nurses, who worked to the care plans and could change them or formulate new ones in the primary nurse's absence. Again, moving forward from the nursing process, primary nursing was all about negotiating care plans with the patient, built around the latter's perception of their needs and problems (Hart, 1991: p. 141). But in its early stages many also saw it as essential that the care planner was also the care giver, i.e. carried out the care presecribed in her own care plans.

The notes kept by a primary nurse were entirely different from the old Kardex system of recording basic details in a largely anony-mous manner. It became common for the nurses' notes to resemble those of their medical colleagues, written in large, individual case files or on specially designed sheets built around the care plan formula. The notes would need to be detailed and descriptive because of the individualised nature of the care given (Ritter, 1985: pp. 16–17). Nursing history sheets, at least as detailed as those obtained by the clerking doctor, would be taken and sometimes accompanied by a nursing diagnosis sheet. Following on from this change from traditional nursing documentation, the nurse was to be at the apex of a new communications structure. Part of the primary nurse's responsibility was to directly communicate with everyone else involved in the patient's care and treatment and where the system has its fullest support from the medical staff, all other members of the multidisciplinary team would communicate directly to the primary nurse.

The consequence of this form of structure and communication was a fundamental and deeply subversive shift away from the traditional hierarchy, with the line management structure effectively flattened out. Communications, for they cannot even be called instructions, were to be made to the most appropriate person, whether that person was a newly qualified nurse or an experienced consultant. Power, in the shape of the authority for decision making, came to the primary nurse as well as the power derived from sapiential authority, for the primary nurse inevitably should know more about the patient than anyone else in the team. It was this power which afforded the nurse greater status within the team. It was argued that this would not necessarily undermine the role and authority of the ward sister/charge nurse. Indeed, her role could be enhanced and enriched as the supervisor for the primary nurses, acting as a nursing consultant or specialist and a point of referral for all disciplines on the primary nursing process. At the same time the administration of the system, the allocating of nurses to newly admitted patients and managing the strategic functions of the ward were all vital to its success.

Primary nursing was never pushed centrally in the way that the nursing process had been. Oxfordshire Health Authority played a key part in its development by supporting a policy of each patient having a named nurse, responsible for that person's care, and sanctioning the development of primary nursing firstly at the Burford Unit, then wards at the Radcliffe Infirmary and John Radcliffe Hospital. The King's Fund Centre, an independent charitable institution aimed at promoting the development of the best practice in all forms of health care, including nursing, also adopted a policy of supporting primary nursing, along with trying to promote a new method of working in a high profile and pioneering fashion. In doing this they had the support of the Department of Health. Oxford was an early focus for this also, as was a unit in Tameside in Manchester.

Nursing development units (NDUs) were designed to push at the barriers of nursing practice, initiating change both in practice and the organisation of nursing from the very bottom up, within individual nursing teams. These new units had the declared aims of:

- Offering the best possible standards of care;
- Monitoring the quality of care and taking appropriate follow-up action;
- Exploiting every opportunity for improving care;
- Evaluating the unit's activities on patients and staff;
- Enabling nurses to develop, personally and professionally;

- Sharing knowledge with a wider audience (Salvage, 1989).

The King's Fund Centre also sponsored a primary nursing network. Although primary nursing was not essential in an NDU, often the two went hand in hand. They had a key element in their task of developing new methods of practice and this was money. A unit selected as an NDU would receive pump priming monies in the form of a specific grant. Cultivating a close relationship with the Department and even ministers meant that their initiative had, at least, official support, as well as government money to support the initiatives.

Jane Salvage, then Director of Nursing Developments for the King's Fund, exploring strategies that could be adopted to pursue improvements in nursing wrote, '(NDUs) appear to be an idea whose time has come' (Salvage, 1989). In seeking greater managerial commitment to developing nursing practice, she again felt confident enough to write, 'At least the times are on our side', citing the need for quality control, addressing the wastage rate from clinical nursing, difficulties attracting new recruits and need for both clinical nurses and managers to demonstrate their effectiveness and efficiency. Primary nursing could be said to achieve all of these objectives. Because of its lack of any overt official push, it was a practice adopted by nurses throughout the health service and beyond, in true 'bottom-up' fashion, adapting it and shaping it depending on their own experience, work and environment, as well as the needs of their respective patients, whichever clinical setting they are in. It has thus become not one organisational system of nursing but many. But while it was developing in discretionary fashion at that local level, on a more strategic plane there were clearly conflicting ideological objectives and claims being set out on its behalf, some of which were articulated by Ms Salvage. Primary nursing was an organisational system born of its time, just like all of its predecessors.

The nursing process in the United States had only made its major impact after being identified as a key tool in quantifying and calculating the cost of nursing input:

> The Joint Commission on the Accreditation of Hospitals, which certifies the quality of hospital services as a basis of Federal and private insurance payments, made the preparation of care plans a prerequisite for its approval of an institution.

Care plans became one of the book keeping devices by which American health planners tried to contain the escalating costs of medical care. They required each item of nursing service to be identified and justified. If an item was not clearly related to the plan or accepted by later reviewers the hospital might be denied reimbursement for its costs.

(Dingwall, Rafferty & Webster, 1988: p. 214).

Those in favour of developing nursing practice were thus advocating a system that, for some managers, could be seen as an ideal way of controlling nursing practice and, through it, expenditure. There was a similar duality about the matter of responsibility and accountability. The developers argued that through 'granting' these to primary nurses, it would enhance nurses' practice and professional status. Yet this individualised the nurse's role to an extent that denied the reality of her work environment and very limited control over it. The complexities of such a notion were never fully worked through, exploring issues of patient safety, the conflict between the nurse's work with her care of an individual patient and its relationship to the needs of the wider patient group as well as how potentially conflicting needs of the unit and the wider institution might affect the individual nurse. All of these factors, as well as relationships between the nursing team itself – including the ways in which the work of one nurse is going to impinge on another – and their colleagues in the multidisciplinary team would inevitably affect the decision making process. Primary nursing's supporters promoted a system that flattened out hierarchies through diffusing decision making and power, enhanced collectivity, teamwork and the wider dissemination of information, and sought to introduce structures that democratised nursing practice (Ritter, 1984: pp. 53–5 and *Nursing Mirror*, 1983: pp. 16–17). But they were describing the same system that could, in other cases, be used to advance ideas about elitist practice and, through the managerial setting of targets, norms and standards, become the foundation of skill mix reviews aimed at producing the most diluted mix of nurses possible to provide cost limited care.

The individualising of a nurse's relationship with a group of patients within a larger work setting has several potential immediate effects. It reins in the nurse's desires to advance her own interests, except through her clinical work. It can divide nurses and, through the use of the individual's responsibilities and acountability, be used to control their activities in pursuit of objectives in the area of pay and conditions. When primary nursing is described as assisting the nurse's *personal* development there are faint echoes that go back to the 1930s and beyond: the vocational spirit has found a new voice, dressed up in contemporary language but still calling nurses ever onward to the greater good of their professional service.

Thus can any system of care be ideologically appropriated. With primary nursing there was no overtly political debate as such; it appeared that there was consensus amongst all parties. It was just the nuances that were different in most cases. But, also, times changed. The boldness, experimentation and expansiveness of the 1960s quickly became the impoverished late 1980s. By the time primary nursing was really becoming established in a lot of units, after the *Nursing Times* had run annual conferences on the subject playing to packed houses, the needs of the service had shifted. The expenditure on nursing was continuing to rise and there had been profound political changes. The managerialists in nursing potentially had a system that could provide improved nursing care on a semi-scientific basis, which had inbuilt cost monitoring mechanisms and would allow for greater control,

Primary nursing was never a trade union issue. COHSE and other nursing trade unions had not had any significant input into the debate, largely as it was not a pay and conditions issue which attracted any particular interest amongst its broad membership, although a lack of resource in professional services would have played a part. As with a number of nursing practice issues, it was only a matter of concern for a minority even amongst the nursing section of the union's membership; many COHSE members who would have been interested would no doubt have fed that interest through either the professional associations or their own service. However, both the nursing process and primary nursing had always been vigorously supported by the RCN, which co-sponsored some of the national conferences to debate the subject and who had many of its leading figures, such as Council member Steve Wright, at the forefront of its development. This close association undoubtedly was one of several factors in the RCN's recruitment success in the 1980s as they helped articulate the aspirations of many influential groups of nurses and the idealism of many students and junior trained staff. The College, most particularly through those directly involved in developing practice, tapped into the radicalism often vaguely expressed by a large minority of nurses, as practitioners talked of equalising relationships with doctors, extending the boundaries of practice and role of the nurse, alliances with user groups and patients and breaking free of the old hierarchies and constraints.

This was a revolution that had quietly been conducted through the pages of the nursing journals and textbooks, in various clinical settings and classrooms. It had not attracted the attention of the outside media and even many nurses and fellow health workers would have been ignorant of its detail in areas where it had not gained any kind of foothold. Nevertheless, it was, in many respects, the starting point for the near revolution that was to follow in a much noisier fashion at the end of the 1980s when clinical grading exploded onto the national stage. The agitation over nurses being accorded improved status through primary nursing, with its themes of authority and autonomy through responsibility and accountability had largely failed. However, nurses were under greater pressure than ever. Not only were they caring for more patients in the form of day cases and in-patient admissions; those patients were more acutely ill and consequently in need of an increased amount of nursing care. This was exacerbated as in-patient lengths of stay dramatically decreased (*Observer* 10.1.1988). It was estimated that the workload of the nurse had increased by 37% between 1962 and 1984 (Carpenter, 1991: p. 45). Added to this were a number of other pressures, with one specifically linked to the concepts of individualised patient care, that coming from managers who were regularly reminding nursing staff of their duty to care as professionals accountable for their practice. The link with primary nursing and pay and conditions was made as some nurses started to voice old demands that nurses should be rewarded for the clinical work they did rather than having to depart the clinical arena to go into management if they wanted material gains.

Failing to Train, Trained To Fail?

The high 'wastage' rate in nurse training has long been a cause for major concern and an indicator to the professionalisers that both nurse training and the practice of nurses have to be developed and improved if nursing is to be perceived as a more rewarding and fulfilling occupation. Inherent in all their arguments is that nursing must have greater status in order to keep nurses in the workplace on a consistent basis and for students to see it as reason to complete their training.

The woman 'suitable' in character, education and social class to be trained as a nurse has, however, proved to be something of a chimera, never there long enough to solve the overriding problem for her sponsors. In truth, this is because the myths have been so wholeheartedly swallowed by the daughters of its original perpetrators, when nurse authors and historians at the beginning of the century, anxious to portray nursing as a homogeneous, educated profession, tended to exaggerate the extent and success of the revolution in nurse training that had taken place. From the outset, at the renowned St Thomas' training school, there were defaulters and probationers being ejected from the course. Between 1860 and 1867 more than 10% were dismissed for a variety of offences, including disobedience, lack of sobriety and not being strong enough. Resignations took the overall loss to approximately 30% (Baly, 1987: pp. 34–44). Even the *Lancet* Commission, writing in 1932 about a loss of, again, 30% of learner nurses, described the need to 'restore the popularity of nursing among educated girls' (Abel-Smith, 1960: p. 149).

Plagued by shortages of nurses, the need to recruit sufficient numbers of people into nursing had always been at odds with the desire to have this elite workforce of suitable women. This was compounded periodically by demographic downturns in the number of young women available to apply for training. From the one year's course initiated by Nightingale, the hopes of widespread reform followed. By the end of the century almost all voluntary hospitals had a training school, often run by a matron who was one of the Nightingale School's protegés. There followed a wave of sackings as older, untrained nurses were ousted to make way for the militant new matron's recruits. Reformers set about the longer term task of introducing training to the workhouses although some enlightened authorities had already initiated their own programmes. But immediately a two tier status for probationers was erected, with the workhouse nurses a poor second, not only in how they were perceived but also how they were treated. Probationers were still cheap labour and were not thus a drain on the individual hospitals. And they could also be hired out (as could their trained colleagues) for nursing people in their own homes.

The numbers of trained nurses grew steadily, although standards were highly variable. Of about 25 000 trained at the turn of the century only about 10 000 would have been trained to Nightingale's standards and only half that number were the lady pupils of the 'right' calibre and social background. Nearly half of all nurses practising in 1901 were over the age of 45; nearly 45% were either married, widowed or divorced (Abel-Smith, 1960: pp. 57–8). These statistics were to change radically as training became more organised and was used successfully as a means of regulating entry into nursing. Florence Nightingale, believing that nurses were born and not made, had opposed the principles of examinations and registration. Neither were as important as the personal qualities and character of the nurse. However, Nightingale saw neither as being the exclusive property of the upper classes as did some of her rivals such as Mrs Bedford Fenwick and these issues remained highly contentious among nurse reformers. But when the battle for registration ended in 1919 the government also created the General Nursing Council. This was made up largely of nurses from the voluntary hospitals and members of the professional associations, the majority belonging to the College of Nursing. It had the responsibility for assimilating all nurses practising at the time of its inception in 1920 as well as determining what would be a suitable period of training but the continuing struggle for power and control on this most crucial of issues between the associations was simply carried on within the elected Council, forcing further government intervention and the threat to repeal the 1919 Act. The Minister of Health also dictated to the GNC the rules for recognising approved training schools and the arrangements for a syllabus and state examination, which was not held until 1925. The nursing organisations had been unable to agree a common strat-egy; the interventions of the government had been designed to protect the 'untrained' nurse, i.e. those who had not been trained in one of the approved schools, and ensure that the registration process was not too restrictive. The pattern for policy making in nursing was set.

Questions about what was a suitable period of training and syllabus for nurses, and what educational qualifications should be prerequisites rumbled on; however, the backdrop to the debate, looming like storm clouds over any attempt to impose strict regulation and stipulations, was the shortage of nurses and the need to keep an expanding service staffed. Equally, any debate about how to develop nurse training was, in reality, how to do this within the parameters of a medically defined model that had helped ensnare nursing into a position subordinate to medicine – unless there was to be a fundamental rethink which would take training out of the hospital environment and completely restructure the curriculum. Even by 1948 and the advent of the NHS, there was no common control over nurse training. The standard, fought for by all the professional associations, of a single portal of entry for registered nurses had not overcome the fact that there were six different parts for nurses in different specialities, including one on the general register solely for male nurses. Some trainings, for health visitors and mental nurses for example, were not even conducted under the auspices of the GNC, while midwives were still controlled by their original statutory body, the Central Midwives Board. Attempts to harmonise training, let alone completely restructure it, were met with predictable resistance from the different specialisms (White, 1987: p. 163).

By the 1980s, the basis of the different syllabuses had to be harmonised with European Community directives. They became more extensive, ensuring nurses received education and practice in a number of specialisms, including community work, as well as more basic allocations such as general medicine and surgery. A new syllabus was introduced in 1982 for mental health to try to improve the standard of training in that field, but all of the syllabuses remained 'skeletons', proposed as models by the statutory bodies. They were still more notable for what was left out of a nurse's training than what was in them (Salvage, 1985: pp. 65–6).

Mrs Bedford Fenwick had long before picked up on ideas about a system of training structured similarly to that of medical students for her cherished single portal of entry, so that nurses would experience a common foundation programme before advancing on to specialist qualifications. This was resurrected, in part, in the Briggs Report, which pronounced unequivocally that nursing and midwifery were professions and gave real hope to the professionalisers that change was at hand, a hope that was yet again to be stifled by the hand of government (The Briggs Report, 1972). The new statutory bodies that succeeded the old GNC, the English National Board (ENB), United Kingdom Central Council (UKCC), with the RCN, continued to press for educational reform in the 1980s and something approaching consensus began to form around a common foundation programme followed by branch programmes, with its educational base moved away from schools of nursing into higher education. It was envisaged that student nurses would be supernumerary, taken out from direct ward allocations and a largely hospital based training where they were under the control of the service side. These changes would give nurse training greater importance and its subjects would have enhanced status against their colleagues from other occupational disciplines. There had been regular complaints that the standard of GNC examinations was deteriorating and set at the lowest educational level possible, part of a prevailing ethos of anti-educationalism within some areas of nursing. The same critics charged that 'the GNC and RCN were influenced by nurses whose prior consideration was the recruitment of nurses to the NHS and who compromised educational standards for the sake of recruiting labour for the hospital wards' (Salvage, 1990 and White, 1987: pp. 163–5). Project 2000, as it was to become known, was designed to change all that.

All is never as it seems, however, and once again nursing's contradictions sneered in the face of the policy makers. If students were to be removed from the service who would take their place? How would the costs be borne? How would students be paid and by whom? What would be the link between the new colleges of education and the hospitals and health service facilities the nurses were being trained for? How would supervision be provided for students on clinical placements when they have extra clinical responsibilities because the students are removed from the ward team? What would be the implications for nurse tutors, many of whom would not be qualified to teach the new curriculum, and nurse educationalists generally, whom some felt were not adequately prepared for the transition (*Nursing Times*, 26.10.1988: pp. 16–17)? Would the vocational qualifications to be introduced alongside the new training merely duplicate the second portal of entry that had been there for the enrolled nurse or would the proposals prove to be too costly and difficult to implement in practice?

Students were taken outside of the service remit, paid a grant instead of a salary and teaching transferred to a higher education setting. But the overall answers and implementation of the proposals were almost all couched in compromise as the needs of the service again had to be recognised and concern about how the whole enterprise would be funded mounted, to the extent that there were fears that the 'whole programme for reforming nurse education' was 'in jeopardy', with RCN president, Maude Storey, telling Council members, 'I'm becoming more and more convinced of a political conspiracy' (*Nursing Times,* 23.5.1990: p. 5).

COHSE, without the strong professionalising and educational lobbies present in the RCN, took a different perspective on the Project 2000 proposals. Its interests were more aligned to its untrained and enrolled nurse membership, both of whom stood to be disadvantaged by the move to a workforce with fully trained and autonomous registered nurse practitioners planning the care to be provided by health care assistants. It had a fine line to tread. It had to be seen to be supportive of the new proposals, which were being hailed as progressive and timely by many influential nurses and for which there was a broad sweep of enthusiasm amongst younger nurses, yet be seen to fight for the interests of its own members. It began a vigorous campaign in defence of the enrolled nurse and set about successfully winning over its members in the debate about working with programmes for National Vocational Qualifications for health care assistants. It also argued in evidence to the UKCC that students should remain on a salary rather than student bursary and expressed concern about potential recruitment problems into the less attractive branch programmmes. The union did not enjoy much success at all in its campaigns, especially in the move to introduce the National Vocational Qualifications for health care assistants. This never materialised in the way that was envisaged and planned for and was a bitter blow after it had expended considerable energy and resources, through its professional officers, on securing a good training package which won over its internal critics.

For the RCN it seemed like a notable victory and the result of successful lobbying and joint work with the statutory bodies and Department of Health. However, the move away from the hospital setting for training, with the loss of the traditional nurse tutors in the school and the ward sister/charge nurse as a constant figure in a student's training, are also going to have major implications for the socialisation process of nurses and, thus, for nursing in the future, as will the influx of large numbers of health care assistants (to be discussed further in Chapter 8). As things stand currently, both the RCN and COHSE/UNISON are engaged in a familiar recruitment battle for Project 2000 students, both offering reduced student rates to members and a range of services specifically aimed at them. However, on several occasions, the RCN has voted not to take health care assistants and untrained nurses into membership, leaving its main rival a free hand to recruit them. The old balance of power in nursing is further likely to be disturbed as the grip of the hospitals – and particularly the high profile teaching hospitals – is significantly eroded.

With nurse training in a state of upheaval there is no clearer indication that the objectives of the professionalisers will be achieved. Project 2000 is being written off as a dismal failure by some. Nurse education has been decimated with large numbers of tutors being made redundant for the first time ever as schools merge or are swallowed up by higher education institutions. Student numbers are dropping and in some areas there are serious concerns about whether or not there will be enough students coming into branch programmes. Problems about supervision on clinical placements are unresolved and students are claiming that they are being used as pairs of hands on their service placements, 20% of their clinical allocation. The wastage rate shows no sign of decreasing from the traditional norms. Perhaps the only ones who can take any immediate comfort are the managerialists concerned with staffing the service. With the consent of almost all strands of the profession they have managed to introduce large numbers of untrained staff into the service; now they are not simply replacing the students lost but, in many cases, the qualified nurses they were previously working alongside (see Chapter 8).

Accountable to a Higher Authority

Five independent statutory bodies were established in 1979, as part of the Nurses, Midwives and Health Visitors Act, to replace the GNC. The United Kingdom Central Council for Nursing, Midwifery and Health Visiting (UKCC) and national boards for England, Scotland, Wales and Northern Ireland were to work closely together on the central task of improving standards of training and conduct (UKCC, 1979). In practice they remained as remote from the experience of most nurses as their predecessor.

The most prominent part of the UKCC's activity for many nurses was its role as overseer of practice, with regular news articles appearing, mainly in the nursing press but sometimes in the national dailies, about nurses being removed from the register, having been found guilty of professional misconduct. However, its role is far more comprehensive and strategic than dealing with individual cases of alleged misconduct – which the UKCC actually define. It has control and responsibility over all forms of training and for placing all nurses on the appropriate register or roll. 'The principal function of the Central Council shall be to establish and improve standards of training and professional conduct for nurses, midwives and health visitors' (Nurses, Midwives & Health Visitors Act, S. 2(i), 1979).

Having gained considerably more authority than in the early days of the GNC, the boards could inspect training schools and the workplace to see that it is a suitable environment for training and, where necessary, remove the training status of an institution without the fear that they would be humiliated by a successful appeal to a minister, as was the case in the 1920s. Removal of training status remained as powerful a tool for reform as it did in earlier decades as hospitals continued to rely on learner nurses to maintain ward numbers. The UKCC and national boards thus have a powerful regulatory function, with large numbers of full-time staff to support the elected members who make up the council and board members, and an important role in discrete nursing policy making, formulating policies on the administration of drugs, ethics and a wide range of practice issues. Two of the most significant policies are its *Professional Code of Conduct* and documents on nurses' accountability.

Harking back to the pre-registration days, a duty listed is the protection of the public, ensuring that people are looked after by safe practitioners and that all nurses, midwives and health visitors are aware that they:

> 'shall act, at all times, in such a manner as to justify public trust and confidence, to uphold and enhance the good standing and reputation of the profession, to serve the interests of society, and above all to safeguard the interests of individual patients and clients'.
>
> (UKCC, 1992).

This has led to an expanding web of rules and regulations governing nurses' training and the practice of students and trained nurses.

But they are still reliant on government for significant policy shifts such as Project 2000, where its role shifts to one of policy advisor rather than policy maker, although the statutory bodies still led the policy formation process. It was because it did not want to remain reliant on central government funding to maintain it, as had been the case since the inception of the GNC, that the UKCC decided to become self-financing, making all qualified nurses re-register periodically. This was a move resisted by many trained nurses but which had the support of the professional associations and trade unions, in the belief that financial independence from government would stop interference from government and mean a better deal for nurses. This support for the UKCC has not always been unequivocal on the part of COHSE. Its 1990 conference, for instance, was fiercely critical, accusing it of being a 'paper tiger with a large appetite for money' and voted for a resolution, backed by its NEC, to investigate its record on cost effectiveness, use of money and accountability to the profession (*Nursing Times*, 4.7.1990: p. 6).

Part of the problem for COHSE and the trade unions has been the historic domination of the statutory bodies by members of the professional associations, the RCN in particular. This is yet another policy making body that the trade unions cannot easily access and through which important relationships are built up with Department of Health officials and ministers. It has also been at odds with the UKCC over what it sees as the growing individualisation of the nurse's role and responsibilities, another facet of which was the Council's pronouncement that each nurse is responsible for her own continuing education once qualified. This manifested itself in the UKCC's proposals on PREPP, a policy for providing a nationally recognised framework for nurses' continuing education. This prescribed a set number of study days that each nurse had to attend within a three year time frame as well as the means for recording these and having them recognised. They were roundly condemned by COHSE for putting all of the responsibility on the individual without putting in place mechanisms to support them in their educational endeavours, although the union strongly supported the idea of statutory opportunities for continuing education.

Equally, trade union stewards at a local level were disappointed that the UKCC and national boards did not seem to be displaying their newfound independence, paid for by the individual nurses the stewards said now needed support in the face of what they saw as abuses by nurse managers, dangerously low staffing levels and unreasonably high workloads. Imaginative campaigners sought to turn the tables on the accountability argument by putting the pressure on managers who were nurses and even the UKCC itself. In Scotland, in the face of reduced staffing levels, cuts in overtime and a 50% cut in the training budget, COHSE circulated excerpts from the *Exercising Accountability* document (UKCC, 1989), advising their members of their accountability to the UKCC and that it was their duty to document and report difficulties in caring for patients because of inadequate staffing levels, calling on managers to rectify the situation. They criticised the UKCC for failing to respond to nurses' requests for advice and guidance on specific issues (Devine, 1990: pp. 30–1). Tom Bolger, then Director of Nurse Education at Camberwell Health Authority and a leading figure in the RCN, was quoted two years earlier as saying, 'I think the profession would have far more confidence in its disciplinary procedure if more nursing managers were brought before the Council. After all, they are the people who allow wards to stay open despite unacceptable staffing levels, very often causing the pressures that lead to errors' (*Nursing Times*, 9.11.1988: p. 18).

The UKCC is trapped in the same Catch 22 as every other body when it comes to nursing. Members of the Central Council have a duty to ensure that professional practice is developed, that training is advanced and progressive, offering the soundest possible academic base on which clinical practice can be built. But they know that managers have to respond to the demands placed upon them by a national health care system creaking under the weight of the contradictions facing it. The issuing of documents such as *Exercising Accountability* and the growing emphasis on the *Code of Conduct* were all linked to the development of increasingly individualised nursing care. Although it was probably not the overt intention of the Council, they can be viewed in the context of the social deconstruction that was part of the New Right's political philosophy and agenda for change. There was no such thing as society, just individual citizens, they were able to claim; similarly, there was less of a nursing occupational group, working to collective principles and shared responsibilities, just individual nurses. Further disappointment came when there was widespread expectation that the UKCC would update their document *Exercising Accountability* to make it easier for nurses who were risking their jobs to speak out. But the new version was seen as being nowhere near strong enough in the face of confidentiality clauses being inserted into trust hospital contracts and the public furore caused by the sacking of Graham Pink, a night nurse who had highlighted inadequacies in staffing levels and their effect on patient care. Perhaps, though, the leaders of the profession are doomed always to disappoint.

Chapter 6

The Anonymous Empire.
Nurses and policy making in the NHS

'Explanations of change have to be able to deal with continuity and change, actions and structures, endogenous and exogenous factors, as well as the role of chance and surprise' (Pettigrew, McKee & Ferlie, 1988: p. 302). How is change brought about in the NHS and what role do nurses and their organisations play? Many would hope that policy making involves interested parties coming together to formulate ideas and solutions to given circumstances or problems but struggles for power are, and always have been, principal factors in motivating change. Obviously, change and the policy process cannot be separated but the rational part of it does not necessarily follow; if power and the struggle for power are a necessary element of change, it becomes clear that in any policy making process there are going to be those who gain and those who do not. Nor is it always helpful to assume that involved parties always act in their own best interests. Three different positions were put forward by Steven Lukes about how people pursue their own interests and power:

> The liberal takes men (*sic*) as they are and applies want-regarding principles to them, relating their interests to what they actually want or prefer, to their policy preferences as manifested by their political participation. The reformist, seeing and deploring that not all men's wants are given equal weight by the political system, also relates their interests to what they might prefer, but allows that this may be revealed in more indirect and sub-political ways – in the form of deflected, submerged or concealed wants and preferences. The radical, however, maintains that men's *wants* may themselves be a product of a system which works against their *interests* and, in such cases, relates the latter to what they would want and prefer, were they able to make the choice (emphasis added)
>
> (Lukes, 1974: p. 34.)

Perhaps it is, then, worth examining not only how the policies are made, but how the problems are identified in the first place, who is involved in defining policy and how it is implemented.

The NHS Runs into an Ill Wind

The NHS was founded on anything but the basis of a widespread consensus (see pages 72–75). The doctors, although they had stood to gain the most from it, fought hardest against it (Tonkin, 1988), with the Conservative opposition unsuccessfully resisting the legislation in parliament. That political dissent was, in part, ideological but there were others, either in the Tory party or whose broad sympathies were with it, who viewed the principles of the NHS as flawed. Nonetheless, as the new service was initiated, the vast majority of doctors signed up for it and actually found their professional dominance legitimised by it (Carpenter, 1991: p. 38). It was extremely popular amongst the people of Britain. But within a couple of years alarm bells were being rung. Largely it was around the issue of escalating costs but as the years progressed wider and fiercer criticisms came to be aimed at it, some from unexpected quarters.

The financial problems of the NHS were, apparently, the most straightforward. Its costs had been projected but the predictions proved to be woefully inadequate, based on the assumption that as the previously unmet needs of the population were addressed the health of the nation would improve and demand would lessen, bringing overall costs down as a consequence. This misconception can be traced back to Beveridge in his original 1942 Report. Concern about 'Socialist profligacy or incompetence' or abuses by a public softened up by Labour rule mounted. Early critics pointed out that, as medicine expanded and more expensive methods of treatment were being developed there was little likelihood that costs would diminish and, in fact, far more probability that they would continue to rise inexorably (Dalken, 1978: pp. 28–34). The subsequent Conservative government of Churchill set up a committee to investigate NHS spending. It was something of a surprise if not outright disappointment to many critics when it not only cleared the NHS of charges of profligacy or extravagance but also declared that rising costs had kept to a minimum in real terms during the years 1948–54. Moreover, because of the neglect of hospital buildings, nearly half of which had been built before 1891, and failure to invest in new buildings in both the voluntary and local authority sectors, Britain seriously lagged behind other countries with a national health service and more money needed to be spent (Bruce, 1973: pp. 70–2).

Criticism of the strain the NHS and other welfare services put on the economy resurfaced in the 1960s and 1970s. They were accompanied by other strands of complaint that, altogether, added up to a comprehensive critique of the NHS and welfare state, both in its principles and practice. Looked at with hindsight, the most surprising aspect of this critique was that, in its early stage, it was coming largely from the political Left. However, the New Right quickly learned the words and tune and sang the song a lot more loudly and to far greater effect. Adding to the arguments, with the arrival of a receptive Conservative government in 1979, they were able to begin acting upon them.

Criticism of the way in which the medical profession dominated health care mounted after 1948. Those who argued that the notion of sickness was a 'social construct' used to reinforce medical dominance in society only saw the NHS as the logical extension of this. The sick were socially deviant and unproductive; to become 'well' it was necessary to enter into the hospital as a sick person, assume a passive role and co-operate with the treatment prescribed by the doctor. This was viewed as relatively benign by those such as Talcott Parsons, but assumed a harsher, more oppressive tone under the gaze of later critics. Attacks on the role of the medical profession and the NHS as an arm of welfare provision were also mounted by a plethora of Marxist critics, although their (sometimes contradictory) analyses varied according to the branch of Marxism they were coming from. The state was seen as '*all* of the activities employed by the ruling class to secure its collective conditions of production', including welfare provision and health care, which were, therefore, 'just as repressive as baton charges. For, to maintain the conditions of production in a class society is itself to perpetuate the oppression of class rule'. Moreover, not only was the NHS repressive but also ineffective and inefficient (Lee & Raban, 1988: pp. 108–10).

A more 'reformist' position was to look at how health care was redistributed and a wealth of evidence emerged, perhaps culminating in the now infamous Black Report, commissioned and then suppressed by the Tories and only published as part of *The Inequalities of Health* (1982), a work by sociologist Peter Townsend. This detailed to devastating effect the failure of the NHS to redistribute welfare services to those in greater need and worse off; the NHS was actually providing qualitatively better care for those who needed it least (Le Grand, 1982; Klein, 1989: p. 52). Tudor Hart described this as the 'inverse care law'. The flaw he cited in the system was a failure to adhere to the original principles of the NHS, with a commitment to primary health facilities such as health centres, where all personal health services would be provided whilst, 'The force that creates and maintains the Inverse Care Law is the operation of the market, and its cultural and ideological superstructure which has permeated the thought and directed the ambition of our profession (medicine) during all of its modern history' (Tudor Hart, 1971). Feminist critics pointed out that women were even further disadvantaged by this failure of redistribution, being discriminated against by policies that were formulated by men. More radical arguments have described how policy has been used to control the lives of women (Wilson, 1983: p. 33) and how women have been subjugated not only as workers in the health service but also as its users. The same thesis has been put forward about the inbuilt racist principles of the service:

> ... heavily implicated in the exploitation and oppression of Black people as an employer (and) depriver of provision or provider of second rate provision, as controller and container of social unrest.
>
> (Williams, 1987: p. 26)

Marxists had described the way in which state welfare provision was used to legitimise the capitalist system but that governments are always hung on the ideological and economic contradictions between state intervention and the market, with one offering hope of a rational, planned system of care provision and the other allocating resources simply according to the pattern of supply and demand. Other analysts saw the expansion of government as being inversely proportional to popular satisfaction, with the increasing unresponsiveness of big government to the needs of the individual leading to frustration, apathy and alienation. All pointed to a collapse in support for the system. On a micro level, for users of the NHS, this was experienced within the service with the same result – up to a point (Taylor Gooby & Papadakis, 1987: pp. 23–5 and Taylor Gooby, 1986). This was coupled with a growing alienation towards the paternalistic structures and systems inherent in the NHS, supporting the medical dominance and undermining any opportunities for democratic participation by staff, users of the service or the local community. Inward looking, its paternalism had left it overly bureaucratic, inefficient and uncompetitive. Moreover, that medical domination had meant that the NHS had absorbed the prevailing models of illness and health, with their methods of treatment and cure in an increasingly hospital based system, which continued to deny nurses and other health professionals the status they were seeking and recognition of their contribution to health care provision whilst disenfranchising the patient and preventing any control they may wish to assume over their care and treatment (Navarro, 1979: pp. 41–6 and Mitchell, 1984).

From other standpoints, questions were raised about the efficacy of the NHS and whether or not it was making any serious impact on the health of the nation. Absence from work through sickness had actually increased steadily; increases in life expectancy and decreases in infant mortality were difficult to attribute to the NHS; more likely they were due to improved social and economic conditions linked to housing, nutrition and education. Some studies suggested that the more doctors there were the worse the mortality figures were (Klein, 1989: p. 167). Awareness of the extent of iatrogenic conditions was growing and no conclusive proof that was not contradicted by an alternative report could be offered to suggest the NHS was contributing to a fitter, healthier nation. The strongest and most radical criticism of professional dominance of health care and the dangers of medicine had come from Ivan Illich, who wrote:

> ... since medicine is a sacred cow, its slaughter should have a 'vibration effect', since people who can face suffering and death without need for magicians and mystagogues are free to rebel against other forms of expropriation...
>
> (Illich, 1975: p. 161)

Whilst the slaughter of medicine may not have played a major part in government thinking in 1979, other matters did. Although criticisms of the financial burden of the NHS had been undermined by the Guillebaud Report, they had resurfaced with a vengeance in the 1970s and been picked up on by the New Right along with all of the other criticisms being levelled at the health service and welfare state. It had long been recognised that health expenditure was in direct competition with industry for subsidy from government and that money that went into the health service would inevitably mean less was available for investment for new industries or to maintain older ones; health service expenditure was also 'unproductive' in that no tangible goods were produced as a result.

In the face of the recession of the 1970s:

> 'no other major economy experienced so severe a crisis, so severe a failure to achieve every economic objective, as Britain. If the NHS has in any way contributed to that decline ... it has a formidable case to answer. The steady absolute and proportional growth in expenditure on the NHS, without any clear evidence of any corresponding economic return, together with the rise in the numbers of staff, some of whom would have been drawn, directly or indirectly, from productive sectors of the economy, creates a prima facie case'
> (Dalken, 1978: p. 158).

According to the body of criticism now coming from the New Right, the National Health Service was an unacceptable financial burden holding back economic growth; it was overly bureaucratic, centralised, inefficient, unresponsive and uncompetitive; dominated by the professions, medicine in particular; it was working to its own agenda and to its own ends. Not only that, but the health service trade unions had been having things their own way for too long. Vitally, on the terms identified for it by its supporters, when it came to redistributing health care to those most in need, it had failed.

Seeking the Holy Grail of the Perfect Managerial System

The agenda for change had been stolen from under the noses of the Left by the New Right, who found greater popular expression for their criticisms and a ready audience. Partly fuelled by the critical debate going on around it, but also as result of people's own experience in relation to using its services, there had been a growing disquiet that affected popular confidence in state welfare during the mid 1970s (Levitas, 1986: pp. 12–15 and Taylor Gooby & Papadakis, 1987: p. 19) even if, paradoxically, the NHS remained a service that showed favourably in poll after poll (Taylor Gooby, 1986). This overall disquiet actually contributed towards changing voting patterns and was one of the factors that paved the way for the Conservative electoral victory of 1979.

The question for the Tories, once they would assume power, was how to effect change? The key was seen as being a managerial system that would afford them greater control throughout the service, but this was not a new objective. Different governments through the previous three decades had wrestled with the same problem, with a belief during the late 1960s and early 1970s that the answer lay in new forms of scientific or industrialised management (Briggs, 1978: p. 449). One of the muddled aims of the 1974 reorganisation had been to achieve more direct managerial control to ensure that policies agreed at the centre would be carried out at a regional and local level. The NHS had enjoyed relative stability until 1974, but the course of events then symbolises one of the problems about policy making as it had affected the NHS. The need for a structural change was identified by a Labour government, who issued two consultative Green Papers under successive ministers in 1968 and 1970 – which proposed the introduction of chief executives and general managers. Further consultation in the form of a Green Paper in 1972 and a White Paper confirming policy in 1973 was carried out by the Conservatives which was then reluctantly enacted in 1974 by the new Labour government. Some alterations were made by Labour, notably introducing elected representatives from the local authorities, but these were marginal and many were unhappy with their implementation of what was seen as the roots of the overly bureaucratic, paternalistic and inefficient service soon to be so heavily criticised. It would have been difficult to completely revamp policy; it would have meant even further delay. But a lot of the core of their 1970 consultative paper was destroyed by the Keith Joseph reorganisation. The only common link between the latter and Labour's proposals was the emphasis on introducing effective management, designed to 'redress the balance in NHS services' and 'between the acute and chronic services in favour of the latter' (Klein, 1989: pp. 91–3). The irony was that, if anything, its structural complexity and tilts towards democratic participation made the whole process of initiating change all the more difficult. National policy in seeking change and moving towards a greater equality of service provision was, as ever, at variance with local policy, where the better off were not willing to surrender services or resources. The equalising method of redistributing funding, the Resource Allocation Working Party (RAWP), introduced in 1976, was never popular or regarded as either fair or scientifically accurate – except by those it rewarded. And costs were no more controlled than before 1974. It remained the classic case that ministers, or central government, could propose, but local politics, particularly as determined by the professionals, would dispose (Glennerster, 1983).

A further change of government whose thinking was shaped by the body of criticism aimed at the NHS as well as its own ideological commitment to the market and minimalist state intervention meant the 1974 changes would be relatively shortlived. A further reorganisation occurred in 1982, removing area health authorities in favour of localised district health authorities. The nursing management structures created as a result of the Salmon Report, which saw the introduction of budget holding chief nursing officers and nurses involved in consensus management at every tier of the service, were dented but this was as nothing compared with what was to come. An era of 'change upon change', had arrived but also one where rational planning and policy making had fallen into disrepute.

Change in the National Health Service – Does Nursing Make an Impact?

The way in which the NHS functions as an organisation is complicated by any number of factors. These are both internal and external. They include its size, interactions between its national, regional and local levels, the number of different occupational groups working within it and their relative status, how those groups interact with external policy makers such as civil servants and politicians, its funding levels and, perhaps most importantly, how its aims and objectives – at whatever level – relate to popular perception of its ability to meet them and its success in doing so. However, for a long time, the process and dynamics of policy making were such an esoteric, guarded process that three RHA chairmen studying it found themselves hampered by a lack of knowledge of how the system worked and no records of the numbers and purposes of interdepartmental working parties (Haywood & Hunter, 1982: p. 143).

The early dominance of the medical profession in the NHS, secured through their syndicalist approach during those tortuous two years of negotiation with Bevan prior to 1948 and the imposition of the culture, values and structures of its predecessor health care systems, would suggest that they secured a privileged position when it came to policy making. If culture can 'shape and not merely reflect organisational power relationships' (Pettigrew, McKee & Ferlie, 1988: p. 302) then immediately the importance of nursing's cultural myths and traditional subservience and subordination to medicine becomes apparent, not just for policy making in the health service as a whole but also within nursing itself. Indeed, that nursing escaped the scathing criticisms aimed at the NHS generally and the medical profession specifically was far less because of any great admiration for nurses or the work that they do; rather it was because of the invisibility of nurses in the policy process.

A study of consultative processes conducted by the academics, Stuart Haywood and David J. Hunter (1982, pp. 142–4), focusing on the 'relationship between (non-Department of Health) groups consulted on policy matters and ministers and department officials', demonstrated that there was evidence of change in the early 1980s in health service policy making. Some of the earlier rigidity had been broken down, enabling more pluralistic mechanisms to work. One of the significant factors in that was the rapid growth in trade union membership in the NHS and the number of different groups within it now jostling one another for position and influence. These pluralistic mechanisms take the form of issues networks and involve interested parties coming together on a specific policy issue. They form and re-form, dependent on the issue, with different participants. However, a firmer network of power relationships was still in existence, indicating that the essential dominance of the medical profession remained, which meant that the participants in the issues networks failed on some occasions to exert the influence commensurate with their involvement. Haywood and Hunter described these latter relationships as 'iron triangles', a pattern of stable, predictable and relatively closed, private relationships between key members of the medical profession, officials at the Department of Health and ministers (pp. 152–4).

Within such models, the beginning of nursing involvement in policy making starts to show itself. If nurses cannot break the iron triangle of civil servant, politician and doctor when it comes to policy making it cannot seriously challenge the dominant position of the medical profession. Clearly, not all policy matters relating to nursing will be determined within this process; in fact, it is likely that more will be dealt with through the issues networks. The coming together of senior nurses, particularly with civil servants from the Department of Health, is a model that has been employed on a large number of policy issues to do with nursing and clinical practice as well as matters relating to pay and conditions. It is not that unusual, for instance, for the Royal College of Nursing not just to be consulted but also to have its senior members, either lay or full-time, seconded to the Department or working with it in the writing of specific policies. For the trade unions, being drawn into the process is more difficult. There have been occasions when they have been able to do so with great effect, whether or not the medical profession have been supportive of the policy, but these have normally been with a Labour government more sympathetic to their point of view but also, importantly, dependent on the support of the trade unions. The battle over private beds was one such occasion (Klein, 1989: p. 117). Trade unions did manage to become involved in policy issues, at least to the extent of expressing an interest, and not only when their members' pay and conditions were affected. Nonetheless, the RCN remained very firmly the dominant force in nursing within the issues networks (Haywood & Hunter, 1982: p. 157).

Rational Policy Making?

'The history of planning warns us against unrealistic expectations of its impact on performance.' So wrote Haywood & Alazewski in

1980 (p. 55). But how rational has recent NHS planning been and how much impact on the service and its performance is it reasonable to expect?

The rationalist models were the ones that dominated 'official' accounts of the planning process described in the early 1980s (Pettigrew, McKee & Ferlie, 1988: p. 308). These related to initiatives that were led from the centre, to be implemented in the regions and/or district health authorities and were thus 'top-down'. Policy cast from the centre, within the structures of the iron triangles, would be relatively easy to identify as rational in that it would have been built up around identifiable objectives agreed on a planned basis by participants who, to a degree, had shared goals. Except that 'the predominant ideology (was) set by the practitioners rather than politicians and civil servants' (Haywood & Alazewski, 1980: p. 65). Nonetheless, such a model assumes that it is the centre that truly rules and that there are no organisational differences: nor that different tiers of the service operate in different ways. Yet the NHS cannot, just as nursing cannot, be described as homogeneous in its structure. It is made up of competing groups, services and levels of organisation, all seeking to exercise power and influence to achieve often contradictory ends.

Consultative processes do, of course, exist within the NHS at a national level in the form of the Whitley Councils, instituted from the outset as a means of addressing policy issues for all disciplines and grades of staff on all matters relating to their terms and conditions (although the Councils are now threatened by the local bargaining that is an integral part of the NHS reforms introduced in the 1989 White Paper *Working for Patients*). Other policy issues, as we have seen, are managed through the wider political structure, although the same rational policy making is, undoubtedly, complicated and made harder because of trade unions. They do not ascribe to the notion of the 'common good' and see their principal task as being one of defending their members' interests rather than assisting in solving the structural problems of the service. Even if they were tempted to join the government or employers in such a task there is every likelihood that the membership would resist. Inevitably, they come into conflict on policy issues and, when they have sufficient power behind them, are able to dictate policy at best, or otherwise resist it, thus maintaining the status quo. This is no different to how the medical profession have acted on key occasions and the formation of the NHS has been quoted as one of them. Thus when it was being planned that the new health service should come under local authority control, it was the objections of the BMA that figured most strongly amongst the issues that led to a change of plan, for as much as they disliked the idea of being 'civil servants' within a nationalised service, it was better than becoming 'municipal officers' within one run by the local authorities (Tonkin, 1988). In such ways are strategic plans thwarted.

However, despite the plethora of committees and groups meeting within the Department of Health and at a local level within the health service, there has always been the issue of non-decision making or the absence of key issues from the policy making agenda. This is in part attributable to the scarcity of resources and high number of competing issues that require progressing through policy making; however, it is also an exercise consolidating the existing status quo and those who derive their power from it (Ham, 1985: pp. 106–13). This takes us back to Lukes' concept of power and interests (1974: p. 43) and the way in which those in power choose either to do nothing and thus support their own interests or suppress action by groups or individuals that could, potentially, threaten the status quo. This they do by using their 'power reputation operating on anticipated reactions' and/or thwarting attempts to raise issues. As a 'policy option' this is one that appears to have operated at national level in nursing and also at unit and even departmental level, where nurses often have the experience of not being listened to or being unable to find a suitable channel through which to make their criticisms heard and try to direct policy. Thus change occurs that is to the detriment of nurses who have not known what the full consequences of change would be: it also occurs when nurses have felt powerless, assuming that any resistance or attempt to effect change on a specific issue would be hopeless – in the absence of any empirical evidence for such an assumption – or have simply been unable to get their grievance legitimately dealt with.

Very often nurses are then blamed – and blame each other – for accepting whatever is thrown at them, even if it is against their best interests, and 'being their own worst enemy'. But the lack of choices available to them, coupled with their apparent desires actually being the product of a sophisticated system that works against them, suggests that nurses are grossly disempowered at every level of the service.

They can also be disadvantaged by mechanisms available to others involved in policy making. Much has been written about whether or not the media influence and shape opinion rather than merely reflecting it. The nursing journals have long been a battleground between both different professional associations and the associations and the unions. The RCN have seen them as valuable enough to ensure that they have always had a mass circulation, commercial magazine serving their interests and, having stopped their association with the *Nursing Times* in the 1960s, now own and publish the *Nursing Standard*. These journals have been used to great effect in supporting campaigns or assisting the process of bringing about change, as was seen in the case of the nursing process. However, their failure to highlight the plight of nurses in certain sectors could have the opposite effect. There was no campaigning in the nursing journals on behalf of the mental nurses and attendants in the early asylums and mental hospitals, despite the knowledge that their conditions of work were bad. A journalist writing about the history of nursing journalism suggests that this slowed the process of necessary change:

> But may not the example of the mental nurses' plight indicate the value of the nursing journals? That asylum attendants lost out partly because the nursing journals were just not interested in them?

> (Dopson, 1985b: pp. 14–15)

It was not just the nursing journals that were not interested in them, however. The professionalising nurses in the voluntary hospitals were busy promoting their agenda and objectives, which were supported by the journals and not the same as those of the attendants. Indeed, the attendants' demands and concerns ran counter to them. This relationship and bias have continued, through their predecessor organisations, to the contemporary relationship between the RCN and COHSE.

A Rational Trade Union Response?

Trade union policy is, according to most rule books, dictated from the annual delegate conference. Certainly this was the case with COHSE. If rational choices need to be made based on the maximum amount of information available, a consideration of the options and then the development of a planned strategy for implementation, then the union's policy was formulated in the most irrational way possible. It was based on five minute speeches putting forward highly subjective opinions on issues that many of the delegates may know little or nothing about and in which they may have little interest. Even if the debate was listened to carefully, it was conducted much more on an adversarial level, with speakers having two minutes to put forward pros and cons to a proposed motion, depending on their own point of view. It was the practice of the National Executive Committee to 'respond' to the debate through a nominated speaker and make a recommendation about whether or not delegates should vote for the motion before its proposer exercised her/his right of reply. The outcome, the winning and losing of the debate, was determined by a vote of all the delegates present in the hall, whether or not they had listened to the debate. This then became the policy of the union.

Within this process several exercises in power would be conducted by the union's leadership. In advance it would be known whether or not they would support a specific motion; they could effectively lobby against its progress and had the choice of making available information which may or may not make its passage easier. The bureaucratic structures and rules of a trade union, as with any organisation, whilst there to democratise its procedures can also be used as an effective means to thwart legitimate attempts to exercise change. Nonetheless, the conference delegates do hold and exercise real power and have in the past used it to halt rational and apparently necessary policy developments, even when adequate information has been provided by the NEC. Moreover, there will also be a process of collusion between all levels of the union when a resolution is passed that the participants know cannot be implemented but which is supported as politically correct. This became the case with COHSE's policy about competitive tendering and the privatisation of ancillary services long after it was firmly established that whilst the Conservatives remained in office it would not be reversed and that even an incoming Labour government would not go back to their pre-1979 position.

Certainly, it is enormously difficult to fashion a coherent set of national policies from a large number of conference resolutions, written by branch officials, many of whom are advancing local issues and/or concerns, perhaps with little understanding or regard for wider, strategic considerations, particularly if their only conduit into the policy arena is the conference floor where style stands every chance of victory over substance. This is, of course, political policy making in the tradition of the Labour movement and British politics as a whole, which has long functioned in an adversarial manner, characterised by the spectacle of the House of Commons. The question the unions have been unable to answer – or even raise in many cases – is whether or not it is the most effective. The reality is that other means are often used to rationalise the process, as unsatisfactory as that is.

The ultimate exercise in power and control is the vigour with which the full-time officers act upon the policy decision of the conference and the union's NEC. Once the lay membership have made their decision they are reliant on the union's officers to turn policy into action. In this, there is common ground with procedures within the RCN, although much else is different. Once passed at the RCN Congress, a resolution is only recommended to the RCN Council, to 'take action "on matters which fall within the established policy"' (Turner, 1992: pp. 16–17). Moreover, each motion submitted must first be chosen by the agenda committee, whereas all motions submitted to COHSE are automatically put to conference unless procedurally incorrect or out of order. The College's Council, by having ultimate policy making responsibility within the organisation, thus exercises ultimate control. However, as so much is decided within the College away from the glare of the public spotlight, this affords its officers more opportunity to exercise influence over the process as well as retain more power either to act or not to act, or act in such a way that nothing happens as a consequence.

The Anonymous Empire

Problems in health service policy making were compounded by the early 1980s as the process became ever more diverse and the number of groups competing and participating within its structures multiplied. These groups weakened the 'iron triangle' process which had so favoured the medical profession but also reflected the growing complexity of the health service and the need, if it were to function anywhere near efficiently, to incorporate other groups. This included users, albeit in the limited shape of the community health councils introduced in 1974. Trade unions as well as professional organisations were being included on nursing issues, but with the RCN and RCM, particularly, almost holding a monopoly on these.

Being consulted and exerting influence is not so straightforward and positive as may initially be thought, however, and can bring problems for a trade union. To be involved in devising policies that could be construed as detrimental to the interests of a particular nursing constituency risks courting unpopularity and losing members. Placing the union in a position where it is likely to be invited in also suggests that it risks losing its critical edge. Why should COHSE or any of the other unions be sought as partners in a policy process of which they are consistently suspicious if not hostile? It is not a dilemma easily resolved but is far less marked for the RCN, committed to a far larger extent with the Department of Health and management generally to a shared set of values. Nonetheless, COHSE has a 'shopping list' of policies, both as a union and as part of the Nurses' and Midwives' Whitley Council, as do the RCN. These have to be pursued within the same framework and networking becomes important within the nursing organisations. Personal relationships are 'paramount' within the trade unions and officers with reponsibilities for nursing matters within COHSE have worked with their counterparts from other organisations far more than with colleagues from adjacent offices but with different occupational responsibilities within their own union. Within the 'closed community' of the Department, personal relationships are also valued. These are built up over time and can be fragile; the last thing to do is rock the boat or jeopardise them, not just for the individuals involved but for the long term working of the organisation represented. Conflict avoidance becomes all important (Haywood & Hunter, 1982: p. 147). The real difficulties for a trade union officer who has to get from the Department the items on the union's shopping list whilst retaining a tenuous position in an issues network that is in a constant state of flux become apparent.

An important part of the regulation of the demand process is the way in which interest groups such as trade unions and professional associations filter out some of the demands made of them, making it more manageable. Thus the demands of a branch are taken to conference in the form of motions for debate. Some of these are unsuccessful and fall by the wayside. Of those that are successful, some will be 'non actionable' other than in the form of issuing publicity materials, perhaps offering support to a particular cause or writing letters containing demands of a general nature. This is particularly so with resolutions passed in support of an international issue. However, even with those which require specific action there has to be some regulation.

One RCN official suggests that this takes the issues networks a step further. It is not just about official groups coming together to debate issues or be consulted on policy. It is described as walking the corridors of an anonymous empire, meeting with departmental figures in a very covert way, contributing to policy making and decisions through non-attributable telephone calls and remarks. Thus the public face does not necessarily have to match the private policy making; working relationships can be preserved whatever the public rhetoric and progress can be made through negotiation, at least as defined by the parties involved rather than the wider membership. Progress on one policy can be sacrificed to further another. What all agree may be too problematic in the contemporary circumstances can be quietly dropped or refused without any great loss of face for either party. Whilst this is a situation familiar to many negotiators in different settings, its effectiveness and use will vary according to the status and involvement of the group within the formal processes. Pettigrew *et al.* (1989: p. 201) describe the best networks as 'the most informal ones, where trust and open communication (have) been established over time'. Thus some groups are not only more adept at exploiting the policy making process but better placed to do so. This can affect the interest not only of one occupational group against another but also within a particular group. Nursing is one of those most vulnerable to this, with its own dominant groups exerting influence, supported by the professional associations – notably the RCN – as well as the interests of the medical profession imposing on its agenda. One simple example of this, already mentioned, can be found in the growth of hospital nurses at a time when all official policies dictated that more resources and nursing personnel should be directed into primary care and community nursing. Again, the media have a part to play and with 'a certain cosiness in relationships between the (nursing) press and the power base at the Elephant and Castle' (HQ of the Department of Health), also tread the corridors of the anonymous empire, deciding what to report and when to report it (Dopson, 1985b: p. 17).

There can be little doubt that one of the primary problems facing nurses is actually identifying what their best interests are and then arriving at strategies for advancing them. Not being a homogeneous group endlessly complicates the process as does their position in the NHS pecking order. The importance of the myths and culture of nursing has been used to try to establish a hegemony for the dominant groups, seeking a wide base of support for their favoured policies, and the 'common good' has held sway for a long time. Whilst the College have dominated the policy making process on many nursing issues, they have only been able to make limited gains when these policies would remove nursing from the influence of the medical profession. Moreover, when they have had clearly identifiable resource implications or flown in the face of recent government policy – when power and control have been the naked issues – they have had no more influence than COHSE.

Chapter 7

Nursing on the supermarket shelf.
The introduction of general management

In 1983 a 24 page letter arrived on the doormat of the Right Honourable Norman Fowler, Secretary of State for Social Services, sent by an acquaintance of Mrs Thatcher. It was no ordinary letter. It was to bring about the most significant change to the NHS since the 1974 reorganisation and paved the way for the fundamental upheavals that were to see it transformed from the service established in 1948. It was also to make the name of its author synonymous with the managerialism that came to characterise the health service of the 1980s and 1990s.

The Government Goes Shopping for a New Idea

The NHS was, according to a variety of diagnoses, in 'crisis' (not a conclusion this author would agree with, as it has been shown that there have been continual problems, tensions and contradictions that have defied resolution for almost as long as there has been a health care system). An almost overwhelming body of criticism had developed over the preceding decade, prompted by public dissatisfaction with welfare services generally, intellectual analyses and ideological considerations/discontent from both Left and Right. If the managerial challenge was how to curtail NHS spending, the Thatcher government did not see the answer in any of the traditional methods of policy making. Consultative papers had been issued in the late 1960s and early 1970s but the subsequent reorganisation had increased bureaucracy without resolving the key problem of how the centre could control spending in the localities. The problem had not been resolved through the 1979 Report of the Royal Commission. The rigid control of policy making within the Department was lost in the amorphous structures of supposedly consensual management permeating throughout the rest of the health service, which in reality only masked the medical profession's continuing dominance. NHS funding was close to its peak in real terms, with no sign of being able to either bring it down or ensure that it was spent as the government wanted it spent. Even the Conservatives' own 1982 reorganisation failed to achieve this. For if the medical profession's dominance remained largely intact it necessarily followed that managers were not the most powerful group in the NHS; they were actually dependent on service providers. Thus it became clear that if change were to be properly effected it must be directed at the total local system for management and not just reorganising the managers (Haywood & Alazewski 1980: p. 148).

It was at this stage that Mrs Thatcher, in true iconoclastic style, called on the assistance of Roy Griffiths, the managing director of Sainsbury's (although he was later to be knighted for his troubles). He was brought in because of his success in retailing, built on an attitude of questioning the cost of everything as well as a track record of speed and effectiveness in decision making. Setting about his task, that of giving 'advice on the effective use and management of manpower and related resources in the National Health Service', he brought with him six assistants: Jim Blyth, the Group Finance Director from United Biscuits, Sir Brian Bailey, Chairperson of the Health Education Council, Michael Bett, Board Member for Personnel at British Telecom, and three civil servants. The results of the inquiry were equally iconoclastic, both in presentation and recommendations. Within just six months they reported back in the form of a relatively brief letter, with a list of 'action points' to be implemented by the Minister (Griffiths, 1983: p. 1).

Nurses Get Caught in the Line of Fire

Hints for the future were omnipresent in Griffiths' method of working. There was no committee work; there was little reference to historical developments in the service; consultation was wide but not formal; no 'evidence' was sought in the shape of official submissions. Consensus was not on the agenda. Nothing new was discovered, however. The final diagnosis was one of 'institutional stagnation' (Klein, 1989: p. 209). The aim of the document was clearly one of establishing centralised financial control through managerial accountability and control and pulling the doctors into the process of management and budgeting. The letter made clear the team's belief that there was a need for a NHS management board in addition to a health services supervisory board, the latter comprising the Minister of State (Health), the Permanent Secretary and the Chief Medical Officer. These would, of course, maintain the formula for an iron triangle of policy making described in Chapter 6. This was, though, to be weakened by 'two or three non-executive members with general management skills and experience'. The role of the management board would be to provide leadership, control performance and achieve 'consistency and drive' over the long term (Griffiths, 1983: p. 3). In seven pages of recommendations for management action by the Minister, nurses were not once mentioned. But did this mean that nothing was happening to them or was it again an exercise in the use of power by not declaring anything and keeping the prospect of change off the agenda until the appointed time?

The impressive sleight of hand about the report was that it appeared to be proposing decentralised management; indeed, this was emphasised throughout. However, because of the managerial structure the line of management spread itself, like a web, out from the centre, covering all aspects of the service. This was only to be reinforced by the implementation of a system of cascading appointments, from the centre outwards, so that appointees of the Secretary of State made the next tier of appointments and so on. There was an equal emphasis on drawing the doctor into the web:

> We believe that urgent management action is required, if Units are to fulfil their role and provide the most effective management of their resources. This particularly affects the doctors. Their decisions largely dictate the use of all resources and they must accept the management responsibility which goes with clinical freedom. The nearer the management process gets to the patient, the more important it becomes for the doctors to be looked upon as the natural managers
>
> (Griffiths, 1983: pp. 18–19.)

In this process, although nurses were not proscribed from managerial posts, with an emphasis on general management skills and experience, obviously, they were immediately disadvantaged. It was a different case with doctors, who had largely avoided positions of prescribed power in the managerial process and did not have line management or budget holding responsibilities, instead dominating the decision making process through other means. Moreover, a number of nurse management positions were obviously going to be lost in the upheaval.

Nurses Left Out in the Cold

The number of non-clinical nursing posts had multiplied rapidly after the implementation of the Salmon Report in 1966 and the 1974 reorganisation. The grade system and the status of a larger number of nurses in managerial positions had been extended but no system of control over the nursing workforce to equal that exercised by the matron had come with it. Salmon had, itself, been in part the government's attempt to introduce some rationality into the structure of nursing, which had been close to chaos since being brought into the NHS (White, 1985a: p. 53). The new structures put in place a decade later meant that nurses now had a seat on management and consultation committees at every level of the service. But there had been no extra training to accommodate the responsibilities handed over to senior nurses and their educational limitations left them cruelly exposed, their roles were never completely clear and any autonomy in decision making did not really materialise (Dingwall, Rafferty & Webster, 1988: p. 212). Often, the role of middle nurse managers was reduced to that of trouble shooting on a shift by shift basis. Even that limited grasp on power was undermined by the 1982 reorganisation, which saw nursing officers (as they were pre-Griffiths) losing their posts in large numbers. Griffiths merely took the depletion of senior nurses on to the next stage.

Any changes in nursing structures could be interpreted as merely coincidental to the overall changes, that nurses were accidental casualties in the process of change. However, this is to ignore the existing policy making structures and power relationships within them. One of the stumbling blocks to nurses assuming more power after 1974 had been the resistance of the medical profession to the advance of consensus management in any way that would weaken their power and influence. The new changes offered the opportunity to further diminish the influence of a rival group. Again, the securing of senior positions within the new management frameworks would inevitably lead to winners and losers, 'disadvantages and casualties' (Maxwell, 1986: p. 5). The emphasis then placed within the new general management structures on cost control and financial stringency ensured that anyone who was not seen to be contributing towards the efficiency and cost-effectiveness of the service would not retain a place.

Nursing officers were an expensive commodity, little valued and with little apparent impact on patient care. They were 'officers', not managers, a leftover from a bygone age and they did not even command the support of their troops. Moreover, the unwritten subtext that leaps off almost every page of the Report is about the need to control the work that nurses do and therefore the cost of the service. That would be achieved in part by drawing in the doctors to take responsibility for managing the resources they had available, but then to have left nurses free – especially as they were busy looking at new and potentially more independent ways of practising – would have undermined the task at hand. Nurses may not have been named in Griffiths' letter but it was as much about them as anyone else in the NHS.

Another factor still very much in everyone's mind was the 1982 pay dispute. Nurses had united around the cause of a 12% pay increase and taken their most militant action yet in a dispute that had run for eight months. They had secured, at its death, a settlement far above that which the government had wanted to concede and an independent pay review body that left the whole costly affair of nurses' pay out of government control for the first time since the formation of the NHS. Not only the doctors but also the nurses had to be controlled.

With the approach taken by the Griffiths team, both the iron triangles and even the issues networks were bypassed. Nurses and nursing organisations were not consulted in any detail on the proposals, to the extent that the then RCN general secretary, Trevor

Clay, was able to declare that they came as a shock to nursing's leaders (Clay, 1987: p. 5). Any attempt to salvage the position of nurses in the policy making and managerial structures was going to have to take place outside them.

The RCN Campaign

In the face of this fundamental change, the nursing unions and professional associations were slow to react. New rounds of trade union legislation, the miners' strike and the continued focus on ancillary issues all initially distracted unions from the potential effects of the Griffiths Report on nurses. Ancillary issues, particularly, were seen as important for COHSE because of the loss of jobs and, as a result, members, as well as the anger expressed within the union at its helplessness as privatisation ran rampant throughout the service. Nonetheless, resolutions were passed at annual conference condemning the changes and the new managerialism: campaigning materials were issued while union officials made public statements about the value of nurse management and of nurses providing patient care as opposed to managers pushing pieces of paper about, but it was all a little sterile and predictable fare. Very little of substance was done publicly although one of the best of the new style of analytical reports was produced in September 1987, detailing the effects of general management and how it failed to address the real needs of the NHS (COHSE, 1987a). Ironically, it hardly saw the light of day as far as many activists were concerned. At a national level within COHSE the feeling was that it was a relatively smooth revolution in getting rid of nursing officers, largely because rank and file nurses, particularly those in COHSE, were not overly concerned about their fate, a situation not entirely of the senior nurses making, perhaps, but a problem nonetheless. They also, as did the RCN, predicted structural problems with Griffiths following on so soon after the 1974 and 1982 reorganisations but there was a significant problem as soon as commentators asked what the nurses' organisations would put in the place of Griffiths. This proved to be a continual problem of the Thatcher years. With so many initiatives and the desire for change coming from government on so many issues, its opponents were easily characterised as 'conservative' and stale, lacking in ideas. The question of whether or not change was actually required or might actually be counterproductive was never at issue, only what kind of change.

Griffiths wrote his letter in 1983. The government did not set about implementing its recommendations for action immediately; initially they went through the House of Commons and were reported on in lukewarm fashion by the Commons' Social Services Committee in 1984. Once they started, however, another significant tactical change emerged. From the outset they eschewed a blanket approach across the country, choosing instead the Griffiths' blueprint of locally devolved decision making – up to a point. Instructions were sent out from the centre about what needed to be done but the implementation was down to local units. Because of the lines of accountability introduced through the Secretary of State's own appointments at regional and district level in the earliest days there was no doubt that the rest would follow.

It was not until 1986 that the RCN made its big move in resisting the change. It was the College that inevitably led on this issue. Not only were the vast number of nurses facing displacement their members, but it was also their own power base, particularly post-Salmon, that was under threat. Their means of maintaining as much hegemony within nursing as possible depended on their control of the managerial structures of nursing. If those structures were decimated by Griffiths, it would affect the internal balance of the College as much as the service.

The RCN's argument was not with the principles of general management but about the cascading effect of the loss of nursing structures. They recognised that their arguments were not going to move the government and embarked upon a campaign of political lobbying and subversion. Tory backbenchers were flooded with briefing materials, with some being targeted for individual attention. Coming in the wake of the miners' strike and the battle that had ensued between the unions and the government not just on industrial and political issues but also cultural and economic values, the RCN now attacked the materialism of the Thatcher government (Naughtie, 1986a: pp. 20–1). Seven regional meetings were held, some attracting as many as 1000 nurses to hear Trevor

Clay decry the changes. Most controversially, however, £250 000 of the College's money was invested in a publicity campaign unprecedented in its history. Full page advertisements were taken out, not just in the nursing press but also in the country's daily papers, including the *Financial Times*.

Investing such a huge sum of money in the campaign was a managerial decision made by the RCN Council. It was unprecedented but regarded as essential because of the seriousness of the threats facing the organisation. Nonetheless, it was not universally popular and was criticised because of a lack of public impact and the fact that many nurses remained apathetic. The newspaper advertisements were much more about affecting opinion formers, however, and here there was clearly some success. Ministers were worried about the effects of the campaign, particularly on backbench opinion, pressing their claims that the reorganisation was a 'success in directing NHS resources to patient care . . . and making life better in every hospital'. Labour mounted continual attacks but the government held firm (Naughtie, 1986b: pp. 22–3). Some nurses felt it was too little too late. 'It was difficult to mobilise the membership and if you're going to achieve anything as a professional organisation, as the voice of nursing, you've got to get the members behind you,' commented one senior RCN official. 'We managed to get them to rise up on issues of nurse management by demonstrating that removing nursing structures affected the provision of direct patient care. That was a watershed in bringing the whole profession together.' There was little evidence of large numbers of nurses rising up anywhere for very long at all, nor of the profession being united on anything. Many may have shared the fears of Tony Breen, an RCN convenor from central Birmingham, who said, 'We may be left with ward sisters and charge nurses and nothing above. And even they could go in the next round of cost cutting' (Chudley, 1986. p. 19). Nursing critics of nurse management, however, saw the new structures offering an opportunity for nurses to change their 'political reality' for a new professional reality and to organise themselves as a counter force to balance the new Griffiths framework. A professional drive for quality would replace the old managerial power with a professional authority based on the work of clinical specialists (White, 1985a: p. 65).

Smashing the Mirror?

Perhaps the biggest sin the nursing officers had committed was twofold: they had given the impression of wielding real power but then not used it to advantage their junior colleagues toiling at the coalface, especially in the hospitals. In many cases nursing officers were not popular with ward based nurses (Davies, 1980 and Mackay, 1989). This, in itself, would not necessarily have been important if they were valued but there is little to suggest that they were. One COHSE national officer supports the thesis that they did not have a good rapport with most nursing staff. Even here, the disparate nature of nursing complicates matters. For the generalist or utilitarian nurses, those to whom nursing was simply a means of earning a living the same as almost any other, nursing officers were another 'manager', someone in authority. For the educationalists and specialists the rift was more fundamental. Managers had compromised on all of the advances the profession required, such as increasing the educational requirements, moving away from an entirely registered workforce and hindered the development of standards of care and individualised nursing practice.

There may have been other factors that affected nurses' reactions. The RCN publicity campaign chose carefully selected images to put before the public, opinion formers and nurses themselves. Young, white women, in uniform, from a general hospital figured alongside Florence Nightingale herself. These were obviously designed to reflect the popular perception of nurses. The other message was about the image still being sold to nurses themselves, with the old vocational ideal, embodied in the suitable young woman apparently still alive and well, eager to walk in the footsteps of the Lady with the Lamp. Except that this was not the case. Griffiths was only the latest addition in a long line of managerial changes; nurses were identifying themselves far more within grades, clinical areas and specialities and through a variety of other means. The old mythical figures and stereotypes may possibly have resonated in some large city teaching hospitals, but not much further than that. Many nurses would have seen a reflection of another mythological representation of themselves that bore little relevance to, or understanding of, their own reality.

The matter was never entirely in their own hands but, perhaps in allowing the loss of their nursing officers without a fight, many nurses were rejecting part of this image of themselves and its use in controlling aspects of their work and the way in which they organised.

General Managers as Cultural Invaders

The struggle for power in the health service has always been as much about creating a cultural dominance as the naked exercise of control. Doctors did not have to stride the corridors of every hospital in the country issuing instructions as they went. Within nursing, the hierarchy and cultural trappings such as uniform and traditional practices represented the internal divisions. The socialisation of nurses, especially through their training and working in a variety of clinical settings, reinforced it at every turn. Everyone knew their place. It was more difficult to establish a cultural hegemony outside the hospital setting, particularly a general hospital, but another hierarchy was in existence at that level and the relationship of any other service to the general hospital was always spelled out in a different way but nevertheless, in the most explicit terms, with funding and allocation of resources.

Although there tend to be more democratic traditions of working as a team in mental health, district nursing, primary care and health visiting, they have to practise in the margins – albeit with those margins representing for the practitioners clearly marked out areas they may well be completely happy with. It is also ironic that mental health is often an area where nursing practice is even more strongly subordinated to medical practice than in general nursing. It begs the question of whether or not the stronger emphasis on multidisciplinary teamwork was simply a mechanism for holding together a potentially fragile structure, supported by a system of *laissez faire* management that, by omission and non-action, still held nurses in a very fixed and subordinated position, but creating the illusion of greater freedom within it. In specialities such as district nursing and health visiting the process of control was further complicated by lack of a grade structure, most practitioners being on a par. The extensive nursing managerial hierarchy was not represented in small community units. However, this was much less of a threat to any cultural hegemony because community staff were safely removed from having any potential influence on their hospital colleagues; indeed, there has always been a strong tendency for nurses who have found the hospital environment stultifying and conservative to move out into community posts or out of general nursing altogether, allowing themselves the opportunity to explore more radical practices, both individually and collectively, away from the potential conflict and constraint they would face in large institutions.

The managerial culture was still one of consensus throughout the health service, a concept that was to become characterised as vague and woolly, management by 'muddling through', leading to stagnation and inertia, by the Griffiths team. It was also to become a term of derision in the businesslike 1980s. Decisiveness, clear objectives, performance targets and control were said to be alien to the consensus philosophy but were set to became the buzz words of the new managerialism (buzz words becoming a vogue term itself in the age of constant change). It was clear that general management was coming, despite the protestations of the detractors. The key individuals who had been performing within the consensus framework were being attacked for all the ills of the NHS – whether real or imagined – and that as the Gamps had been more than a century earlier, they were being pilloried as part of the softening up process to make way for the reformers who were to follow. They were now facing the options of remaking themselves in the new image of the manager rather than the old administrators or moving aside. Many were replaced by managers appointed from industry and commerce, whose lack of health service experience and ignorance about health care management was seen as an asset.

The cultural battles could only be waged once general management had established a foothold in the service. Griffiths emphasised the links and similarities between business and the NHS (1983: p. 10) and these were made real by bringing in outside managers. With them would come a completely different world view and way of examining the problems of the service. One person being charged with decision making and then held accountable for them was a change in itself, but it would not have a major impact on the culture of the service if it rested there; that was to be achieved by a process that would devolve this concept down to the lowest level. The blueprint was for a service that would ultimately be made up almost entirely of mini general managers. Even ward sisters and charge nurses would be budget holders. This was an important distinction from being a budget manager. In the case of the former, nurses had the responsibility of ensuring that their ward operated within budget. They did not have the authority of a budget manager, who could make decisions about how the budget would be spent, nor were they involved in any negotiations about the setting of the budget. They were given an abstract sum of money tied to their existing staffing establishment and stock items such as dressings, catheters etc. – if they were lucky it was reasonably accurate – and instructed to ensure that they did not overspend. They had no extra authority or opportunity to use their initiative. They could not, for instance, restrict admissions if the staffing costs were going over the limit. In effect, they were the gatekeepers of expenditure, at ward level, for the general managers. It was nurses at ward level policing other nurses and rationing stores. If doctors had been accused of exercising power without responsibility then nurses were being dumped with responsibility without power.

Essential to its continued success was to be its author's insistence on instituting a system that would ensure a 'constant search for major change and cost improvement' (Griffiths, 1983: p. 13). Its fluidity and adaptability at local level were, again, designed to bring cultural change, introducing a localised relevance, coherence and legitimacy for its introduction. But it also had the added effect of making it very difficult for its opponents to mobilise against it at a national level, which left the unions and professional associations confused locally and even more impotent nationally.

Was it knowing the price of everything and the value of nothing that led general managers to question the validity of cherished and innovative clinical initiatives? Or was it merely the new broom sweeping away the cobwebs of inertia and the old professional dominance? Whichever was the case, general managers gradually asserted their authority. But the vast majority of NHS staff, nurses included, stubbornly refused to accept the business culture that they were trying to impose. The sharpsuited managers who came and went from one senior position to another were undoubtedly in charge, answering Griffiths' overriding question. But they were more like an army of occupation than conquering heroes.

The Big Bang That Didn't Quite Happen

The intention of the implementation of the Griffiths Report was to initiate something akin to a 'rational–comprehensive' reorganisation. It looked at clear values it wanted to instil, the objectives or ends it was to achieve and then the means to achieve it were explored. However, it moved away from this theory of policy making in its classic sense by deliberately eschewing a comprehensive analysis, where every relevant factor is taken into account (Lindblom, 1959). In fact, it was only partially successful and became part of an incremental process of change, being added to over a period of time both with developments to the general management process and new pieces of legislation. Nor did it hit its principal targets with any real force. In fact, the attempts to draw in the medical profession to the management process, holding them responsible for the day-to-day management of limited budgets, largely failed. The direct confrontation some in government wished to see as a result of the Griffiths Report failed to materialise and, although substantially weakened, the dominant role of the medical profession in policy making remained. Thus the battle against rising costs was left unresolved. Doctors were forced to change as a result of the changes, particularly by introducing clinical audit (Klein 1989: p. 212). In order to stave off outside interest in their affairs they also had to develop a more self-critical gaze and new initiatives such as resource management were carefully examined as ways of doctors becoming more involved. But the big bang left the doctors standing.

Nurses, whether accidental casualties or not, were not so lucky. The campaigns of various bodies, principally the RCN, did succeed in retaining a great number of posts for nurses, but most lost their 'officer' status, with discrete budgets of their own to manage. Chief nurses, directors of nursing and nursing officers' posts were lost all over Britain. Trevor Clay may have overstated the case when he wrote that, 'The Griffiths Inquiry of 1984 (*sic*) signalled the demise of professional power in the NHS' (Clay, 1987: p. 57), but many senior nurses would have echoed the sentiment. In their place came advisers' posts and, lower down, senior nurse managers, clinical nurse managers and ward managers. The significant change was that at the top of the nurses' line management tree perched not a nurse but a general manager, even if professional supervision and advice were available from a displaced senior nurse. Nurses had also lost their tenuous grip on policy making at all levels. Whereas they had found a place reserved for them at the tripartite table of consensus management after the 1974 reorganisation with the administrators and doctors, now that was gone; they were waiting to be called to the table to offer their advice and depart again to await the decision of the general manager. The fear that 'anyone' could be employed as a ward manager, whether or not a trained nurse, proved groundless . . . eventually; the revolution did appear set to progress that far at one stage, however. Another avenue displaced nursing officers were being directed into was quality but this was, again, one they were ill-prepared for. It was not going to bring about any significant change in the internal politics of nursing. Nor was it ever going to be a rallying point for hardpressed nurses in face-to-face caring roles with patients. Besides, the educationalists and clinical specialists were moving in a different direction entirely as they were exploring and developing individualised care and advanced nursing systems such as primary nursing. The only real point of overlap between those pushing the new nursing and those introducing general management was the mutual insistence on accountability.

There were, nonetheless, two policies being developed in parallel. One, regarding nursing practice, involved high level discussion between the professional associations and nurses heavily involved with the development of clinical practice. The other, aimed at the NHS at a whole, did not simply ignore the voice of nursing; it sought to undermine it and recast its audience in its own, new, image.

Many of the old administrators did apply for jobs as general managers, with varying degrees of success, as did a sprinkling of doctors and nurses. Importantly, performance related pay came to be introduced for senior managers, meaning that they were financially rewarded for implementing policy as dictated to them in the form of personal objectives. That was the carrot; the stick was fixed term contracts offering no security of employment for the first time at that level in the NHS. Nonetheless, there were still enough people in the NHS who valued the old culture and the objectives of consensus style administration – the running of a service rather than the management of people – to mitigate the impact of the new managerial modus operandi. At a higher level there were real problems with a new power struggle being enacted by the management board – introduced as a result of the Report and the civil servants at the DHSS – aided by those who advised and worked with them from within the NHS. The first chief executive resigned amid controversy about political interference from ministers and, ironically, uncertainty about roles.

The web of control was woven out from the centre to local level through general management but it was still not sufficiently sophisticated to draw the clinicians all the way in. Money was still flowing into the NHS, although in real terms it began to decline quite dramatically in the mid 1980s and the Social Services Committee estimated the accumulated underfunding as being at £1.325 billion in 1986, rising to £1.896 billion in 1988 (Klein, 1989: p. 230). If 'productivity' had increased in the form of more patients being treated and operations performed, waiting lists were still growing. And expenditure on nursing was still the largest factor in NHS funding. Regardless of whether or not the head had been lopped off, the body still required regular and massive nourishment. Advocates of the management changes, noting that there was farther to go, identified the need for quality of care and staffing level assessment initiatives such as 'GRASP' and 'Monitor'. These would, if used properly, offer greater control over nursing practice. However, there were those who recognised that the acid test for any government's commitment to a fully industrial mode of management would be whether or not they were prepared to make significant attempts to restructure nursing along the lines of a small number of highly trained nurses supervising a variety of semiskilled workers performing a limited range of patient care activities (Harrison, 1988: pp. 147–9).

The introduction of general management would facilitate such a change. But the changes it had already wrought were beginning to have a decisive effect. Thrusting more work of a managerial nature at ward sisters and charge nurses, removing them from work alongside their colleagues of a clinical nature, particularly providing advice and supervision, meant a greater weight of responsibility was falling to staff nurses, many of them relatively newly qualified. Tension around locally devolved budgets mounted. The notion of the 'common good' was being refined if not completely redefined. Nursing was on a collision course.

Chapter 8

'490 000 Nurses Will *be at work today'*.
Clinical grading

By the time that the Conservatives won their landmark third consecutive electoral victory in 1987, general management was becoming increasingly established in the NHS, particularly in general hospitals. The NHS had featured as an issue in the election, with the Labour party campaigning on what it had put forward as the government's poor record on funding, privatisation and the introduction of more and more managers to the detriment of medical treatment and nursing care. All had been to no avail. Polls may have shown that people believed the NHS was underfunded and were willing to pay more in taxes, but this did not translate into votes. For the Tories, the time seemed ripe for putting into action their most radical agenda yet. There was talk of further reforms to the health service. Then, in the autumn of that year, a storm blew up out of nowhere.

Not Enough Nurses – Still

One of the demands of the new managerialism was that everyone should work harder. There was a fundamental problem if doctors worked harder, however. They inevitably saw and treated more patients, which meant more nurses were required to care for those patients. But more nurses – even if they could be found – would mean more cost. In the autumn of 1987 this old conumdrum exploded into a national issue when a Birmingham baby died awaiting treatment he could not have because of a shortage of suitably trained nurses. This was followed by a succession of similar stor-ies appearing in the national press. Immediately an air of crisis descended on the health service – again. The problems of the past had been exacerbated by the cash limiting introduced in the late 1970s, a policy brought to the fore in the next decade and which led to an inevitable focus on nurses' pay. With the introduction of the nurses' PRB, great arguments had arisen about 'who' would pay for increases, even though the government had not always accepted the PRB recommendations in full and either staged awards or not implemented them in full. In 1985 and 1986 this had been the case. Cash limiting meant that there was a certain percentage of funding allocated for wage rises; if the nurses or any other occupational group were awarded anything in excess of this, the money had to be found from health authority budgets. Any other rising costs not accounted for in the annual allocation also had to come out of authority budgets unless exceptional reasons could be given as to why extra money was necessary.

Inevitably, in a system that was becoming increasingly localised, there was an uneven picture. Under the RAWP formula, some health authorities were gaining while others lost; health needs varied enormously from area to area; some local management initiatives were resulting in more efficient service provision and less financial pressure. However, the overall picture, fuelled by health professionals, trade unions and, perhaps surprisingly, managers, was one of diminishing resources in the face of growing demand. Health service managers even went as far as to issue a joint report for the House of Commons with the RCN, the BMA and NIHSM, highlighting the limited effect further efficiency savings could have (NIHSM, BMA & RCN, 1983).

The financial problems were not the only factor. One of the few references to nurses in the Griffiths Report, and possibly its most quoted comment, was: 'If Florence Nightingale were carrying her lamp through the corridors of the NHS today she would almost certainly be searching for the people in charge' (1983). Four years later, on the same journey, she might have been looking for the exit. Many nurses were. Even with extra resources the shortage of nurses would have been a problem, a point made with increasing emphasis by the staff side of the Nurses' and Midwives' Whitley Council throughout the 1980s. Over a five year period in the mid-1980s, the numbers of students entering training fell by nearly 30%, with the drop-out rate remaining high at 35% for RGN courses and 30% for enrolled nurses. Predictions were that the situation would steadily worsen as the number of young women leaving school – the principal recruiting 'pool' – was in rapid decline until, by 1992, almost one third of all female school leavers would need to be recruited to maintain contemporary levels. Hospital nurses were bearing the brunt of increasing managerial tasks *and* clinical workloads year by year, with this being passed onto community nurses as patients were discharged earlier or only taken in as day cases when they would previously have had a brief spell on a ward. Equally, midwives were subject to the same demographic downturn and vacancies, at 16.5% nationally, were regarded as unacceptably high, although trained nurse vacancies in London hospitals were even higher, averaging 20%.

No Masks This Time

News that the Department of Health were recommending to the PRB that nurses' special duty payments should be stopped leaked out in early January. Within days, 37 Manchester nurses, all members of NUPE, had staged a 24 hour strike (Lewis & Hildrew, 1988). Their faces were on the front page of most of the national papers and spread throughout the pages of the nursing press for the next fortnight. Like their 1937 counterparts they were hailed as heroines by many; however, there were no masks in evidence. Moreover, they clearly were not going to be isolated in their action, even though they were the first. Their strike was branded as 'misguided' by the *Nursing Times*, which also pointed out that '11 were actually auxiliaries' (and, therefore not real nurses) and condemned outright by the RCN's general secretary, Trevor Clay. The action was described as being of dubious value and a distraction while it was noted that 'The prime responsibility of any nurse must be to her patients' (*Nursing Times*, 13.1.1988: p. 3). But further stories continued about 'Tragic toddlers who must wait in vain' (*Observer*, 10.1.1988). By the following Wednesday the Minister for Health, Tony Newton, had 'Backed down over nurses' money' (Naughtie & Hildrew, 1988), withdrawing the threat to remove special duty payments.

Nurses had a new image by then. It was of a group of women standing together under a Manchester night sky. They were a relatively small proportion of the workforce, made up of different grades. By turns they smiled confidently out from their photographs or looked grimly determined, carrying placards bearing the legend, 'Official Picket.' It was an image that was to resonate throughout the country (Plate XV).

Clinical Militancy

A somewhat complex issue had arisen that had a unifying effect on large and significant groups of nurses, whatever their background or location. It was pay, but set firmly in the context of the work that nurses did – and what they could not do. The complexity was that it could be looked at on different levels and appear to be about one or the other, depending on how it was articulated and by whom. However, it was apparent to some at the time that this was different from the 1982 dispute in that it was not just about pay; nor was it simply 'a feeling that something has to be done to stop patients suffering,' as Mick Jackson, a charge nurse and RCN member, stated (Pownall, 1988: p. 18). Using the advantage of hindsight it is clear that both of those issues were on the nurses' agenda but with something else. They were concerned with how they were treated and how they were perceived, regardless of whether or not they were going to take industrial action as a means of addressing those issues. The industrial had become inextricably interwoven with the 'professional' and clinical militancy was born. Contemporary news reports showed how nurses were consistently linking the pay issue to their conditions of work and patient care:

'Members have seen the health service decline and services deteriorate at the hospital over the past two years. In the past few weeks they have begun to react. They have voted with their feet to tell the Government they have had enough. Many nurses have voted with their feet by simply leaving the health service.' (Ian Morton, COHSE Branch Secretary)

(Sherman, 1988)

Feelings here are running very high. The vote for strike action . . . was absolutely unanimous. We want the full percentage pay rise we are asking for, plus £1,000 London weighting. We also want to ensure that there will be no more cuts affecting patients. Enough is enough.

(*Evening Standard*, 20.21.1988).

The *Nursing Times*, facing a backlash after it criticised the Manchester nurses in its editorial three weeks before, ran six pages of articles about nurses either preparing to go on strike or resolutely staying at work. There was more than a page full of letters and eleven news items, plus their editorial, all about nurses' pay, protests and related matters. Nurses from both sides of the divide were saying virtually identical things as they diagnosed the deep malaise affecting nursing:

> Nurses are extremely angry and bitter about the state of the NHS and frustrated that they cannot deliver the care their patients need. They are fed up with the closures of wards and cuts in services, with staff shortages, with moral blackmail and exploitation, underfunding of pay awards . . .' (Lesley Fisher, a night sister at St Ann's Hospital, explaining why she was planning to go on strike)
>
> (Fisher, 1988: p. 22)

> . . . Like them I go home totally exhausted and frustrated with the level of care I am able to give. . . All the betrayals of nurses' hopes, all the stress, all the bad pay and conditions, privatisation and staged pay awards still do not justify action which affects the patients. (Sally Colter, a ward sister at St Thomas' Hospital)
>
> (Colter, 1988)

Protests were being mounted almost all over the country, with 34 London hospitals taking action. Moves were afoot to try to force an extraordinary general meeting to discuss Rule 12 of the RCN's constitution which forbids members to go on strike. It was now clear that the DHSS were opposing large, across the board pay rises for nurses, instead favouring regional pay variations that would supposedly help recruitment and retention. National pay would be based on the newly agreed grades as part of the clinical grading review.

The next major 24 hour strike was on February 2nd at London's Maudsley Hospital. Again, new radical images were being created. Those on strike were psychiatric nurses, not wearing uniforms, but who were working in a prestigious teaching hospital more akin to the old voluntary hospitals than the asylums. They were all in COHSE, women and men from different ethnic and class backgrounds, with support from ancillaries, administrative staff and, during a much publicised lunchtime break, doctors. They came together on a picket line (Plate XVI), where 'grim messages of crisis failed to crush the carnival atmosphere' and 'tooting horns of support competed with the music and chanting, and cheering pensioners joined in' (*The Times*, 3.2.1988). The interest sparked by the Manchester strike prompted the media to turn out en masse and the tone was set for the early stages of the dispute.

The issues were complex and the ambivalence strongly felt, perhaps best summarised by a description of Staff Nurse Lisa Smith, 'standing on a picket line with a placard in her hand and an emergency bleep in her coat pocket. The placard is to proclaim why Lisa, like thousands of nurses all over Britain, is striking for the first time. The bleep is in case there's a crisis so acute on the wards of the Maudsley Hospital that some nurses must go back in' (*Daily Mirror*, 3.2.1988). Again, pay and conditions as well as issues about standards of care were cited as reasons for Lisa's decision to support the action. TV bulletins reported on the progress of the Maudsley strike throughout the day. Labour MPs Harriet Harman, Tony Benn and and Denis Skinner all visited. More significantly, Hector MacKenzie, COHSE's general secretary, arrived and gave a virtual press conference from the hospital, announcing that no progress had been made in that morning's discussion with Mr John Moore, the Secretary of State for Health. 'I bring no message of hope. The Health Secretary is wrapping himself in a blanket of statistics while the NHS is crumbling around them' (*The Times,* 3.2.1988). Mr Mackenzie declared the union's unequivocal support for the action and predicted more to come. Another feature of that day was the support of the patients and the spirit of co-operation between COHSE and RCN nurses, two of whom worked double shifts so that their friends in COHSE could go on strike (*The Times*, 3.2.1988). This was not a spirit to be maintained at a national level but was shared in many workplaces.

The next day, further 24 hour strikes hit hospitals all over Britain. In a rich irony, many of the nurses who had taken action in London that day made their way to a meeting organised several weeks previously by the pressure group, London Health Emergency. Instead of the couple of hundred expected, the Camden Centre was engulfed with more than 2000 nurses, some of whom had unknowingly retraced the steps of the masked nurses from 1937. Fifty years later the nurses were not just bold enough to march through the streets unmasked, they were blocking the traffic in the busy Euston Road and singing songs of defiance as they went to a meeting held on the same site as the St Pancras Town Hall meeting.

Events were moving at such a pace that no one could keep up with them, least of all trade union officers. Organisation was often chaotic and lacking in any formal understanding of structures. At Guy's Hospital, no vote was actually taken about whether or not to go on strike despite repeated calls for immediate industrial action and the spontaneous circulation by RCN members of a petition calling for a change of Rule 12. 'Union officials have underestimated the strength of feeling and it will be difficult to contain nurses who were told that "even the union was stamping on anger"' (*New Statesman*, 29.1.1988). Nurses who were involved in taking action spoke of a feeling of having control over their work for the first time. Negotiating emergency staffing levels – even though they often complained these were better than their normal staffing levels – and identifying what clinical work was a priority and refusing to do 'non-nursing' duties was a new experience. They were willing to discard their 'angelic' image and state their needs and demands. Perhaps it was this that led some newspapers to have banner headlines declaring, 'Angels who nurse a death wish' (*News of the World*, 31.1.1988), '"Deserters" Jab at nurses' (*Today*, 3.2.1988), '490,000 nurses *will* be at work today' (*Daily Mail*, 3.2.1988).

Sporadic industrial action continued throughout February, including more 24 hour strikes by nurses who were, by now, dominating not just the nursing press with the issue but the media as a whole. It was an issue of prime national concern. It was in no way a static situation. What had started as 'a ferocious and climactic confrontation about funding' (Klein, 1989: p. 232), with doctors in the forefront, had been transformed into a struggle about what work nurses do, how they do it and their place in the structure of the NHS. Now, it was gradually being transformed into a traditional nurses' pay battle.

Any attempt at consensus betwen the nurses' organisations at a national level was rapidly falling apart. The RCN and *Nursing Times* maintained a line of saying there were legitimate grievances but criticised the tactics used by many nurses. The College, particularly, made much of the fact that they believed there were few qualified nurses taking part in any action, especially at a controversial march on Downing Street where a trained nurse had been arrested. They were also scornful of the Manchester nurses, stating that NUPE had orchestrated that strike and manipulated the nurses involved. The RCN further stoked the fires of controversy by denying media led reports that nurses were deserting the College for the unions, especially after Paula Morrison, a Maudsley charge nurse, resigned on BBC TV in direct response to comments from Trevor Clay about her colleagues' action. They claimed more than a thousand extra applications per week. Increasingly, senior figures from COHSE and NUPE were retaliating in the face of Trevor Clay's outbursts; he was also facing trouble from within his organisation, particularly around the Rule 12 issue. One senior lay activist and former Council member, Tom Bolger, criticised his refusal to hold a general meeting to debate the issue. 'I think he has avoided a general meeting because he would be criticised for his laid back approach. Nurses I have spoken to are very unhappy about the RCN profile on the NHS' (Turner, 1988: p. 19). However, Hector MacKenzie was facing a different kind of pressure, with rumours circulating that the TUC's health services committee wanted him to get COHSE nurses into line and stop taking action unless it was co-ordinated and planned. Clearly, there were serious concerns amongst some union leaders that the militancy might get completely out of control.

For this reason, if no other, it made sense to try to shift the emphasis to pay. There were other advantages to such a strategy. A pay campaign was a clear win or lose situation rather than trying to tackle the more abstract issue of NHS funding and trying to create a 'feel good' factor for nurses working in the health service, both of which would be extremely difficult to achieve. Pay was certainly the issue for many of the traditionalist nurses, historically COHSE's main bulk of members, who focused on their general conditions far more than on professional issues. DHSS statements had also focused a lot of nurses' attentions on pay as they had recommended the loss of special duty payments and the loss of a national pay structure.

However, COHSE developed a two-pronged attack on government policy and did nothing to stop their nurse members protesting or taking action, despite the pressure from the TUC. They retained their focus on pay, especially London weighting claims and enhancements for those working in elderly care and mental health, but at the same time tried to channel the unfocused concerns of radical nurses into a coherent campaign aimed at increasing NHS funding. This was the '2p For Health' campaign, started in late February 1988. It concentrated on Chancellor Lawson's much vaunted tax cuts. With widespread speculation that the government were preparing to make a 2p reduction in the basic rate of tax, COHSE produced campaign material claiming that if this were abandoned and that 2p used instead to bolster the NHS, the estimated deficit of almost £2 billion would be wiped out.

In addition to all of the spontaneous protests going on throughout the NHS, the South East Thames Region of COHSE planned a 'day of action' for the Monday before budget day, joined by other parts of London. Already the TUC had organised one of the largest marches and demonstrations ever seen in support of the health service on March 5th, when crowds estimated at anywhere between 120 000 and 2 000 000 marched to Hyde Park.

There was one more factor in the union's concerns about keeping the pay issue to the fore. Over the past two years representatives from all the nurses' organisations had been working with the management side on their Whitley Council to introduce a new clinical grading structure which looked as if it was slipping away from them.

What *is* the Problem?

Nurses going on strike were not just a problem for the employers. It was as if the sight of nurses walking away from the patients unleashed a deep psychological anxiety in all around them. For the trade unions there were obvious concerns of a straight political nature, with the potential damage that could be done to their own members and the credibility of the unions themselves if it turned into another 'winter of discontent' – and Margaret Thatcher and her ministers had already made several scathing attacks on striking nurses 'who desert their patients' (Today, 3.2.1988) – but it went further than that. One of the regular comments coming from government commentators was that this was militancy that had been whipped up by full-time officers and Left wing agitators, a theme echoed by sections of the RCN. However, the trade unions themselves knew this to be untrue and also recognised how little control they had of the situation as a result. For many it was difficult to understand how it had blown up so quickly, particularly when it did, just months after the Conservatives had won such a resounding victory at the polls.

Public support for the nurses was traditionally recognised as being high, but was often seen as being reliant on the nurses promoting their vocational devotion to duty and self-sacrifice, on their being 'angelic'. However, poll after poll revealed that this support was undiminished by the nurses taking industrial action, both in support of their own pay and in support of the NHS (Cole, 1988: pp. 18–19). Even 67% of Conservative voters supported the nurses taking strike action, only marginally less than the total of 79% of all voters questioned (*Daily Telegraph,* 3.2.1988). Yet for those close to them, the anxiety about their action remained, even when public support was obviously high. The reason for anxiety on the part of nurse managers was obvious. Any defiance by nurses in the form of industrial action, literally making themselves unmanageable, was the ultimate denial of the myths, tradition and culture that had bound them; for the professionalists and educationalists, industrial action meant nurses turning their backs on the patients, thus undermining the image of mature, caring professionals who should have equal status with other professionals. The professional associations would adhere to both analyses but probably with more emphasis on the former. For the trade unions it should be a different story, but even amongst some of their number there was an underlying anxiety. Perhaps it was a fear of what might happen if the patriarchal systems of control were abandoned; perhaps there were deeper fears stirred up about abandonment and neglect, mixed with the threat of crisis and complete operational breakdown of the service. Certainly, there was no evidence whatsoever of patients being harmed through nurses taking industrial action.

One of the charges made regularly by both the RCN and government ministers was that it was only a small minority of the workforce on strike or becoming involved in demonstrations. This was, to a large extent, true and not particularly surprising. Such a large number of people in a single occupation were bound to reflect the wider electorate, one which had just re-elected a Conservative government. However, that was with a minority vote and though nursing remained generally conservative with a small 'c', there was a feeling of disenfranchisement from those who had voted 'the wrong way' for a third time, that no matter what happened, they were powerless to change anything through legitimate means. This was not just a feeling about the wider political processes but also the internal policy mechanisms within the health service. The feeling of things getting worse and no one in authority doing anything to lighten the burden on nurses was strongly present in the comments of many nurses at the time. Moreover, there was a suspicion that general managers were going to make things a lot worse, with nurses expressing resentment at the growing number of non-clinical staff at a time when they were having to work harder than ever, with staffing levels being perceived as wholly inadequate.

Within nursing there had always been a radical minority which varied in size, depending on any number of external variants. They found different ways of expressing their radicalism: through attending splinter meetings of radical nurses, midwives or health visitors, thus separating themselves out from the rest of their colleagues; channelling it into developing clinical practice; leaving the service altogether; sometimes through trade union activism. Late 1987 and 1988 was a time when this latter occurred. The radical minority, agitating for change, had tapped into the mainstream of nurses' thinking and articulated the frustrations of a generation, just as happened 50 years previously.

The Clinical Grading Structure

None of this should really have been necessary. A policy had been devised to meet nurses' immediate aspirations on pay and extend the grading structure, which would, ultimately, benefit the employers. It had actually been the subject of detailed consultation and joint working between the two sides on the Nurses' and Midwives' Whitley Council for two years.

The PRB had decided in 1985 that it wanted a new,

comprehensive structure because of the inflexibility of the existing one, which did not reward nurses for the work that they did. The aim of such a structure would be to reflect and reward the work of nurses more accurately as well as provide better incentives and a career structure, to keep nurses in the clinical arena. The DHSS made early moves to devise a structure but the staff side wanted to become more involved and were highly committed to it from an early date, as Hector MacKenzie pointed out in early 1986 (*Nursing Times*, 29.1.1986: p. 60). One senior COHSE official involved described it as a 'massive exercise'. Over 1300 question-naires were sent out to individual nurses, followed by structured interviews. Both sides brought in outside experts to help them analyse the results. This provided hard information about what nurses were doing; after that came the task of fitting definitions and a pay structure to nurses' responsibilities. A joint secretarial group, made up of members of the staff and management sides, met almost daily to do this, with the lead being taken by the joint secretaries. All involved felt the process was going well, until in mid August 1987 the different staff side organisations were reporting to their nursing members that 'considerable progress has been made ... The staff side are hopeful that agreement can be reached with the management side in order to put evidence to the Pay Review Body in November' (COHSE, 1987b).

It was not until September that hints came that anything was wrong. The staff side had wanted a 12 point structure but at this stage the management side said they wanted two structures, one for qualified nurses and the other for unqualified staff. When the staff side refused, management's next offer was of a six point structure. What followed was serious and hardnosed negotiation, but some on the staff side remained suspicious and disappointed at the about-turn from the management side, believing that it could only have been prompted by 'momentous government inter-ference', with the Treasury asking for preliminary costing. Despite the difficulties, by the end of the year a nine point structure had virtually been agreed. There had been, and were still, points of dis-agreement within the staff side but compromises had been reached. Most pointedly and with remarkable foresight as things turned out, the RCM believed they should have a completely dif-ferent structure.

There was still the problem of attaching pay scales to the new structure, which was the job of the PRB. The nurses' organisations put in strongly worded evidence, published just before Christmas, concluding that, 'It is time to face the realities of a demoralised, shrinking and over-stretched workforce. Unless the facts are faced now, the future of the profession and of the NHS cannot be assured' (Staff Side Evidence, 1987). Much emphasis was placed on comparability between nurses, firefighters and police constables, showing how far behind nurses' pay was lagging, with a student nurse's starting salary nearly £5000 less than a probationer police officer's; a newly qualified staff nurse was about as far behind a police constable of the same length of service. Each of the organisations put in their own supplementary evidence, as usual reinforcing their own particular concerns, with the RCN focusing on clinical specialists and the number of nurses consistently working unpaid overtime – estimated at 60% – while COHSE concentrated on the low paid and unqualified staff. It was estimated that 40% of nurses were earning less than the Low Pay Unit's threshold of £132.27p a week. The overall demand for a salary increase was 20%.

Gross Annual Earnings	£	
Police constable	13 520	
Teachers	12 220	
Firefighters	11 440	
Welfare workers	9724	
Lab technicians	9412	
Nurse (average)	7800	
Enrolled nurse	6250 – 7750	⎫
Staff nurse	7300 – 8600	⎬ basic salary only
Ward sister	9000 – 12 000	⎭

The new clinical grading definitions were published by the DHSS in March 1988, before the PRB reported on its recommendations about pay levels. No one knew whether or not the PRB would see the value of the nurses' case or if the government would then accept the recommendations in full but, after several months of the most virulent unrest in the NHS since 1982 – and, in some cases worse because of its spontaneous and unpredictable nature – the PRB's recommendations were, for once, fully accepted, with an immediate 4% rise to be followed by a further increase dependent on where nurses fell in the new structure. Indeed, the new clinical grading had become the panacea to cure all of nursing's ills.

Politics Takes Over

It has long been established that the London teaching hospitals can, to an extent, subvert the policy process by creating a feeling of drama or crisis in the face of proposed changes, most especially when they perceive themselves as threatened or potentially disadvantaged; in such cases the senior consultants often act as front-line spokesmen, putting out statements that would be difficult for an administrator or manager to make. In 1987 there was certainly an element of this, with doctors from a number of prestigious hospitals joining in. Their agitating was soon overtaken by the nurses, in a much more radical way. It was the doctors who had put them at the centre of the debate initially, but in highlighting the nursing shortages they were placing them in the context of the problems it posed for them and the way in which it stopped them from working. Once the nurses were actually taking action and the storm grew rather than blew over, it became clear that the 'problem' had to be seen to be resolved. The two issues – of nurses' pay and NHS funding – had to be dealt with separately but had forced their way to the top of the domestic political agenda. The latter was accommodated by an almost throwaway line by Margaret Thatcher under intense questioning from David Dimbleby on the *Panorama* programme in January 1988, who said that there was to be a ministerial review of the NHS. The former involved a lot of money and was therefore subject to slightly more thought.

The clinical grading structure was thus drawn into the process of solving all of the problems of nurses' pay. This fitted with the non-nursing media perception of what a lot of the nurses' action was about and fed into the trade union officials' instincts of how to make the most of the situation, both for their existing nurses and in recruiting new members. But for the government, the old problem of cost and funding came back to haunt them with a vengeance. In agreeing to a nine point grading ladder and then accepting the PRB's recommendations on pay scales the government had solved a short term political problem but committed themselves to an overall structure which was completely uncosted. This was done when a 1% increase for nurses would cost the Treasury approximately £35 million. That was just the start of the problems. Nurses everywhere had had their expectations raised to the roof, partly by the national press hailing massive increases for nurses as a great victory for their militancy, but not least by their own ambition and the audacity and boldness of their actions over the previous few months. John Moore, Secretary of State for Social Services, had crowed that this was a major step forward for nurses, with an average rise of 15.3% but with some nurses receiving an increase of 60%.

If the government now had a serious problem, it was very swiftly passed into the hands of local managers and the regions who, in turn, were going to do their best to pass it on to the unions. The new structures had to be implemented at a local level. As soon as the new pay scales were announced it was immediately apparent that there were vast inequalities in the pay rise that would be attached to individual grades. There was enormous disappointment and anger that nurses at the lower end of the new scales, notably the 'A' and 'B' grades for untrained staff, were going to receive the lowest increases, with the highest being reserved for those at the top end and the new 'E' and 'G' grades. The new structure had its immediate critics in COHSE who, despite Hector MacKenzie's enthusiasm, saw it as divisive and ultimately damaging. This was particularly true of older traditionalists within the union who saw that constituent areas of key historical strength would be undermined, such as the two charge nurse system in mental health. But many nurses, in all branches of nursing, were scrutinising the definitions and saw themselves as finding a place in the new structure that would reward them.

The Time for the Work Nurses Do to be Valued

The procedure for allocating nurses to grades should have been relatively simple. It was worked out after further detailed negotiation between the staff and the management sides, after which guidance had been issued. Each nurse was to be interviewed about her job and the nature of the work that she did; tick sheets with a list of definitions were to be filled in, indicating whether or not the individual nurse had specific responsibilities such as contributing to the care planning process, being a primary care giver or taking charge of a ward. The areas of responsibility being looked at were both clinical and managerial, with the nursing process and primary nursing becoming key factors in determining the differentiation between 'D' and 'E' grades as well as whether or not a nurse was in charge of the ward regularly. For charge nurses or ward sisters, 'F' or 'G' grades, the key differential was whether or not they had continuing responsibility for their ward – a concept that was not much employed prior to clinical grading at that level. For nursing auxiliaries it was a question of working unsupervised or not. Clinical nurse specialists had key criteria about providing clinical advice, formulating policies and research, or the management of more than one ward or equivalent sphere of nursing, midwifery or health visiting, or being nurse teachers in clinical settings. The 'I' grade was primarily for nurse managers managing more than one ward or equivalent sphere but was also applicable to clinical nurse specialists and nurse tutors in a clinical setting. Perhaps the key grade was that placed at scale 'F' which, as well as being applicable to ward sisters or charge nurses, was clearly meant for experienced staff nurses who would have some experience at what was defined as the new scale 'E'. There was some overlapping of all the grades: untrained nurses could reasonably expect themselves to be placed within the grades 'A' to 'C'; enrolled nurses from 'C' to 'E' (although there would be very few who should have been placed at the lower end); staff nurses on 'E' or 'F' (although many argued that 'D' was applicable if they were not regularly in charge, with 'regular' constituting once a week or more) and ward sisters on 'F' or 'G'.

A timetable was worked out for completion of each stage of the grading, with 31st October 1988 the deadline for all nurses to be assimilated onto the new scales.

With the benefit of hindsight it is easy to wonder how the staff side could have been so naive as to expect the process to be carried out smoothly and within the letter of the agreement given the track record of the employer, be it government, a board of guardians or the worthy governors of a voluntary hospital, when the key question of money was raised. By July of 1988 it was clear that the agreed procedure was not being adhered to. Shorter timescales were being imposed at authority level, preventing the completion of the criteria. Nurses were being told they were being placed on the lowest possible grade for their post and would have to compete for higher grades – some were even being told they would have to reapply for their own posts. Job descriptions were unilaterally changed by managers, retrospectively, so that individual nurses would not meet the criteria for a specific grade. Consultation with local staff sides was not occurring as it was meant to and trade union officials were being excluded from the process of contributing to decision making; the issues of supervision and continuing responsibility were emerging as key in what was happening for nursing auxiliaries and ward sisters respectively. These were, obviously, the worst cases and in many instances the grading exercise was carried out properly, sometimes in the face of pressures being placed on honourable nurse managers by their general manager bosses. However, there were enough horror stories to exercise a widely held sense of grievance and injustice.

Unusally, this was not the health service localities subverting planned national policy in the way that had prompted such drastic managerial change in the recent past. Evidence began to emerge of collusion between the centre, the DHSS and those charged with the responsibility of implementing clinical grading at a local level. It became clear that cash limits were secretly being imposed on authorities, that the management side had prescribed that there could only be one 'G' grade per ward, whatever work was being done by individual nurses, and that guidance around supervision was deliberately being manipulated. The 'G' grade issue was reported as 'Scandal of the ward sisters given £20 a year rise', as all nurses would get a basic 4% increase, regardless of grade, which meant that those going onto scale 'F' would get virtually nothing more while their 'G' grade colleagues would receive a pay rise of 28%. It was also estimated that the exercise could cost £150 million more than the £803 million government had allocated (*Observer*, 17.7.1988). Labour calculated the potential underfunding as potentially as high as £360 million, which would equate to bed losses of 14 000 and it was clear that nurses were preparing to 'go back to the front line':

> The euphoria which greeted the nurses' pay award in April has all but vanished. There is now a climate of hostility in hospitals nationwide.
>
> (Brindle, 1988a)

The Measures Taken

The drama was far from over. A polite letter from Val Cowie of the RCN and staff side secretary to her counterpart within the management side conveyed the concerns of the staff side if not the anger. But back in the workplace, nurses were increasingly restless and unable to contain their fury. What had been meant to be an exercise in rewarding them by recognising the importance of their work and paying them accordingly had been pulled away from under their noses by the very people to whom they were supposed to remain most loyal, their senior nurses. Relationships at every level were becoming strained to breaking point, whether between the unions and professional associations, the staff side and DHSS officials or nurses and their managers.

The issue now, most definitely, was one of pay. COHSE branch secretary, Ian Morton, who six months ago had led his branch on strike as much over staffing levels and patient care, was clear: 'Nurses have learned over the past year that the way this government behaves is very much dependent on how it perceives what nurses are doing. They have massively misjudged the mood.' His COHSE branch were about to vote on an indefinite strike 'over the national pay and grading dispute'. However, claims that the action was being union led were thrown into doubt when a Leeds meeting only attracted 50 nurses out of a potential 2000 and regional officer Glyn Robinson said, 'The nurses are angry and frustrated, but we are not too big to go along with the membership if they don't want to take action' (Brindle, 1988b). In fact, far from being union led, the action that was breaking out up and down the country, as in February and March, was unco-ordinated and lacked any great national focus.

The staff side was desperately trying to hang together. It had already survived an August walkout led by COHSE's Judith Carter and the RCN's Val Cowie, while Hector MacKenzie and Trevor Clay had been on holiday. This was in protest at the Department's intransigence on the definitions of continuing responsibility and supervision. In some respects, the ability of the two major nursing organisations to carry on presenting a united front rested on the personal relationship between Clay and MacKenzie. For although they could be publicly abrupt, insiders from both organisations felt that their rapport had been able to hold things together whenever the organisations' clashes threatened a real split. COHSE was recommending branches lodging disputes and the passing of resolutions through branch meetings calling for industrial action if the structure was not properly implemented. The RCN, as ever, took a more measured tone and condemned industrial action wherever it occurred, advising that the procedural mechanisms be used (Buchan, 1988: p. 9). The matter of industrial action dogged the internal relationships within the nursing unions and associations throughout the year. Trevor Clay had eventually agreed to a ballot on Rule 12 rather than an extraordinary meeting but 'the ballot paper was strongly condemned for its wording, which many felt urged members against strike action'. The RCN made much of the fact that the membership followed the College's advice and Rule 12 remained (*Nursing Times*, 28.12.1988: p. 17). But the Royal College of Midwives, despite a similar 'no strike' ruling, was close to abandoning it as pressure from midwives reached boiling point.

Nursing negotiators within the staff side were extremely disappointed at what they perceived as the RCN's 'cold feet' when the management side breached the agreements reached. COHSE officials believed that gave the government what they were looking for – a rift in the staff side, which weakened their ability to wring concessions from the government. Many within the RCN, however, had taken a cynical view of the nurses' unrest from the outset, believing it to have been carefully manipulated. Although criticised for the wording on their ballot they believed that, again, the silent majority had made their feelings known since there were only 67 complaints formally lodged about it; moreover, theirs were the nurses who saw no issue on which to take industrial action and had remained with the patients. One officer described the RCN Council as confident in the officers' ability to get the 'best deal' for the members in terms and equity, as quickly as possible. RCN insiders also believed the PRB report was all that had been asked for, the culmination of 'Towards A Professional Nursing Structure', an RCN campaign arising from a document outlining a proposed structure for nursing.

Many within the College had believed the grading criteria were reasonable – as did their colleagues in COHSE – and were genuinely taken aback at subsequent events. But not to the point where they believed it warranted industrial action that would undermine what they saw as their negotiating strength, their commitment to the patient, a line apparently reinforced by Margaret Thatcher when she stated, 'These nurses would never have got this (pay) award but for the no-strike policy reaffirmed by the RCN' (Vousden, 1988).

Regardless of the RCN's position, further strikes and protests by nurses occurred throughout 1988 and into early 1989, amid all sorts of allegations of 'fixing' the process, including regional cartels of senior nursing managers meeting to fix grades together on a cash limited basis and being instructed by DHSS officials what percentage of each grade they could afford. The nurses' action was now aimed at forcing more money from the government and securing proper implementation of the structure from local managers and senior nurses. The longest lasting twelve days in September was at London's Maudsley Hospital. The increasingly beleaguered John Moore had disappeared during the early days of the dispute, to be replaced in July by the bullish Kenneth Clarke when health and social security were split as Whitehall departments. Mr Clarke promptly went on holiday, refusing to return whilst the crisis was heating up and remained unrepentant throughout the vicissitudes of the coming months – until October, in time for the Tory party conference, when he almost casually announced a complete political about-turn. After almost a year of saying that there was no extra money for the nurses, enough was found to make an increase of £138 million for the funding of the clinical grading review. That was followed the next month by an extra £1.8 billion NHS funding for the forthcoming year, almost exactly the figure by which it was estimated the service was underfunded (Klein, 1989: p. 235).

By November the arguments about supervision and continuing responsibility were still unresolved. When it appeared that things could get no worse the decisions about individual grades were announced. It was yet another signal for nurses' anger to erupt and for further walk-outs. The next tactic used by nurses was to 'work to grade', carrying out tasks as close as possible to the criteria and definitions within their newly designated posts. This was most straightforward for nursing auxiliaries, refusing to work without the direct supervision of a registered nurse.

Midwives, who as a group felt more disillusioned than any other, balloted for the first time in 100 years on whether or not to continue the existing RCM policy on industrial action (there was a narrow majority in favour of retaining their policy, but with a large number of midwives not voting at all). They were anxious that, as with a lot of staff nurses, newly qualified midwives were going to be put on 'D' grades inappropriately and that many hospital midwives the RCM believed were entitled to 'G' grades would be amongst those held down to a grade 'F' because of the Department's insistence that continuous responsibility was only about management and not clinical responsibility (Turner, 1988a: p. 19). Many midwives joined in the working to grade but this was strongly discouraged by the RCN who claimed that nurses were being suspended without pay for doing so – although no cases were reported. They restated their belief that any form of industrial action would fail to break the deadlock. 'As the situation becomes more polarised the scope for solution becomes narrowed' (RCN, 1988). However, working to grade did seem to achieve results in places like Banstead and Horton Hospital, where 70 night nurses were upgraded without appeal, and Doncaster, where midwives were regraded as a result of their action. Midwifery, however, was pronounced as being in crisis after 44 staff midwives resigned from the North Middlesex Hospital in protest at the grades they were given. Justifying their lower than expected grades, District General Manager David Hirst made it clear that he wanted to use clinical grading to introduce a hierarchical grading system and seemed oblivious that his managers should have been grading the posts according to the work the midwives were doing in April 1988, regardless of his own service agenda (Hirst, 1988: p. 19). The political reaction became ever stronger, with Kenneth Clarke using his familiar robust language to try and half ridicule, half bully nurses, urging health authorities to take disciplinary action against any staff who used industrial unrest to protest against their grades but it was the arguments now emerging publicly between the unions and professional associations that were of most concern to nurses.

120 000 Appeals

It was estimated for Radio 4's *Today* programme that 120 000 appeals were eventually lodged by nurses against the grades they were awarded in 1988. The implication is obvious, that clinical grading was a failure of enormous magnitude on the part of the nurses' organisation and that nothing had been gained from one of the most bitter years in nursing history, when thousands of nurses and midwives had taken industrial action, some had resigned their posts and, overall, forced the government into more than one humiliating climbdown. It had all been for nothing. Or had it? What exactly was the legacy of clinical grading?

Clearly, politics had taken precedence over sound policy making. What had been a well thought out, well intentioned policy initiative in 1985, designed to solve the long-standing recruitment and retention problems, had got lost in the process of answering the question of whether or not the government were paying nurses enough and funding the NHS adequately. The policy had originally rested neatly within the issues network/iron triangle formula, involving the nurses' organisations at every step until funding became the key issue, at which point it became an exercise in power and they were excluded. For the trade unions and the professional associations, their conflicting philosophies and objectives were papered over while they were involved in detailed work with the management side on the Nurses' and Midwives' Whitley Council, but exploded out as the dispute became increasingly bitter. Trevor Clay's attacks on 'handfuls of nurses destroying the profession's image with silly banners' were equalled by his denunciations of the 'traditional industrial unions' and their tactics but rebutted by Hector MacKenzie, who had become Clay's public sparring partner. His declaration that Clay needed to decide whose side he was on, the nurses' or the government's, was a lot more pointed than his oft quoted allegation that the RCN was willing to roll over and let Kenneth Clarke tickle its tummy (*Nursing Times*, 21.12.1988: p. 24).

Behind the animosity was a concern about recruitment and their principal constituency groups in the context of the winners and losers from clinical grading. Both COHSE and the RCN were claiming to have recruited thousands of nurses during the year, many coming from the other organisation. There is no doubt that it was COHSE's most successful year in recruitment terms since 1981 and had arrested a five year decline. But the RCN recruited 14 000 new members – nearly 4000 more than COHSE. There was undoubtedly a drift from the College to COHSE by nurses wishing to take part in industrial action. Many of them who made the move were very public in doing so. Those who shifted in the opposite direction were probably fewer and were certainly less vocal about it.

Another consideration had been about how clinical grading fitted in with the overall strategy of the different organisations. As has been shown, midwives were badly served and the RCM very hostile as a result of it, justifiably arguing that it potentially worsened the structural deficiencies in their service that had led to high vacancy levels. Health visitors managed to let most of the troubles pass them by with the vast majority of their members content with their grades.

COHSE officials at a national level had been as committed to the development of a clinical grading structure as any of their colleagues from the professional associations. But the union was representing a large number of nursing auxiliaries who were furious with what had been awarded for the lower grades initially and then had that compounded by how the criteria were manipulated to ensure that the majority were graded at scale 'A', the lowest possible grade. Although, as a union, it had a long tradition of campaigning on health service issues, opposing cuts in services and bed closures, at its heart lay the simple knowledge that those were more important to its officials and lay activists than to many of its members, who were most interested in what would be in their take home pay at the end of the month. Many of them were low paid, a large number below the Low Pay Unit's definition of poverty, and such concern was understandable. Made up largely of traditionalist or generalist nurses, many of whom still held some degree of collectivist or class tradition, they saw themselves as part of a large workforce with a right to be paid for the work they did, just as any other worker. If the work became more complex, with more responsibility and they had to work harder, then they should be paid more. It was this constituency that felt most aggrieved within the mass of nurses, whatever their working background.

Taking any form of industrial action always carries risks in terms of the union's relationship with its members and for COHSE these were threefold: some nurses were critical that they had done so at all; others would have regretted the fact of 'having to become involved in it' if they had not benefited personally and saw the action as a failure; many lay activists were critical of the fact that no nationally organised demonstrations had been called and the action had remained locally focused, even when the issue was occupying the national stage.

The RCN had been much more concerned about ward sisters and charge nurses; it was always known that the issue of continuing responsibility would be difficult but once they had won concessions from the Department and increased the percentage of senior nurses placed on a 'G' grade they could feel that they had accomplished at least a large part of their objectives. Individualised nursing care, in the shape of primary nursing, formed the hub of the clinical grading criteria for the middle range of nurses, whether through enrolled nurses contributing to care planning or staff nurses acting as primary nurses. Thus a quiet revolution that had started towards the beginning of the decade had come to its full and final fruition and been integrated into the very grading structure that defined nurses by the work that they did. Additionally, the specialists could feel pleased because there were now grades that gave them a real reward and career structure for their work in the clinical arena. It was no longer a case of remaining as ward sister or charge nurse, becoming increasingly bogged down in ward management or going into senior nurse management. A real alternative had at last been created. Nonetheless, a lot of RCN nurses were of the traditionalist or generalist background and were as frustrated as COHSE nurses at the outcome. Many of the RCN's more radical nurses who did remain within the organisation were obviously angry at the College's refusal to endorse any action at all and many saw Trevor Clay as 'bashing' nurses with the government when he should have been bashing the government (*Nursing Times*, 21.12.1988: p. 19).

The irony was that it became very difficult for any trade union official or anyone from the College to say publicly that clinical grading had been a great success. From a government position of wanting to remove special duty payments, introduce regional pay and hold the overall pay bill down, they had been forced to accept the new grading structure, honour the PRB's recommendations in full (for the first time in four years) and then, despite their determination not to, put in additional money to meet the shortfall from their original financial estimates. Overall, the increase was 15.6% and many nurses were vastly better off than they ever would have been.

Perhaps this reluctance was because something of great significance had been lost in the process. The open and public acrimony between the different nurses' organisations had eventually percolated down to ground level. The campaigns about funding, staffing levels and patient care – the things that had originally stirred so many nurses together – had not been articulated by national officials in the same way and, eventually, been lost. The competition between organisations for members came to be mirrored, in a perverse way, by the rivalry experienced between different nurses aspiring for particular grades. Staff nurses were placed on different grades, as were ward sisters and charge nurses, enrolled nurses and nursing auxiliaries. The uniformity that so many nurses had found in their clinical militancy, fighting on issues about their work, the NHS and their role within it, was largely lost. They were more split than ever before. Some were happy with the results and how they had been achieved. Others experienced increased alienation towards their managers, whom they blamed for downgrading them, and felt disillusioned with their national unions, whom they saw as having colluded in the policy process. The 120 000 appeals were as much a symbolic continuation of their rebellion against all that had happened as it was a legitimate pursuit of justice. For the local activists who had to represent those nurses it was a nightmare and resulted in the loss of a generation of shop stewards who became burnt out trying to pacify angry members and sustain themselves in the face of cynical managers who would turn down obviously legitimate appeals, appeals still being heard at regional and national level five years on.

Perhaps the most sinister legacy of clinical grading came out of its overall cost. The whole exercise had cost a government publicly committed to cutting public spending almost £1 billion. Moreover, with the passing of each month, each successful grading appeal goes off like a financial time bomb, damaging ward budgets as nurses win what is now thousands of pounds in back pay, all adding to the final bill. In those extra hundreds of millions of pounds lay the seeds of the future undermining of the registered nurse. Clinical grading simply priced nurses out of a job.

Chapter 9

The coming of the consumer.
The White Paper *Working for Patients*

A Gut Reaction?

Harry Enfield, a popular contemporary comedian, appeared at several benefits for COHSE nurses during the disputes in 1988. He also had a regular slot in a TV show, *Friday Night Live*, featuring several characters, one of whom was Stavros, a kebab shop owner. In the inimitable style of this comic character, Enfield was able to sum up the position of the NHS in 1988: 'The NHS is sadly bugger up. Is underfunded and under-peeped' (*Nursing Times*, 28.12.1988: p. 20). Although Mrs Thatcher probably did not quite agree with this analysis, she had promised a ministerial review back in the January of that year, largely to deflect the mounting criticism being fuelled by the nurses' action. The purpose of the review in this context was to assure the public that the government remained sensitive to concerns about underfunding, shortages of nurses and a lack of responsiveness to conditions requiring urgent treatment. They were listening to the complaints of nurses and medical staff. However, there was a second reason for signalling the need for a review, this being to reassure her own Right wing backbenchers that the whole system of NHS funding would be carefully scrutinised, as had been talked about very early in that parliament. With this debate occurring against a backdrop of a growing budget deficit at a national level and a serious decline in the manufacturing base, there was a sense of urgency about the need to achieve this.

After John Moore's mysterious disappearance, the task of co-ordinating the review fell to Kenneth Clarke. Nothing was heard of it for more than a year as the nurses' campaigns undermined the Conservatives' political authority on the NHS, although the very fact that it was on the agenda prompted almost every health service policy analyst to rush out a pamphlet or article detailing an agenda for even further change. When the results of the review did surface, however, it was clear that it had been conducted without any consultation with any of the nurses' organisations whatsoever. They had been completely excluded from the policy process.

There was no doubting the radical nature of the proposals. They were based on the work of the American economist Alain Enthoven, who had noted that there were very few incentives for efficiency within the National Health Service. Without an environment of competition, efficiency and consumer choice could not be stimulated and there were widespread variations in performance throughout the service between hospitals and districts. Enthoven suggested keeping what he saw as the popularist elements of the NHS, such as universal access and having it financed through the tax system, but instituting an internal market to produce the missing ingredients. The White Paper, *Working for Patients*, had these principles as a starting point and then took them further (Robinson, 1989: p. 298). It contained seven key proposals:

1. More delegation of responsibility to local level;
2. Self-governing hospitals;
3. New funding arrangements;
4. Additional consultants;
5. GP practice budgets;
6. Reformed management bodies;
7. Better audit arrangements (HMSO, 1989).

These were framed within claims of enormous government achievement since 1978, with the need for (further) change arising from the expansion of services and staff since then, plus the cost of those staff providing those services. The answer, the White Paper stated, was not simply to throw more money at the remaining problems. So what had started primarily as a review of funding made the leap of faith into becoming a blueprint for a complete reorganisation, more far reaching than anything put forward since 1948. A principle common to that of the Griffiths proposals on general management was the double bind of greater local responsibility coupled with even greater accountability to the centre, thus affording even tighter control than had been gained through general management.

The Doctors Remain Untamed

The very fact that the White Paper had followed on so soon after the introduction of general management indicates the latter had not been a total success. This was partly because of the way in which administrators and doctors had continued to subvert central policy at a local level. It was also because general managers had been sent in to accomplish an almost impossible task in the circumstances. They had been expected to control expenditure whilst increasing productivity and efficiency. Difficult enough. But they did not have control of medical staff, who were still employed by the regional health authorities and had job protection schemes that would have been envied by the old Fleet Street unions; moreover, it was their activity that was the basis for all other health service spending. Money cascaded out from the work that doctors did, most especially in hospitals. They put forward strong arguments for ever more costly hi-tech equipment that benefited relatively few patients and they were a long way from agreeing to take a major responsibility for their own budgets and limiting their own spending. Finally, the public still trusted them. Managers and government ignored them at their peril. When the doctors said they needed more resources because they could not treat sick children, people wanted to know what would be done.

There were problems of a more functional nature, too. General managers had completely inadequate financial and operational information systems. Hardly anyone knew how much anything cost or what the accurate state of budgets was, be they for staffing or non-staffing costs. And the nurses had hammered home how central policy could be smashed if the key actors were not involved and signed up to the process. Managing was not just a matter of introducing ideologically driven changes; there was a necessity to completely redevelop systems within the existing functional services and establish structural changes that would bring the professions under control through other means.

Who's Consuming Whom?

As indicated in the White Paper's title, *Working for Patients,* its popular thrust was to give the user of health services a greater say in the type of services they would receive. But there was a degree of ambiguity about who exactly would become the consumer.

The age of consumerism was, of course, one of the hallmarks of the Thatcher years. People travelling on British Rail or other transport services ceased to be passengers, instead being transformed into customers. Many in health care fields such as community mental health had already started describing patients as clients, in common with many working in social services, as part of an attempt to alter the balance of power within what many viewed as a paternalistic relationship, intimating that the user was exercising choice. Indeed, society had, in the words of the Prime Minister, ceased to exist. The individual consumer now reigned supreme. Of course, this philosophical view of the world matched the change from a manufacturing economy to a service economy. In the same way, the health service would now be made up of those who provided a service for those who purchased it, with the objective of getting as many levels of the service involved in being both purchaser and provider, introducing this form of commercialism right into the heart of the NHS.

District health authorities were to be changed into purchasing authorities. Their relationship was to be redefined on a contractual basis, buying health services from provider units, whether new self-governing hospitals, independent of health authority control, or hospitals still 'directly managed' by the authority. The authority would no longer be bound to obtain services from the nearest hospital but could 'shop around' for the best deal, according to price and efficiency. Similarly, GPs were to have the option of becoming fundholders, able to buy hospital services from whichever hospital offered the most cost effective deal. Any money left in their budget at the end of the financial year could be ploughed back into the practice. The concept of 'money following the patient' was born, the idea being that efficiency and cost effectiveness would mean that the hospitals that met these criteria most succesfully would treat the most people and thus generate the most income. Those that were inefficient would lose out. Where was the user of health services in this new equation? It was difficult to ascertain who was the consumer – patient, GP or purchasing agent.

Consumerism in welfare was not a new concept in 1989. It was seen as an answer to many of the complaints and criticisms that had been formulated by both Left and Right more than a decade earlier, especially the Right. If the zenith of health service paternalism had been seen in the 1970s, both from consultants and trade unions, many had not liked what was on offer. The idea of providing people with the 'freedom of choice' was an endlessly attractive one for the New Right, who believed that this would drive the market to produce the highest quality, efficient and cheapest services possible. But there was no clarity about the use of the term 'patients' choice', certainly around how service users would be able to participate in the exercising of choice and decisions affecting the provision of their services, which is what makes welfare consumerism truly meaningful. Nor was there any consideration about whether or not it actually was a 'good thing'. Consumers are necessarily in competition with one another, all seeking the best level of service or the best 'deal'. In all forms of welfare provision it had already been seen how articulate, wealthier groups were able to secure the best provision of services through a variety of means, disadvantaging those from poorer backgrounds, often in greater need of services which were then unavailable because of limited resources (Cook, 1987). With the lower socioeconomic groups also less well placed to make detailed assessments of quality they would also be further disadvantaged, as they would be if choice of hospital location became an important part of the consumer agenda. Those with lower incomes, working long hours and possibly shifts would be far less inclined to choose to receive treatment at a better hospital outside their locality. Trevor Clay, arguing for a shift of emphasis to health promotion and illness prevention, pointed out that plans for setting up self-governing trust hospitals was far more about management initiatives than health and did not create any options for choice for the consumer (Clay, 1989: p. 16).

The issue about whether or not the consumer at large – the public – wanted the changes in the first place was another question never given an airing within the White Paper. The self-interested groups, the medical profession, nurses' organisations and trade unions had already entered into confrontational campaigns highlighting their opposition to the proposals when opinion polls began to show trends of approximately 70% of respondents being against the White Paper's reforms. Ballots of local communities and staff were ruled out by the government although when organised by local people, with or without trade union support, they confirmed the public's general opposition.

In reality, the consumers were to be GP fundholders and purchasing authorities, although many authorities did begin to consult more widely with groups representing users and community health councils on what sort of services they might wish to see provided.

Can the Market Actually Work?

The purchaser/provider split was the mechanism for introducing the market into health care but this did not mean that there would be an unlimited amount of money that providers could draw upon. They would still be working within a strictly cash limited service, with that money being allocated to the new purchasing authorities in a new funding arrangement. This meant the abandoning of the old RAWP formula and represented another significant change. The Resource Allocation Working Party [RAWP] had introduced its formula of giving the population weighting factors for, prinicipally, age and mortality. It was introduced in 1976 but had been the subject of great controversy throughout its history, as it facilitated the reallocation of funding from areas that, according to its formula, were less deprived than others, with parts of the apparently affluent south-east, for instance, losing out to places like Trent (Klein, 1989: p. 82). *Working for Patients* outlined a system of capitation funding, or an allocation of monies per head of population within a given health district. This would hit inner city areas particularly hard, as they had relatively small populations but contained a large proportion of people with special health care needs. Because of this a weighting formula was to be devised and transitional funding available for a limited period as the new purchasing authorities and provider units got to grips with building their services around the changed system. Further costs were built in for provider units through the government placing far greater importance on the efficient use of buildings and capital assets, introducing capital charges on them rather than treating capital as a 'free good'. Effectively, hospitals would have to pay interest charges for all their buildings. Again, this would drive up costs for inner city services. These two factors created enormous problems for major teaching hospitals – almost all located in inner cities – who would also find that extra costs associated with their teaching functions would not be borne by their local health authority purchasers.

The government had made it clear that they wished to introduce a market in health care but the White Paper was not proposing to do this. Some of its innovations were market oriented, such as the elimination of cross subsidies, preventing service providers or purchasers from balancing a service that was overspent (or underfunded) with another which had underspent, something that had become fairly standard practice in the NHS. However, other elements essential to the success of the market were not included. Because of the nature of hospital care, local monopolies were still going to exist, health care was still a business that was highly regulated by government and there was not the kind of homogeneity of 'product' to allow the market to function efficiently. Perhaps most important, at least in the early days of the new changes, was a lack of information. Ideally, for the market to operate, consumers must have prefect information or knowledge. Certainly, if the consumer was the patient they could not be expected to know who was the best surgeon for a hip operation or the ward that had the best recovery rate for patients with a myocardial infarction; Even GPs and/or health authorities would not possess the necessary levels of information, producing a reliance on the local provider and monopoly (Le Grand & Robinson, 1984: pp. 38–9). Either that or they would be basing their judgements on inadequate information – something that was to plague the market as purchasers became bolder in their decision making. Moreover, as has been noted, the information systems in the NHS were inadequate in themselves and there were not the trained, experienced personnel to operate such systems. This meant bringing in new computer systems and relatively large numbers of new managers and staff to make the contracts and information systems work, diverting much needed money away from clinical services.

The question of demand and efficiency was one of the central issues that the White Paper was designed to address. Increased demand had plagued the NHS since its inception. Increased throughput of patients had meant more people being treated annually but, at the same time, waiting lists were still growing. In traditional economic theory growing demand would give power to the supplier or provider but would also be affected by the price of the product, rising as the price falls, falling as the price rises. However, health produces a situation of inelastic demand. The incidence of ill health does not fall or rise with the market. Demand therefore would only be a factor that would arise out of a purchaser's willingness to buy services from a particular provider. It would have little to do with the morbidity of the local population. Higher turnover, or greater efficiency, had been achieved by improving throughput rather than increasing capacity (Flynn, 1989) and that had been at a cost, particularly to nurses, with increased turnover of staff and all that had been encompassed in the unrest of 1988. There was also going to be a limit to how much further throughput could be increased without a severe effect on the quality of care provided.

Just as the demand side was inelastic, so was the supply side. Hopes raised by the White Paper that hospitals and service providers would be able to function more as autonomous business units and raise their own capital were quickly found to be unrealistic; if there were the potential to expand a successful service it could only be done as far as the physical limitations of buildings allowed – and, because of the winners and losers inherent in any market system, would only be funded if that money, which was coming from a fixed overall NHS budget, was taken from elsewhere. Thus it would not be a matter of expanding the overall service; rather it would be depriving Peter to fund Paul.

Thus the whole premise of the internal market was undermined before the project was even begun (Webb & Charles, 1986) and the speed of the changes being put forward in the paper were also going to generate their own inefficiencies (Barr, Glennerster & Le Grand, 1989: p. 123). But another problem was to be the cost of introducing the changes, variously estimated at between 10% and 15%, for which no additional funding was provided. The Resource Management Initiative, also proposed within the White Paper, never fully materialised and the downward pressure that was to be exerted on drug prescribing was only a limited success.

There was a major political question that underlined the introduction of such radical reforms. Within the pages of the White Paper was a prescription that would alter the map of health care provision far more than any act of parliament since 1948. Effectively, it declared the National Health Service dead, at the very least as it had been known up until then. Potentially, the White Paper proposals, whatever their stated aims and objectives, could create strains that would destroy it completely, depending on how it was implemented (Barr, Glennerster & Le Grand, 1989: pp. 117–18). Strategic planning at even a regional level would be a thing of the past. Education for both doctors and nurses would be transformed as hospitals and community services became market oriented, providing services which the purchaser wanted to buy rather than in a unified pattern at least partly designed to give students a comprehensive education. Coupled with Project 2000 pushing nurse education out of the schools of nursing, the White Paper signalled a complete break with the past. The market would also mean that, with the exception of certain core services, areas could be deprived of a particular clinical service if a neighbouring – rival – unit could provide it at a more attractive rate. Alternatively, if it were proving 'uncompetitive' to provide a certain clinical service, there was no longer an onus on the provider unit to continue with it unless specifically contracted to do so by the purchasing authority. However rare in practice, even the objective of developing rationally planned, comprehensive, integrated and holistic services was abandoned. The possibility arose that anything could happen, if it was the will of the market. Even world famous teaching hospitals could be forced to close if they were uneconomic and no longer viable. If that did happen, it would be possible for the first time in over 40 years for the government to state that this was not their responsibility, but was the action of the local decision makers based on what was best for local people. The question was, would they let the market, in the form of their local purchasing authorities, go that far? There were far too many questions to be answered in simple terms and a series of working papers supplemented the original White Paper.

A Return to Local Bargaining

There were two other elements to the proposals that were designed to improve efficiency and cost effectiveness, both of them necessary for a government committed to cutting the costs of the country's most expensive labour force. One was the introduction of local pay bargaining, the other 're-examining the work of nurses and other professional staff so as to secure the most cost effective use of their skills' (HMSO, 1989).

The introduction of local pay bargaining into the NHS would have enormous organisational implications for trade unions and professional associations that have been built as much around their national functions as anything else. It would mean that the much criticised Whitley Councils would largely cease to have a purpose and, with them, a loss of role for national negotiators. If the emphasis shifted to local bargaining, the spotlight would inevitably fall on both local managers and shop stewards, involved in detailed negotiations to set pay for anything from a couple of hundred to several thousand staff. This would mean a complete restructuring of relationships between trade unions and managers at a local level, not just on issues of pay and conditions but on policy making generally. The promise of the White Paper is to devolve policy making of all kinds to a local level, meaning effective consultative and negotiating machinery has to be in place. It is extremely time consuming for managers, charged with numerous extra responsibilities, but for trade unionists who have a full-time job (and often family responsibilities) it is an onerous position to even contemplate.

Once it became apparent that this was an integral part of the White Paper, speculation arose about no-strike deals, single union recognition agreements or the setting up of management controlled 'staff associations' similar to those that existed in some hospitals in the early part of the century. It also threw the future of the pay review body into doubt, with inconsistent signals from the government on the matter, with each minister seeming to take a contradictory position on it from their predecessor.

Within the trade unions and professional associations there was, understandably, considerable debate about what all of this might mean for them. It might be perceived that the RCN and RCM, with inbuilt no-strike rules already in place, would be well placed to take advantage of local deals in the way that the government claimed they had been favoured nationally during the 1980s (Buchan, 1989: p. 20). However, a lack of a meaningful shop steward network with negotiating skills would militate against being able to achieve that. Another problem for the professional associations is that nurses and midwives do not join them in order to be negotiators on such issues. Both Colleges thus made it an early priority to strengthen their industrial relations departments centrally. The RCN also launched a recruitment campaign for new shop stewards but their organisation in the workplace remained relatively lightweight. Although it might have been imagined that COHSE would welcome the opportunity to negotiate pay on a local basis the cautious enthusiasm of national officers was met with reluctance from lay activists who believed that an increasingly powerful management would be able to bully them into submission. There was also intense suspicion about how they would compete with the College at a local level, where it would have close working relationships with management.

Local pay bargaining is not an entirely unknown quantity in the NHS, however. It has its antecedents in the introduction of incentive bonus schemes for ancillary workers in the early 1970s which, as has been shown (page 78), prompted an explosion of trade unionism, with the unions recruiting new members in massive numbers, supporting shop stewards who were negotiating directly on their behalf. The remedy if the membership were unhappy with what was on offer – either from the management or the representatives – was also close at hand. There was no need to go through the time consuming, cumbersome, often disempowering process of trying to influence national policy as a means of seeking redress. Whether or not nurses would react in the same way is very difficult to assess. The worst recession since the war has clouded the opportunity to judge how health workers generally will behave as the job market has been squeezed ever tighter and local bargaining has yet to become a reality, despite the rhetoric of many NHS trusts and government ministers. There has also been a greater degree of unity amongst trade union officials at a local level than many would have predicted after clinical grading. Recognition agreements are being signed. But, with only a few exceptions, all the unions previously representing members in the workplace are being included. Most managers have taken an extremely cautious attitude to local bargaining and not wanted to be seen to be the first to open this particular Pandora's Box, fearing that it might become an all-consuming monster, taking up enormous amounts of time to negotiate relatively trivial matters as well as pay, the 'big one'. There is also a fear that, with a change in the economic climate, they could find themselves facing localised action and a disastrous downturn in industrial relations as well as the loss of potential income. For, as is the case in any market, nurses and other health workers now have the ultimate threat to hang over the employer's head: they can stop the means of production.

Nursing in Retreat

It was, perhaps, a supreme irony that Trevor Clay's successor as general secretary of the RCN was a general manager. Christine Hancock, a former midwife and then ward sister at the National Heart Hospital, was appointed whilst serving as district general manager in Waltham Forest (Snell, 1988: pp. 16–17). Clay had announced his impending retirement in the midst of the clinical grading conflicts but remained in post for a year and was thus involved in formulating the College's early responses to the White Paper, including setting up its own Commission into the NHS, chaired by Rabbi Julia Neuberger. Again, a priority was to ensure that nursing had a 'voice'. The demise of health authorities, as they had been constituted at a regional and district level, was explicit within Clarke's proposals. They would be replaced by the purchasing authorities, with trust or management boards for the provider units, much more oriented to a business method of working, with no elected members or outside professionals. Five executive members would have key posts within the trust, five non-executive members would be appointed externally, with the chairperson appointed by the Secretary of State. All local authority representatives and representatives from the professions would be lost. With so much policy making to be devolved to local level this would mean that the professions as well as the trade unions would face exclusion from key decision making. The preservation of a nursing voice at different levels of the health service had been an RCN objective, both before and throughout the years of the NHS, and had been a mainstay of their attempts to ensure that nurses maintained a managerial role at the highest levels. However, there were long-standing doubts about their efficacy and the quality of the advice they were providing and, as ever with nurses, questions were raised about whether or not they had contributed to their own downfall rather than looking at the political framework in which the changes were taking place (*Nursing Times*, 22.3.1989: pp. 50–1).

One thing was completely clear, however, and that was that the nurses' organisations were seen as completely marginal. To an extent, Clarke had also tried to marginalise the medical profession, with the BMA not enjoying their usual place at the policy making table, but the forcefulness of their campaign made it clear that they were not going to knocked over that easily and, before too long, it was easy to imagine that Clarke's Hush Puppies were going to have to tread softly through the corridors of BMA House.

The RCN lobbying machine was put into full swing, suggesting amendments and utilising 'the links that have been built up with government' (*Nursing Times*, 9.11.1988: p. 17), largely engaged in what many officials saw as an exercise in damage limitation. But they were very limited in their effect. More radical voices from within its ranks were harshly – and publicly – critical of the White Paper:

> The NHS White Paper is such a preposterous set of proposals that without the experience of ten years of Thatcherism it would be impossible to believe that the Government means to implement it in the face of almost unanimous opposition, natural justice and common sense. While the principles behind it are inhumane, most of the content is simply unworkable.
>
> (Gooch, 1989: p. 42)

At this stage, those like Sally Gooch began to think about new ways of campaigning and saw the value of working alongside service users in the hope of frustrating the process of opting out and exposing the protagonists. 'Be subversive' was her message. Trevor Clay had seen alliances with users in a different light, writing, 'I believe we will only win if our focus is on making the health service work for the patients and clients, and not making the rights of those who work in it our only priority' (Clay, 1989: p. 16).

Devoid of any opportunity to exploit links with government, COHSE's campaign was straightforward and oppositional from the outset. 'The future existence of the NHS is at stake', it wrote out to all branch officials in May 1989. A substantial memorandum of evidence opposing the proposals was submitted to the Social Services Select Committee and political lobbies of parliament were organised. An extensive education programme was organised to help branch activists campaign as effectively as possible but at the same time prepare for the changes. A comparative study of the American health care system was commissioned for lobbying and publicity purposes. The overall campaign had a clear objective, to stop or substantially modify the White Paper proposals and it was decided to revise and update its 'Charter for Health' to counter possible allegations that it had nothing positive to say. However, almost all of its attention was focused on so-called opting out hospitals, those preparing applications to become self-governing trust hospitals and GP fundholders. The make up of trust board membership was no more than one aspect of the general concern about the changes and the loss of an independent nursing voice from the old health authorities barely rated a mention from COHSE. Calls for industrial action at the union's 1990 annual conference were not supported and, again, it failed to make a major impact, either on the policy process or in terms of sustaining a profile for its national campaign. The government did make some concessions and alterations. The method of funding remained through taxation and principles of universal access, free at the point of need, were re-emphasised. But those changes that they were most keen to see implemented went ahead: the purchaser/provider split, GP fundholding, the introduction of the Audit Commission, serious medical audit and the involvement of medical staff in the process of management through putting consultants into clinical directors' posts, new managerial structures and information systems, devolved responsibility and greater accountability, the ability to introduce local bargaining and greater pay flexibility as and when they were ready.

Nurses seemed generally confused by what was happening. In part this was no doubt due to Sally Gooch's diagnosis. It was difficult to believe that the government were seriously intending to proceed with their proposals, partly because they did seem unworkable as well as promising such radical change, but also because there was such widespread opposition to them. Perhaps everyone was watching the campaign being waged by the BMA against the changes. It was high profile and featured regular confrontations between senior members of the medical profession and Kenneth Clarke who, for once, did not seem to be getting things all his own way. It was becoming progressively personalised, to the point where a series of billboard posters went up all over the country asking, 'What do you call a man who refuses to listen to medical advice? Answer: Kenneth Clarke'. Before too long he was involved in direct negotiations with the doctors.

The BMA's campaign was never going to help nurses, however. Although they had genuine concerns about GP fundholding, the financing of the NHS, the needs of the patient and maintaining a degree of clinical independence, their primary concern was to ensure that doctors would hold positions of influence within the new structures. It was also difficult to maintain a sense of the reality of the promised changes when working from day to day inside the NHS. Clarke published the outcome of the review in February 1989 and it was almost like a phoney war until April 1991, when the changes came into effect with the introduction of the first wave trusts. Then the plethora of news stories about the problems of the opted out hospitals, especially the supposed 'government flagship', Guy's Hospital, seemed to merge into a prolonged propaganda war that became increasingly surreal. The news that the Department of Health had established a 'good news unit', specifically to counter bad publicity about the NHS should have come as a shock but didn't.

The Conservative government had been in obvious and steady decline as they were rocked by ministerial resignations, continuing financial disasters and mounting opposition to the poll tax, one unpopular policy too many. When Margaret Thatcher was ousted in 1990 it had seemed as inevitable as the punishments she had so casually meted out to her many opponents in the previous decade. A change of prime minister seemed to promise changes in policy but there was no relenting on the health service. The government carried on regardless with the White Paper changes. There were minor storms, around GP fundholding especially, some local campaigns against opting out which gained a high profile, notably at by-elections, and Labour's shadow health spokesperson, Robin Cook, gave his ministerial adversaries regular bloody noses in parliamentary exchanges. But all to no avail. The second wave trusts came into being on April 1st 1992 during a fiercely fought election campaign but one in which the Tories seemed to be on the ropes. As it had in all of the previous three elections, the NHS seemed to be one of Labour's strongest issues but confusion about whether or not it would maintain the purchaser/provider split and allow opted out hospitals to remain 'out' was compounded by problems of news management over one particular story that became infamous as 'Jennifer's Ear'. When John Major's Tory party won a surprise victory, many senior managers in directly managed units (DMUs) in the NHS acknowledged that, despite their own misgivings and opposition to the *Working for Patients* inspired changes, they would have to submit applications for opting out in the next wave. Within a year there would barely be a DMU left in London.

Nurses were now, more clearly than ever, excluded from the policy making process except on issues of clinical practice. They could continue, primarily through their professional associations, to have direct access to departmental working parties and policy groups, with COHSE's professional officers also becoming involved, albeit to a much lesser extent. The Whitley Councils carried on their work at a national level but lacked real authority as key sections of the General Whitley Council agreement, governing the terms and conditions of all NHS staff, were being undermined by increasingly confident local managers or, in one case, unilaterally thrown out by the government. Increasingly nurses, as with other NHS workers, saw their own managers as the employer, particularly as the modern phenomenon of nurse unemployment became a prominent concern in many areas. Many newly qualified nurses were affected, with, unsurprisingly, the cost of successful clinical grading appeals being cited as one of the reasons for difficulties in filling vacancies (Thompson, 1990: p. 18).

Chapter 10

Why let things be difficult when, with just a little more effort, we can make them impossible?
Towards the millennium

It is nothing new to imagine that we are living in an apocalyptic age. It is one of the strange quirks of the human condition. The end has been nigh for a very long time. We are not now witnessing the end of the registered nurse, as some have predicted, although it is almost certainly entering into a post-industrial stage. There is every likelihood that major change is not very far off, including substantial alterations to the training of those working in the fields of mental health and learning difficulties, perhaps eventually moving nurse training into a more generic framework. Despite the upheavals resulting from Project 2000 it is quite possible that further reforms will occur in general nurse training.

Looking back on how we have got to where we are now, particularly after the changes of the 1980s, it does appear that we are in the process of turning full circle. The drive towards registration that occupied the early part of the century, followed by the preoccupation with training, failed to deliver a cost effective nursing service that could meet the needs of the nation's requirements. Moreover, the development of 'modern' nursing, more than a century ago, occurred at a time when Britain was expanding its role as an imperial power, seeking out new trading markets in the world and undertaking a series of great engineering projects, both mechanical and social; now, in a time of economic decline, nursing and the service to which it is inextricably tied are viewed increasingly as a burden the nation can ill afford. The pressure for a reduction in the cost of that service is growing. The way to achieve it is through cutting the number of trained nurses and students being trained.

An Educated Workforce – Theory and Practice

The issue of education has always been one that deeply divides nursing. Sceptics on the service side, particularly nurse managers, criticise the educationalists for putting forward idealistic and impractical theories about nurse education and practice, disregarding the realities of nursing life in an underfunded, understaffed service. Furthermore, they have accused the theorists of avoiding the difficulties the implementation of their theories would cause by maintaining a divide between education and the service, which is rarely crossed by those from the education side. The educationalists, allied with the professionalist or specialist group of nurses, have countered that the future of nursing is dependent on the quality of training given to nurses; a more theory based training provided for nurses with a strong academic background better prepares them to develop practice once they are qualified. If the arrival of Project 2000 would seem to have been the realisation of the aspirations of the educationalists, early reports of its difficulties have done little to smooth over the old divisions or resolve the debate either way. Research commissioned for the English National Board confirmed what many already knew or suspected. Tutors and practitioners were ill prepared to accommodate Project 2000 students, who were often left to work alone and unsupervised. Confusion about the roles of teacher, supporter, supervisor and mentor was compounded by short and interrupted placements and 'the task of making connections between theory and practice was formidable'. The overall problem was that the timetable for the introduction of the new training had been 'unrealistically short' (Gilbert, 1993: p. 5). Problems were also being reported about enough students progressing onto the specialist branch programmes after completing the common foundation programme. The development designed to complement Project 2000, a system of national vocational qualifications (NVQs) available to health care assistants brought in to do the work previously undertaken by 'old style' students, is a revolution that has almost not happened. Although now established on the health care map it is nowhere near as widespread as was originally envisaged and is another initiative fractured by the drive towards a market oriented service.

Problems about a new system of training, especially one as radically different for nursing as Project 2000, can be overcome in time, if the climate is receptive and commitment is there at all levels of the service. However, other trends in nurse training highlight different priorities. Some colleges of education have shown reductions in contracted levels of students of 25–40% for April 1994. 1630 nurse tutors have gone from the health service, out of a total of 8200 working in 1986 – and not all to higher education by any means. Tom Bolger, the RCN's director of education, has pointed out that the switch to a reliance on market forces now means there is no central database for information on education which has increased the trend towards developing workforce plans based on short term expediency (Bolger, 1993: p. 18). Nationally, the number of students will fall from 23 949 in 1992–3 to 17 733 in 1994–5, making a cut of 26% in two years.

For the UKCC, the educational problems have mounted. Its proposals on post-registration education and practice (PREP) drew the fire of UNISON, the RCN and the HVA, all of whom advised them to go back to the drawing board. But at almost the same time as Tom Bolger was describing the proposals as 'unrealistic' (*Nursing Times*, 6.10.1993: p. 5) an RCN consensus conference was calling for an all-graduate nursing profession, with degrees earned either pre- or post-registration.

Any further changes to a better educated workforce have to confront the contradictions that would occur in practice, however. The issue of nurses' pay in comparison to that of other occupations is still a live and dangerous one. When a newly qualified nurse earns 16% less than a police constable at the same level and as much as 30% less than someone starting work in a bank, salary costs and the money to fund them are not matters that can be ignored. A more competitive labour market than we have in the recession drained 1990s will offer graduates a wider range of job opportunities. But if they can be attracted into the service, better educated recruits experiencing a longer or more costly training programme both pre- and post-registration will inevitably lead to fewer nurses unless the funding priorities of government significantly shift. That is not going to be the case with a Conservative administration carrying a £50 billion deficit.

The obvious, if usually unstated, corollary to the professionalists' argument is that they support a smaller, elite workforce, planning and evaluating nursing care to be carried out by predominantly untrained staff. Either that or they have completely misread the economic history of nursing.

Too Many Nurses – What is to be Done?

Those nurses who have consistently argued for improved standards of care and a scientific base to nursing practice have seen many welcome advancements in recent years. The work of the King's Fund in promoting both primary nursing and nursing development units has made great strides, with NDUs being set up throughout the country, which receive sizable grants from the King's Fund and the support of its full-time workers. Its primary nursing network, although suffering from a lack of resources and organisational support, is nonetheless established and primary nursing is now regarded as a progressive form of practice, used by nursing teams in any number of clinical settings. Support was evidenced by funding through the King's Fund and favourable ministerial utterances, reinforced by work done in the anonymous empire of the Department of Health's policy making networks. Although it became apparent that he had misunderstood the term and its implications, John Major even went on record as saying that his government would ensure that every patient would have a primary nurse (quickly changed to a 'named nurse,' it was ultimately a policy that was developed as little as it was thought through). This clumsy attempt at a top-down initiative also belied the support for primary nursing and related methods of organising care. Without official guidance and instruction at a national level it is a system that has spread, being taken up and developed by nursing teams themselves for all of the complex reasons explored in Chapter 5. It has, in some cases, even been done without the support of managers or medical staff.

The closure of Beeson Ward, of the Oxford Development Unit, in 1989 was a bitter blow to the cause of highly professionalised practice. The ward used a variety of nursing and organisational innovations. Health care assistants were introduced to supplement the work of its primary nurses, domestic and catering staff had a more generic role and nurses were not bound by either nursing or hospital policies or by medical control. Research based, it lay outside the management structure of the hospital. Its key innovation was the use of nursing beds – with nurses making decisions about whether or not people came into hospital (Pembrey & Punton, 1990: pp. 44–5). It was eventually so severely undermined by key medical staff (although strongly supported by some) that the health authority closed it because of 'shortage of money'. As well as the anger expressed at the time of its closure, there was also a lot of surprise. Looking at it in the context of everything else happening in the NHS at the time the surprise possibly should have been that it got started in the first place and then survived three and a half years.

While the loss of Beeson Ward was being analysed, another ward, operating in an unorthodox fashion specialising in the care of the elderly, was being opened (Dopson, 1990: pp. 46–8). This was one staffed entirely without nurses, a policy adopted because it was believed that nursing staff had become too reliant on performing tasks and not providing the holistic care needed for the ward's elderly residents. Using a key worker system, with staffing levels of five for an early shift, three for a late shift and two or three at night, the care workers and ward manager could call upon nursing advice, the same as if they needed a doctor, as any carer would if they were looking after a relative at home. There was a nurse manager, outside the ward's establishment, as with any other ward and the staff were being trained in the practical skills of nursing – or caring. Although an important part of the reasoning for the project was seeking an alternative to caring for the elderly that would break the doctor/nurse/sick patient circle, cost and projected shortages of registered nurses were also considerations. The ward manager was paid at the equivalent of an 'F' grade, her deputy at the equivalent of scale 'E'; the rest of the staff were either on grade 'C' or 'B'.

Research by Lois Thomas into the work of qualified nurses and nursing auxiliaries in the care of the elderly field showed that:

The most important differences were found across organisational modes, with qualified nurses and nursing auxiliaries within organisational modes engaging in similar patterns of work. Nursing staff in primary (nursing) wards were found to spend more time in direct patient care and communication and less time in supplementary patient care and staff activities than their team and functional counterparts. Team and functional subjects, on the other hand, spent more time with patients in domestic and administrative activities.

(Thomas, 1993: pp. 45–8)

Ms Thomas's findings suggested that ward culture, philosophy and work practices influenced nursing practice more than methods of care organisation and that there was a role for nursing auxiliaries as carers which 'argues against the professional ideology which proposes classifying work so that nursing is given only by nurses with a statutory qualification'.

The debate about nursing practice has then, in many ways, returned to the same issues that concerned the protagonists a century ago. What is the role of qualified and unqualified nurses and what can be afforded? How can the best standards of care be delivered? A backdrop to those questions has been a far less overt problem. How can an improved status for nursing be attained? This has largely fuelled the educational and professionalising lobbies, even if that has not been the principal aim of nurses in nursing development units or introducing initiatives such as primary nursing. To a large extent, those issues have never left the agenda, but are simply more prominent now, taking the form of shared concerns because of the new managerial culture and the way in which cost consciousness – and control – has been pushed down to ward and service level. Few nurses are unaware of the cost constraints facing their own team and these are usually relayed now through the ward sister or charge nurse.

Nurses have to carry on with their basic task, however, that of caring for those who use their service, whatever the system of care, whatever the clinical setting. Often it is still in a task or team oriented framework, far away from the glamorous vision of primary nursing's advocates. More than ever, it is in difficult circumstances, either environmentally or practically, as many health service premises deteriorate through a lack of capital funding and the workload for nurses increases.

Between September 1989 and September 1991, the NHS lost

almost 5850 nursing posts; the staff side of the Nurses' and Midwives' Whitley Council discovered that 1200 more were declared redundant within the first nine months of 1993 and there were 17 720 nurses unemployed. In the same period, the 'throughput' of patients has risen by 9% and the number of day cases treated went up by 23%. Scotland's loss of 3500 WTEs in two and a half years from a smaller workforce was equally worrying (Turner, 1993a: pp. 14–15). Nor has it been a case of a shift from trained to untrained nurses. Over 1400 untrained nurses' posts were lost between September 1991 and March 1992. A further 7000–10 000 nurses' jobs could go with the dramatic losses of hospital beds recommended in the Tomlinson Report on London's health services. The inexorable logic of these job losses is that, even if the numbers of patients seen and treated remained static, nurses would be working considerably harder; as it is, with that figure rising steadily but still insufficient to keep pace with growing demand, their workload is simply becoming almost unmanageable. The reduction of students being taken into training, coupled with the consistent 'wastage' rate from nursing and its regular turnover of staff, mean that these shortages are to be further compounded within another three years. This will coincide with a period when 1762 extra nurses will be needed just to maintain existing staff–patient ratios in elderly care because of the growing number of people living longer.

All of this might seem a familiar scenario. Nursing shortages are nothing new. What *is* different in the 1990s is that neither the government nor health service managers are complaining about insufficient numbers of nurses to do the work required. There is no possibility of a modern day equivalent of the Athlone Committee being appointed to look into the reasons for a 'crisis', because no such calamity is perceived. Part of UNISON's first set of supplementary evidence to the PRB took the form of a poll to highlight nurses' reasons for considering leaving their workplace (UNISON, 1993). In the light of its findings, it is worth re-examining the results of the *Nursing Mirror*'s 1937 poll to see how it reflects against current concerns. There are direct similarities between the two, but also some sharp variations:

1937	1993
1. Hours of duty;	Managers' treatment of staff;
2. Rates of pay;	Having to compromise on standards of care;
3. Petty restrictions;	Staff shortages;
4. Lectures in off duty hours;	Unfair grading;
5. Prospects for advancement;	Levels of pay;
6. Interchangeable pensions;	Problems with patterns of working hours;
7. Compulsory living in;	Conditions of service;
8. The gap between the school and the hospital (*Nursing Mirror*, 1.1.1938).	Inadequate maternity and childcare provision (UNISON, 1993).

UNISON discovered that 53% of their respondents had considered leaving nursing/midwifery altogether, whilst 48% had thought about leaving the NHS. 35% had considered this very seriously. Nearly a quarter were still in their job only because they could not find anything else. Perhaps paradoxically, 60% had remained in their job because they still enjoyed it.

Nurses' perception of how services to patients had worsened related directly to some of the key changes of the previous decade:

1. Cutbacks in staffing levels	81%
2. Increases in administrative duties	70%
3. Management attitudes	60%
4. Reorganisation of services (UNISON, 1993).	48%

There is in place now a system for delivering health care that the government feel largely comfortable with. The necessary mechanisms for controlling expenditure are firmly set, even if it has taken an increase in managers of 236.2% in the four years from 1989 to achieve it (*Labour Party News*, 1994). Short term contracts for senior managers, a web of appointments from the centre outward and the removal of any system of democratic accountability within trust boards or health authorities means that, in government terms, those given the responsibility of managing the service can concentrate on just that. They are directly responsible and accountable to their paymasters. Nursing has not been an accidental casualty to that process but a victim of what has been seen as a very necessary evolution, driven by both pragmatic and ideological considerations and for the first time nurses are not managed by nurses. General managers, having initially taken a questioning attitude to the value of qualified nurses at all levels of the service, have shifted ground. Apart from redundancies and reduced intakes into colleges of education, so-called skill mix reviews have been instituted in many services, ostensibly looking at the work being undertaken by various grades within a nursing team and then exploring whether or not the current mix of grades is the best to deliver care. In reality these reviews have been used far more to reduce the number of trained nurses in relation to untrained staff (*Nursing Times*, 26.2.94, 1992: p. 22) without clear, reasearch based conclusions to support the action taken. It is clear that it is expected that far more of the work that qualified nurses have done will, in the future, be carried out by untrained nurses. Even if there were an immediate change in national policy on this issue it would take long enough to filter through to leave a period when unqualified nurses will have to take on an increased role in the delivery of care. However, there is no change in sight. Academics and senior health service managers at a national level, such as Duncan Nichol and Eric Caines, have made it clear that they believe there are too many nurses and that the redundancies of the 1990s are simply the effects of the market 'shaking the NHS tree'. Roger Dyson, director of the Clinical Management Unit at Keele University, has argued that the nursing profession has not tackled the problem of 'over supply' because of the erroneous belief that it is a temporary phenomenon brought on by the recession. It has, he says, failed to recognise the radical change in the NHS, with fewer and fewer services being provided within hospitals and hospital beds being dramatically reduced (Dyson, 1993: p. 20).

Clinical grading. Two words in the UNISON evidence to the PRB that stalk contemporary debate on nursing like Banquo's ghost. Five years on, 44% of UNISON's respondents cited unfair grading as a reason for considering leaving nursing. That 43% of RCN nurses surveyed in 1989 (Buchan *et al.*, 1989) reported dissatisfaction with their grade shows the depth of feeling that has endured. There is little doubt that the lingering sore of appeals has kept that sense of grievance alive. The irony is that many services have simply ignored the clinical grading criteria over the last two to three years – if not from the outset – placing staff nurses and enrolled nurses who are in charge of wards regularly on scale

'D' rather than 'E', as are primary nurses. Ward managers are being appointed at scale 'F' while scale 'G' nurses are being expected to take charge of more than one ward. Having waged such a fierce and bitter campaign, nursing has seen its gains taken back on an incremental basis ever since.

The Search for Constant Change Leads to Continuing Chaos

Integral in the Griffiths Report of 1983 was the assumption that the search for constant change would prevent the NHS from slipping back into a state of inertia and stagnation. However, if his prescription for the introduction of general management did not take the process of change far enough, it was to be the foundation on which further change could be built. For there is no doubt that the changes introduced in the White Paper, *Working for Patients*, could not have been made unless the Griffiths advance guard were already there to lead the process. General management actually only made proper sense once the reforms were enacted.

There was hardly any change after April 1991, when the reforms were officially introduced with the advent of first wave trusts although, immediately, the impact of the new managerial regimes became apparent with the emphasis far more on finance and job losses being used to reduce costs and attempt to balance trust finances, as each separate 'business' could no longer maintain a deficit at the end of the financial year. It was not until the internal market really began to take an effect, with contracts being set between purchasing authorities and provider units, whether trusts or not, that the effects of the changes could be felt throughout the service. By 1993, with the third wave of trust applications having been approved and the services opted out of direct managerial control of the NHS, the market was in full swing. London and the major cities felt its impact most sharply, because the competition for services to be purchased by relatively few health authorities from a large number of provider units was greatest. Wards were being closed, staff made redundant and operations stopped because provider units were completing their contracted number of cases before the end of the financial year, with no money to continue providing a service; moreover, purchasing authorities and GP fundholders outside London who had traditionally referred patients to the London teaching hospitals for specialist treatment – or simply out of preference – either reduced the number of cases they were willing to pay for or stopped altogether. London's hospitals were also having problems getting payments for extra contractual referrals (ECRs), admissions that are not provided for in a contract set up with a purchaser authority, either through a reluctance on the part of the purchaser or inadequate financial, information and administrative systems. The situation was becoming increasingly chaotic.

In an attempt to bring some rational planning into the process of deciding what happened to London's health services, the government commissioned a report to be prepared by Sir Bernard Tomlinson. The Tomlinson Report (Tomlinson, 1992) and the government's response to it, *Making London Better* (HMSO, 1993), contained plans for a radical shake-up of the capital. Hospital beds were to be drastically reduced. University College Hospital merging with the Middlesex Hospital, St Thomas' merging with Guy's and Bart's Hospital closing featured amongst the headlines of various closures, mergers and reductions. The money saved, Sir Bernard proposed, would go into developing new primary health care facilities which everyone acknowledged were sorely lacking in London. The loudest and most voiciferous opposition to the Tomlinson proposals came from COHSE, particularly its London Region and its Regional Secretary, Peter Marshall, although they concentrated on its effects on health care provision as a whole rather than what it might do to nursing in the capital. The RCN gave it a lukewarm welcome, with Dee Borley, its senior officer in its North West Thames region saying, 'The Tomlinson recommendations are a good thing if it means that no individual loses their right to be cared for by a qualified nurse and that no nurses lose their jobs as a result of it' (Reid, 1993: pp. 41–5). However, its critics pointed to the Report's flawed methodology, the haste with which it was prepared and its failure to consider the special circumstances of London, particularly its ethnic mix, the deprivation factors, transient daytime population and the enormous problem of homelessness in the capital, accounting for up to 30% of patients treated in some inner London services. With the national figures for waiting lists topping 1 000 000, there was also concern about the 130 000 people on London's growing waiting lists, the existing problems with bed shortages that sometimes left patients waiting on A&E trolleys for hours while doctors tried to find a bed and, most fundamentally, Sir Bernard's theory that the amount of hospital admissions required would sharply fall in correlation to the number of new primary health care services set up. Many argued that increasing the number of GPs and health centres would actually have the converse effect. Having been quietened by the government over the introduction of the reforms, the BMA resurfaced with renewed opposition to the government's proposals post-Tomlinson but, again, retreated into the background after long meetings with the Minister.

There was also opposition from the Right, who argued that, having set the market in train, it would be wrong to interfere as soon as it started to work. There were few initially, apart from COHSE and London Health Emergency, who argued that London's health services did not need 'a shake-up' which included a loss of beds and shift of emphasis to primary care (Reid, 1993: p. 43) although Labour, NUPE and the other health service unions quickly made clear their opposition to the plans as they stood. The government's problem was how best to achieve it. They had instituted reforms aimed at redefining the country's health services through introducing the market; then they had returned to a system of planned change. This was further emphasised when reviews of specialist hospital services, such as neurosciences, plastic surgery and burns, renal and cancer services were undertaken by a separate group, again at the behest of government. Their recommendations in some cases contradicted Tomlinson but were, again, at odds with the principles of the market. The report that came out of the specialty review recommended reducing the sites for various services, moving them onto single sites and, in some cases closing them down completely. Whilst the government prevaricated, the situation moved forward sharply. A host purchaser, Camden and Islington Health Authority, issued proposals to remove its contracts with its local providers, University College London Hospitals (UCLH), incorporating University College and the Middlesex Hospitals, a move the hospitals' chief executive, Charles Marshall, and a number of health policy analysts agreed would mean their effective closure. The sole reason given was that they were convinced they could buy a cheaper service from neighbouring trust hospitals. Quality, patient choice and the massive hole that would be left in London's health care provision with the loss of the A&E department at UCH did not figure in their calculations at all. The reaction of the local UNISON branch to that and the UCLH management's plans to close the main inpatient building in order to reduce its costs and make it more competitive was to ballot on industrial action. With nurses taking a clear lead, UNISON mounted the most high profile health service strike since 1988 and firmly focused everyone's attention on the internal market. It lasted six weeks and, at its end, the health service and, particularly, the future of London's hospitals were again top of the domestic political agenda. Units were being closed to save money, the new funding formula was forcing some purchasing authorities to impose drastic budget cuts to provider units (*Health Service Journal*, 7.10.1993), hospitals stopped operations unless the patient came from a fundholding GP (*Guardian*, 9.9.1993) and West Midlands Regional Health Authority decided to ask the public to choose which south Birmingham hospitals should close (*Birmingham Evening Mail*, 28.9.1993). UCLH itself was accused of starting a 'price war' by announcing its reduced prices for the financial year 1994–5 (Cresswell, 1993: p. 4).

The plight of UCLH stood as a symbol of the chaos created by the market. Having apparently survived two government initiated reviews, albeit only after merger, the hospitals faced closure directly as a result of the internal market. Despite UNISON's strike, public protests and campaigns, Health Secretary Virginia Bottomley left its fate hanging in the balance. More was to come. The regional health authorities and Department of Health outposts were to be replaced by a smaller number of intermediate tiers (*Health Service Journal*, 21.10.1993: p. 3). When Mrs Bottomley publicly announced the fate of UCLH, saying that it was to survive and receive funding to get it over its immediate problems, she also confirmed that whilst Bart's and the Royal London Hospital were to merge, Bart's A&E department was to close. Within weeks she was seeking an exploration of the possibility of merging UCLH with the Hospital for Sick Children at Great Ormond Street and the National Hospital for Neurology and Neurosurgery. Even the NHS Trust Federation, representing the majority of health service trusts, was in 'disarray . . . split by internal disputes' and its credibility damaged 'even, allegedly, among ministers' (Butler, 1993: pp. 11–13).

Examining the management of change in the health service, academics Andrew Pettigrew, Lorna McKee and Ewan Ferlie drew a number of conclusions (1989: pp. 200–2). Perhaps unsurprisingly, they concluded that the soundness of a policy and its coherence could be crucial; attention to organisational processes of negotiation and change were important, as were the values and acceptability of the policy; leadership of change was crucial but may fall to different leaders at different times and building unity from diverse constituencies was a part of that process. Importantly, they recognised the difficulty of describing the NHS as having a single culture. By its very nature it was pluralist. Perhaps most telling, they reminded readers that 'effective change, paradoxically, may require a degree of stability and continuity in policy, priorities and personnel'.

The only thing that could be relied on in the health service of the early 1990s was Griffiths' stated desire for change upon change (1983), introduced in an increasingly contradictory and chaotic policy framework. Attempts to fulfil the desire for pragmatic and necessary reform at the same time as soothe the clamour from the Conservative party's ideological wing and new radical Right have floundered and, particularly during the years of the John Major administration, it is hard not to think that a mix of basic, oldfashioned incompetence hasn't combined with policy drift and weariness to contribute to the picture of chaos and structural decline that has so rapidly eaten away at the framework and core of what was a national health service.

A Political Vacuum

The changes to the National Health Service symbolise a wider decline in Britain's institutions. The claims of medical science as a rational means of explaining our world are severely dented. Sickness and ill health are seen to be phenomena that doctors are often powerless either to prevent or cure. Whilst medicines and

medical/surgical treatments can stem the progress of many diseases or be a palliative against the worst symptoms, this has only
resulted in a large population of chronically sick who do not benefit from any further medical intervention. The medical system,
of large hospitals supported by expensive research and training
facilities, has been subjected to the most careful public and intellectual scrutiny and is suffering a crisis of faith.

The changes experienced by many of our public services, once
highly regarded, have been matched by massive changes to the
country's industrial base. It is not just the health service but local
government, transport, education and housing that have all been
dramaticaly reshaped over the last 15 years. Industries nationalised after 1945 have been sold off, withered and, in many cases,
died. When Margaret Thatcher first started declaring that the
NHS was safe and that more money was being put into it than
ever before, she said so knowing that it would have been unacceptable for a government to be publicly advocating cuts in a
modern, relatively affluent society. However, a decade later, the
position of the NHS is seen in a completely different context.
Whilst Virginia Bottomley still wants to rattle off statistics that
show how well the health service is doing in terms of funding and
government commitment, her colleagues in government, particularly from the Treasury but also including Social Security Minister
Peter Lilley, are busy emphasising the need to make drastic cuts
into a national deficit of £50 billion. The cuts, they reiterate at
every opportunity, have got to be made somewhere and no service
can be immune. People have long perceived that cuts are being
made to the health service but are now being told that there is no
alternative. Perhaps this is one of the reasons Virginia Bottomley
was polled as the least sincere minister and John Major to be even
less trusted with the NHS than Mrs Thatcher just before her fall
(White, 1993: p. 22). If the NHS could be seen as an obstacle to
the growth of the economy in the 1970s, when Britain's industrial
base was intact, there are even greater problems in sustaining it
20 years on without any major industries generating the necessary
income to support ever more costly public services. Nursing's
expansion and development over the past 40 years can be viewed
as a problem in this context, particularly after clinical grading
pushed the pay bill up so severely. The irony is that as nursing

began to establish the possibility of a basis for itself beyond its traditional subordination to the medical model, it was subordinated ever more tightly to economic constraints.

The NHS was also founded on a wave of political support for a Labour party that was able to overcome all opposition to both its principles and framework. The consensual approach of both major parties to social policy issues in the next 30 years guaranteed its survival. But that consensus was based on economic assumptions of relative growth. North Sea oil and revenue from a rolling programme of privatisation during the 1980s masked the difficulties any government would have in funding such a costly service as economic decline set in. That it coincided with the arrival of a particular government so ideologically distant from what the NHS was about meant that solution only compounded its problems.

The dominance of the Conservative party in British politics over a 15 year period has meant that serious debate about change has become decidely sterile and muted. There is no clarity about what sort of health service is wanted, just as there is uncertainty about what kind of society we want to live in. Too much has changed, and too fundamentally, for the country to move backwards. But when there is opposition to government health reforms, it is often rooted in terms that place far too much emphasis on the 1948 model of the NHS, with no vision of what is needed for a population vastly different to that of almost 50 years ago, living in a society that has undergone vast technological, social and political change. This lack of vision, again, is not restricted to concerns about the health service and nursing. The virtual collapse of the intellectual Left, as well as the defensiveness of the Labour Party, has given the New Right almost total domination of the political agenda. Overwhelming parliamentary majorities have meant that, until the 1992 election at least, the government have been able to pass one piece of unpopular legislation after another; the demoralisation and loss of confidence of some opposition forces steadily progressed to the point where it has become possible for many to contemplate whether or not we were witnessing the death of politics. It seems that every proposal from Right wing academics, government think tank, civil servant or minister, no matter how wacky, has apparently found serious consideration in one government circle or other, sapping the energy of opponents constantly having to respond or put forward counterproposals.

In the face of this, the Royal College of Nursing's position of political neutrality has left it better placed to try and influence the government wherever and whenever possible. Their sophisticated lobbying techniques and visible access to the corridors of power have benefited them even if they have not been able to exert influence on key health policy issues that go beyond nursing alone. When introducing the *Working for Patients* reforms, the ease with which the opposition from the professional associations – the BMA excluded – and trade unions was swept aside demonstrated a major change from 1988 but strongly suggests that it is only on issues of pay and conditions that nurses' organisations can unite long enough around agreed objectives to make any sort of meaningful impact on finance and/or organisational driven policies where the government are determined to have their way.

Unified in UNISON?

It is highly unlikely that the confrontational, polarised relationship between the present government and health service unions will change. The latest trade union legislation, which requires the employer to obtain, from every trade union member, written authorisation to continue deducting their subscriptions, presents UNISON and other unions with a logistical nightmare and the potential loss of thousands of members. It is, perhaps, the least subtle of the government's attempts to undermine the organisation and strength of the trade unions and a clear signal that the ideological onslaught of the 1980s is not over. The RCN, with most of its members paying by direct debit from their bank account, as is the case with most of the associations, will be relatively unaffected. The arrival of UNISON does offer opportunities, however. Within the Department of Health and the National Health Service Management Executive there may be some movement as UNISON is able to lay claim to representing almost as many nurses as the RCN, whilst its position as the country's largest union gives it the opportunity to stamp its authority in the health service generally. The loss of confidence in the wider trade union movement has not passed over its constituent groups in the health service. The relative powerlessness within, and alienation from, the policy process has been as acute in health as anywhere else. Thousands of members have been lost in the wake of policies that the unions have waged costly and disruptive campaigns against, particularly privatisation. The trend of membership decline and concommitant reduction in income was undoubtably one of the factors in the merger between UNISON's partner unions, COHSE, NALGO and NUPE. Together, they will not have to compete with one another for a shrinking potential membership in the public sector and should, through achieving economies of scale, be able to make better use of their not inconsiderable combined resources. For nurses, it raises old questions. They will be members of a general union, one far more like the old NUPE than COHSE in that respect. UNISON's structure allows for service groups, however. One of these is in health and within the health group there is a nursing sector. As with COHSE, there is a regional structure, which includes a regional health group, meaning that nurses and other health workers have a structure in which they operate directly relevant to their own employment whilst having general regional councils and a national union that allows them to participate in wider, non-health care issues. With 240 000 nurses, the nursing sector will form the largest part of the health group which, in turn, will almost certainly be the highest profile group within UNISON, whatever the merits of its local government, gas, water and electricity groups.

UNISON's higher profile, born of the strength of its membership base and the pooling of the resources of three separate unions, with the different skills and experience of their respective officer groups, completely changes the landscape for COHSE. Whilst it had a position of relative strength within the health service, it was almost non-existent in local government where increasing amounts of what was once traditional health care are going to be provided; within the TUC and Labour party, it was one of the middle league unions and only able to exercise limited influence. With very finite finances, its impact through publicity and lobbying techniques was equally constrained and its officers and staff were vastly overstretched in trying to keep up with the workload brought about by the changes in the health service. In that sense, they shared a direct and common burden with nurses. UNISON should be able to focus its resources and energies more successfully. The new union will, of course, also be ideally placed to look at health care issues and represent nurses' interests as the transition is made for community services from the health service into local government and the voluntary sector, as will be the case for many mental health, learning difficulties and elderly care services. The fact that its nurses will form such a substantial part of the largest affiliate to the TUC and Labour party will not be insignificant although, as ever, relevant only insofar as those institutions carry influence at a national level. The greatest challenge facing UNISON, however, will be of integrating the three separate unions – all with very separate cultures and traditions – at every level throughout its organisation and developing a clear, unified vision during a period of such widespread and rapid change in the services where its members work, calling upon the resources and energies of the union. The risk is that one will be sacrificed for the other or that it will fall between the two stools, either being seen as too contemplative and introverted as its members come under increasingly intense fire in the workplace or ignoring its own organisational needs which will leave it structurally weak for years to come.

The competition between the RCN and UNISON is likely to be even fiercer than it was between COHSE and the College, largely because the new union poses more of a threat. In the same week as UNISON unveiled its nursing sector, the RCN proclaimed its 300 000th member (Turner, 1993b: p. 22). The issues are likely to be broadly unchanged from when COHSE was facing the College, trade unionism versus a professional association, striving for status through improved pay and conditions or developing clinical and educational expertise, pushing the boundaries of nursing practice forward. It returns to the old but serious question of whether nursing is truly a profession or a craft, theory or practice based, which lies at the core of the differences between them. Sometimes this is argued out in the form of amusing, caricatured polemic:

> So at last the so-called leaders of the nursing profession have woken up to the existence of developments in vocational training ... Nursing was once based on vocational training methods. It

could, if it had not been for the desperate desire on the part of educationalists, theorists and careerists at the UKCC, have developed
vocational training in health care to higher standards and become
the body which controlled the NVQs. However, because of the
head-in-the-sand approach to training known as Project 2000,
nursing is rapidly becoming an academic pursuit rather than a practical one . . . Bring on the NVQs: patients deserve a competent and
trained health care worker and not an elite of sherry-sipping, pearl
necklace rattling theorists.

(Marshall, 1991: p. 14).

I do love to see our senior union officials articulate their viewpoints
with such objectiveness and balanced argument . . . I presume that
as sherry, pearl necklaces and theory are anathema to Mr Marshall,
he must endorse strong lager, gold medalions and a propensity for
doing without thinking.

(Lloyd, NT, 26.6.1991: p. 23).

More than ever, though, this key issue is skirted around as both
the trade unions and professional associations seek to encroach
upon each other's territory. Both the RCN and UNISON will be
trying to emphasise their own strengths and the other's weakness
and the College has, while proclaiming itself as the voice of professional nursing and a nurses only organisation, pointed out the
irony that, despite UNISON's commitment to proportionality and
being a woman friendly union it has, in Bob Abberley and his
deputy Malcolm Wing, men as head of health and the nursing sector respectively. In return, UNISON will highlight the strengths of
representing nurses of all grades along with other health workers,
particularly in the increasingly business oriented health service
where the attraction of employing generic workers is likely to be
an option employers wish to pursue. It will be able to provide a
voice for nurses across the different sectors of health care and
more in the way of professional advice and services to nurses than
COHSE was ever able to. Nonetheless, it knows its effectiveness
on pay and conditions issues will still be the crucial criterion on
which it is judged primarily. It has sharply pointed to the fact that
the gender of nursing leaders was never an issue when Trevor Clay
was general secretary of the College.

At a local level, as old COHSE branches combine their membership with NALGO and, particularly, NUPE, UNISON will
undoubtedly be able to exert far greater influence than any of the

partner unions did individually, particularly if/when trusts begin to tread the precarious path towards local bargaining. This will give UNISON an advantage in competing with the College as will the latter's reluctance to recruit health care assistants, of whom there are clearly going to be an increasing number in the health service and other sectors providing health care generally, especially as the numbers of qualified nurses both in work and being trained declines.

No One Likes Us, We Don't Care – Or Do We?

It is ironic that, despite the 'angelic' image and vocational commitment that engenders such strong popular support both from the general public and other trade unions in times of industrial unrest, nurses are probably least popular with other health workers, for a variety of reasons not all of which are consistent with each other. Indeed, it is not unheard of for nurses to decry their colleagues as an occupational group. Animosity to nurses amongst other health workers is nothing new. They were accused of 'snobbishness' by the TUC in the 1930s and were already drifting away from other groups of staff in the early Poor Law institutions as soon as they began to formulate their own occupational loyalty. More recently, during the 1982 pay dispute, accusations were made about nurses not supporting the unions and the health workers directly involved in taking action, echoing splits which had occurred in 1979.

There are those nurses who complain of their nursing colleagues behaving in an oppressive manner to ancillary workers, a view that is shared by some – but by no means all – ancillaries, but which goes beyond the caricature of the starchy ward sister. The resentment felt throughout nursing's ranks about the treatment meted out by nurses in a more senior position is as deep as it is widespread (Mackay, 1989). Again, this wrongly panders to the idea that nurses are a common occupational group, bound by particular attitudes and codes of behaviour; it also presumes that they can behave out of context with the situation they find themselves in and that they always act in accordance with their 'wants'. Medical staff, particularly consultants, are often heard to praise nurses; very few, however, make any effort to alter the balance of power or relationships between nursing and medical staff. Attempts at nursing innovation or independence have often been thwarted as a result of medical intervention. Having ensured that nursing is in a subordinated position, it is clear that the medical profession as a whole is not going to relinquish its power easily. Now nurses are managed by general managers and there is no evidence that they are well disposed to the occupational group who account for the biggest drain on any health service budget and who have shown a worrying trend to give the appearance of being unmanageable at times (Clay, 1989). Policy makers in health care have consistently shown their disregard for nurses who, at best, are treated as if they are invisible. Changes that have major implications for them, their work and the patients they care for are imposed on them with little reference to them, their needs or interests. This is reflected in most of the social policy literature on the NHS and health services, where nursing is rarely referred to in any depth, if at all. The demurely worn mask of the vocational, subordinated myth is all that is seen – and passed over.

The pace of change in health care is unlikely to diminish during the lifetime of the current government. The logic of that change has been built up over the past 15 years and gives us some idea of where it is leading. It does not look as if it is heading in a direction in which the majority of nurses wish to go. Ray Rowden, the first nurse to head the influential Institute of Health Service Management and one of the RCN's more radical figures during the 1980s, sees a future where the 'district general hospital as we know it will be dead in ten years' time' but is nonetheless 'full of brilliant possibilities' (Rowden, 1993: p. 21). He rightly points to the way in which hi-tech medicine can be taken into primary care settings and the likelihood of further demarcation lines in health and social care dissolving, giving the employers the opportunity of placing the same groups of care staff into different settings as well as having qualified nurses in both hospitals and local communities planning, supervising and evaluating care to be implemented by untrained staff.

The problem for nurses is that the debate about how their work should progress is largely taking place around them, only further reinforcing their position as a disempowered, subordinated workforce unable to control its own destiny. It is yet another irony that user empowerment in health services has become such a strong contemporary issue, following the rise of the consumer, as a progressively organised user movement tries to create something tangible for itself rather than a neat headline for service providers and politicians. The notion of empowering service users necessarily means taking that power from someone else. The problem for nurses and midwives is that they are often viewed by the users as the ones having that power, no matter how disempowered they may themselves feel. COHSE tried to address this issue when publishing its guidelines for user empowerment in mental health, with the authors of the document, Jan Wallcraft and Jim Reid, arguing that empowering users is part of the process of nursing staff empowering themselves and that there is a mutuality of interests that can be served (Wallcraft & Reid, 1992). This was a view taken by such figures as the RCN's Sally Gooch when calling for alliances with users around the introduction of the internal market. It would be easy for nurses to react defensively to the user movement's demands and try to subvert them in the belief that they are only being further criticised for failings in the system that are not of their making (Higgins, 1993: p. 31). There is also the fear of what effect a perceived loss of power would have on nurses' status as well as concerns about whether or not 'expert' knowledge, skills and experience should be given up, about who really does know best.

User empowerment is about seeking a quality service where people's rights are protected, particularly the most vulnerable. It seeks to provide the right of advocacy and to have advocates, drawn from within the ranks of users, speak on their behalf as individuals attempt to gain or regain control over their own lives within a collective process. Again, this takes away an important part of nurses' self-image, for nurses have long seen themelves as the patient's advocate, protecting and speaking up for the helpless, particularly in the face of harsh doctors or uncaring managers. To recognise that users do not need that and that it can, in fact, have a detrimental effect on them is something that many nurses are having to come to terms with. It means they have to reassess their own relationship with the person they are caring for and also their relationship with medical staff and others in the health care system. Because user empowerment addresses people's strengths and abilities, as well as their rights, rather than deficits and needs, it takes the individual out of the victom role (Gibson, 1991). It involves the process of negotiation, of looking at differences, both in terms of prescribed role and the wants and interests of both parties. In acknowledging the power and control that nurses have over patients, particularly those hospitalised, it allows it to be questioned; it does not necesssarily mean that nurses surrender everything and agree to the individual's every whim or desire. Far from it. But in seeking partnership as a goal and being open and honest about the difficulties entailed in that, it allows nurses to acknowledge their own limitations and those of the service they work within. The user empowerment movement is also, to a degree, a collective response to the way that people's relationship to society has been privatised through consumerism and, from that, there are lessons to be learned by nurses as their collective traditions continue to break down.

Now nurses need to decide whether or not they see health care as a service or a business, recognising that the world in which they work is deeply politicised and that this is what is fuelling the rapid changes threatening to engulf them. The move to a market oriented system was an ideological decision in large part, ignoring the evidence of a theoretical experiment in East Anglia that resulted in chaos and the NHS going bust, as well as the empirical evidence of the failure of the pre-NHS market, when the voluntary and local authority systems were brought to the verge of collapse because they could not cope with the rising demand and cost of providing services – with the cost of nurses a key factor in the equation. Paradoxically, although now robbed of all strategic planning, the health service has become increasingly centralised in policy making but with devolved responsibility and the web of accountability holding all local managers in its grip, something nursing mirrors professionally. The arrival of performance related pay for nurses (PRP) further threatens to individualise nurses' relationship with the employer as well as their work, when nurses are apparently to be judged on the strength of their individual performance gauged against key objectives. But this comes at a time when PRP is largely discredited in industry, being seen as a demotivating factor because, of course, most people will inevitably have to fall within the 'average' category, as statistically they do in PRP schemes, and this rarely equates with how individuals perceive themselves, particularly when they are having to work much harder, with fewer colleagues with which to share the burden. One thing is clear; having struggled to recover from clinical grading, health service managers are not going to introduce anything that would dramatically push the pay bill up again.

In creating the myths that would conquer the image of the Gamps, the nineteenth century pioneers started nursing off on a path that was strewn with contradictions and conflicts. They have resulted in a 'profession' that is fragmented and vastly different in its constituent groups, partly as a result of the way nurses were placed together at key historical moments, such as 1948 and the formation of the NHS, partly through the evolutionary processes of distinct health care services. The pursuit of particular objectives that were of more importance to certain influential sections has dragged nursing along in its wake but it is extremely difficult to see where those sections, or groups, begin and end. If a map were drawn around nursing and its different constituencies, its borders would be ragged and movable. For nurses' loyalties and their aspirations, as well as their means of identifying with others within their nursing group, do not necessarily conform to the simple boundaries of where they work or the type of nursing they are involved in. This is most obviously reflected in being a member of a specific organisation, be it a trade union or professional association, but it straddles a wide variety of other factors. A nurse working in a surgical ward may see herself as a worker earning a living the same as anyone else, just as a community psychiatric nurse does; a nurse providing care for the elderly may identify herself as a specialist, as would a paediatric nurse. Some will believe they have achieved improved status through getting a large salary increase, others by being given recognition for a particular area of their work or being given extra responsibility; some will wish to see nursing move closer to medicine, taking on extra duties once associated with the doctor's role, as opposed to those who want to take it further into the bounds of social care. All of this ignores the more concrete boundaries between nurses, such as the specialty they work in, their grade and regional differences, as well as those of gender, race and class.

The 'connectedness' that nurses experience is constructed both by the nurses as they look to where they identify themselves and in the way some of these groups are put together. Equally, feelings of 'connectedness' can be deconstructed. Thus nurses may feel that, as professionals, they have little in common with other health workers or, for instance, workers in industry. But all are subject to the same political divisions based on economic priorities. Nurses have aspirations, as does any other group of people, but they do not always coincide with their common interests.

The professional ideal will not disappear from nursing. Far too much has been invested in it, at every level of nursing and not least by its professional associations. Its hegemonic grip is far too powerful. But it would seem to be facing severe damage from current health economics. If Roger Dyson is correct, the changes affecting nursing are both more radical and lasting than many in nursing have assumed (see page 251). The domination of the hospital nurse may also be in terminal decline if those health economists who predict the sudden death of the district general hospital are correct. Pursuing the professional ideal, whether it has been in the form of the suitable woman, a fully qualified workforce or through attempting to impose a common vocational/professional ethos on such a large and diverse workforce has, apart from being unrealistic, been detrimental to nursing's wider interests and probably hindered the development of better nursing practice overall. Nurses do still need to resolve what forms of care they are going to provide within the context of what is *needed*, not by the market, not by doctors, but by the people who require nursing care. In so doing, there are many areas of commonality in nursing but also many differences. If nurses are to make real progress in both achieving status and better pay and conditions, it is unlikely to happen unless those differences are openly acknowledged and recognised whilst the areas of commonality are strengthened. Clearly, initiatives in practice can have unexpected consequences and the connection between workload, responsibility, accountability and pay is one that nurses and all of their organisations cannot ignore in the future, particularly when trusts are very clearly going to be attempting to mask it.

There are, as ever, more questions than answers surrounding nursing practice. Is Project 2000 nurse training the best way to prepare people to work in areas such as mental health or is a more generic approach aimed at creating a mental health worker no longer described as a nurse the most appropriate? What is the right mix of theory and practice? Is the current body of knowledge appropriate to nurses if they are to break free of their medically subordinated position? Or will it simply perpetuate it? What do nurses want? The government inspired changes do offer opportunities, as do the changes in practice of the last 15–20 years, which suggest nursing can have a future separate but complementary to the medical profession. But nurses will have to look beyond the boundaries of their own occupational experience if they are going to see real and lasting change. Their fate is too closely linked with wider political issues for them to be able to make fundamental changes in their work in isolation from political change.

There can be little realistic chance of a coming together between the RCN and UNISON whilst there are those within the ranks of each respective organisation for whom such a prospect would be anathema. They will carry on representing opposite ends of the same continuum; but the middle ground may come to be of increasing importance in the struggle for members and influence, particularly if the same vacuum persists in government policy following the recent changes in the health service and nursing becomes even more marginalised, as is a real and distinct possibility. Within the chaos that has filled the health policy vacuum, UNISON faces the enormous challenge of trying to evolve a series of coherent policies of its own, as well as a means of formulating those policies and decision making processes that will enable it to confront the problems of the 1990s. It will also have to decide if it is going to have a health group that will be a vehicle for local organisaion rather than trying to match the RCN as a 'consumerist' organisation providing an increasingly sophisticated range of services to its members.

It may be that the latest crisis will focus nurses' collective consciousness on its need to find a greater degree of unity than ever before, enabling them to tolerate their differences whilst forging links on broader, important issues. But, again, there is little evidence to support such a theory. If all of this seems to paint a bleak picture for the future, there are rays of hope which lie in nursing's buried past. Very often, a key task of the nurse is to hold on to hope for a patient who cannot see anything positive as a result of her/his condition. Throughout nursing history there have been those nurses who have fulfilled that role for the rest of the nursing workforce. They have recognised that change is a possibility and fought for it, even when not appearing to make any immediate progress. Change is possible, but only as a result of how nurses perceive and then organise themselves, identifying how their aspirations are often the product of a system and tradition that works against them. This implied use of power recognises that nurses can alter the balance and begin working for policies that will serve their true interests.

References

Abel-Smith B (1960) *A History of the Nursing Profession.* London: Heinemann.

Alexander Z & Dewjee A (eds) (1984) *The Wonderful Adventures of Mrs Seacole in Many Lands.* Bristol, Falling Wall Press.

Allan M (1939) Nurses Lose Jobs In Thousands. *Daily Herald,* 13 December 1939.

Allen P & Jolley M (eds) (1982) *Nursing, Midwifery and Health Visiting since 1900.* London: Faber & Faber.

Appleby J and Brewins L (1992) Profile Of A Profession. *Nursing Times,* 88:4 (22 January 1992).

Association of Nurses (1937) *The Association of Nurses, Why It was Formed and What It Hopes to Achieve.* London: Association of Nurses.

Athlone Committee Report. 1939.

Baly M (1987) Nightingale nurses: the myth and the reality. In: Maggs C (ed.) *Nursing History: The State of the Art.* Kent: Croom Helm.

Barnard K & Lee K (1977) *Conflicts in the NHS.* London: Croom Helm.

Barr N, Glennerster H, Le Grand J (1989) Working for patients? The right approach? *Social Policy and Administration,* 23:2.

Beardshaw V (1981) *Conscientious Objectors at Work.* London: Social Audit.

Bell L (1987) Shortages of nursing 1928–1935. *History of Nursing Journal,* 3:5

Bellaby P & Oribor P (1980) 'The history of the present' – contradiction and struggle in nursing. In: Davies C (ed.) *Rewriting Nursing History.* London: Croom Helm.

Bent E A (1982) The growth and development of midwifery. In:

Allan P & Jolley M (eds) *Nursing, Midwifery and Health Visiting Since 1900*. London: Faber & Faber.

Bolger T (1993) Cutting classes. *Nursing Times*, 89:43 (27 October 1993).

Bond M (1982) Do you care about your colleagues? *Nursing Mirror*, 20 October 1982.

Bosanquet N (ed.) (1979) *Industrial Relations in the NHS – The Search for a System*. London: Croom Helm.

Bowman G (1967) *The Lamp and the Book*. London: Queen Anne Press.

The Briggs Report: Report of the Committee on Nursing (1972). London: HMSO.

Briggs A (1978) The achievements, failures and aspirations of the NHS. *New Society*, 23 November 1978.

Brindle D (1988a) Nurses Go Back To The Front Line. *The Guardian*, 21 July 1988.

Brindle D (1988b) Nurses Threaten Indefinite Strike. *The Guardian*, 18 August 1988.

Brown C (1984) *Black and White Britain, The Third PSI Survey*. London: Heinemann.

Bruce P (1973) *The Rise of the Welfare State*. London: Routledge & Keegan Paul.

Buchan J (1988) Making the grade. *Nursing Standard*, 6 August 1988.

Buchan J (1989) The hidden agenda. *Nursing Times*, 22 February 1989.

Buchan J, Waite R and Thomas J, Grade Expectations. *IMS Report Number 76*. Brighton: November 1989.

Buchan J (1992) Running To Stand Still. *Nursing Times*. 88:4 (22 January 1992).

Butler P (1993) How fare the crusaders? *Health Service Journal*, 30 September 1993.

Carlisle D (1990) Racism and nursing. *Nursing Times*, 86:14 (4 April 1990).

Carpenter M (1980) Asylum nursing before 1914. In: Davies C (ed.) *Rewriting Nursing History*. London: Croom Helm.

Carpenter M (1988) *Working for Health*. London: Lawrence & Wisehart.

Carpenter M (1991) *Nurse Subordination in Health Care: Towards a Social Divisions Approach*.

Carr E H (1961) *What is History?* Harmondsworth: Penguin.

Charles S & Webb A (1986) *The Economic Approach to Social Policy.* London: Wheatsheaf.

Childs D (1986) *Britain Since 1945. A Political History*, 2nd edn. London: Routledge.

Chudley P (1986) On the campaign trail. *Nursing Times*, 5 February 1986.

Chudley P (1988) Strained relations. *Nursing Times*, 84:50 (14 December 1988).

Clark J (1988) Striking attitudes. *Nursing Standard*, 19 March 1988.

Clay T (1987) *Nurses, Power and Politics.* London: Heinemann.

Clay T (1989) Winning the argument. *Nursing Standard*, 3:20 (11 February 1989).

COHSE (1960) *Fifty Years of Progress.* Manchester: COHSE.

COHSE (1983) *The Mallinson Report.* Banstead: COHSE.

COHSE (1987a) *The Impact of General Management and General Managers in the NHS.* Banstead: COHSE.

COHSE (1987b) *Nursing News.*

COHSE (1991) *Recruitment Strategy for the 1990s.* Banstead: COHSE.

Cole A (1987) The Writing Is On The Wall. *Nursing Times.* 83:50 (16 December 1987).

Cole A (1988) Nurses On Strike: What The Public Thinks. *Nursing Times.* 84:6 (10 February 1988).

Cole A (1989) Without A Voice. *Nursing Times.* 85:12 (22 March 1989).

Colter S (1988) Should Nurses Strike? The Case Against. *Nursing Times.* 84:5 (3 February 1988).

Cook T (1987) Participation. In: Clode D, Parker C and Etherington (eds) *Towards the Sensitive Bureaucracy.* London: Sage.

Coote A & Campbell B (1982) *Sweet Freedom, The Struggle for Women's Liberation.* London: Pan.

Cowell B & Wainwright D (1981) *Behind the Blue Door. The History of the Royal College of Midwives 1881–1981.* London: Baillière Tindall.

Cowie V (1982) Organised labour. In: Allan P & Jolley M, (eds) *Nursing, Midwifery & Health Visting Since 1900.* London: Faber & Faber.

Cresswell J (1993) London's hospitals fight for survival with a price war. *Health Service Journal*, 14 October 1993.

Dalken B (1978) *The NHS – The First Phase 1948–71 and After*. London: Allen & Unwin.

Dangerfield G (1966) *The Strange Death of Liberal England*, 2nd edn. London: Paladin.

Darbyshire P (1987) The burden of history. *Nursing Times*.

Davies C (ed.) (1980) *Rewriting Nursing History*. London: Croom Helm.

Davies C (1987) Making History: The Early Days of the HVA. In: *Health Visitor*. 60.

Davies N (1994) The Casualty Still in Ward Four. *The Guardian*, 12 February 1994.

Davin A (1978) Imperialism and Motherhood. *History Workshop Journal*, 5.

De La Cuesta C (1983) The nursing process: from development to implementation. *Journal of Advanced Nursing*, 8.

Devine J (1990) Exercise your rights. *Nursing Times*, 86:21 (23 May 1990).

DHSS (1976) *Making Whitley Work (The McCarthy Report)*. London: HMSO.

Dickson N (1988) The Battle That's Beyond Our Ken. *Nursing Times*. 84:51 (21 December 1988).

Dingwall R, Rafferty A M & Webster C (1988) *An Introduction to the Social History of Nursing*. London: Routledge.

Dopson L (1985a) The Radcliffe Martyr. *Nursing Times*, 12 June 1985.

Dopson L (1985b) *Nursing Journals and The Development of Professional Nursing*. Paper presented to the RCN History of Nursing Group, May.

Dopson L (1986) Leading Light. *Nursing Times*, 29 January 1986.

Dopson L (1990) Nursing without nurses. *Nursing Times*, 86:14 (4 April 1990).

Doyal L (1979) *The Political Economy of Health*. London: Pluto Press.

Dyson R (1993) The numbers debate. *Nursing Times*, 89:41 (13 October 1993).

Edwards J (1987) *Positive Discrimination, Social Justice and Social Policy*. London: Tavistock.

Ersser S & Tutton L (eds) (1991) *Primary Nursing in Perspective*. Middlesex: Scutari.

Ferriman A (1988) Nurses To Quit Over Broken Promises. *Observer*, 17 July 1988.

Fisher L (1988) Should Nurses Strike? The Case For. *Nursing Times*. **84**:5 (3 February 1988).

Flynn N (1989) Commercial care. *Health Service Journal*, 27 April 1989.

Foucault M (1961) (trans. R. Howard) *Madness and Civilization*. London: Tavistock.

Foucault M (1986) In: Ed. *The Foucault Reader*. Harmondsworth: Penguin.

Fyvel P (1992) *English Penny*. Devon: Stockwell.

Gamarnikow E (1991) Nurse or woman: gender and professionalism in reformed nursing 1860–1923. In: Holden P & Littlewood J (eds) *Anthropology and Nursing*. London: Routledge.

Ganz C (1985) Preparing for battle. *Nursing Times*, 27 February 1985.

Gibson C H (1991) A concept analysis of empowerment. *Journal of Advanced Nursing*, **16**.

Gilbert J (1993) P2000 Research Study Confirms Worst Fears. *Nursing Times*, **89**:39 (29 September 1993).

Glennerster H (1983) *Planning for Priority Groups*. Oxford: Martin Robertson.

Gooch S (1989) White Paper whitewash. *Nursing Standard*, **3**:28 (8 April 1989).

Graham A (1987) State of the nation. *Nursing Standard*, 10 October 1987.

Green D (1985) *Working Class Patients and the Medical Establishment*. Hants: Gower.

Griffiths R (1983) *NHS Management Inquiry*. London: HMSO.

Ham C (1985) *Health Policy in Britain*. London: Macmillan.

Harrison S (1988) *Managing the NHS*. London: Chapman & Hall.

Hart C (1991) Close enough to touch. In: Ersser S & Tutton L (eds) *Primary Nursing in Perspective*. Middlesex: Scutari.

Haywood S & Alazewski A (1980) *Crisis in the Health Service*. London: Croom Helm.

Haywood S & Hunter D J (1982) Consultative processes in health policy in the United Kingdom: a view from the centre. *Policy Administration*, 69.

Hegyvary S T (1982) *The Change to Primary Nursing: A Crosscultural View of Professional Practice*. St Louis: C V Mosby.

Higgins R (1993) Raised voices. *Health Service Journal*, 20 July 1993.

Hirst D (1988) The Manager's View. *Nursing Standard*, 3:12 (17 December 1988).

HMSO (1989) *Working for Patients*. London: HMSO.

HMSO (1993) *Making London Better*. London: HMSO.

Illich I (1975) *Medical Nemesis: The Expropriation of Health*. London: Calder and Boyers.

Jerrome K (1992) *Anatomy of a Trade Union Merger*. Unpublished dissertation.

Jolley M (1982) Retrospective: Pre-1900. In: Allan P & Jolley M (eds) *Nursing, Midwifery & Health Visiting Since 1900*. London: Faber & Faber.

Kirp D & Halsey A H (1982) Doing good by doing little. *New Society*.

Klein R (1989) *The Politics of the NHS*. 2nd edn London: Longman.

Labour Party News, January 1994.

Lancet Commission Report, 1932.

Lathlean J (1987) Who is the new nurse? *Nursing Times*. 83:47.

Lee P & Raban C (1988) *Welfare Theory and Social Policy*. London: Sage.

Leeson R A (1973) *Strike, A Live History, 1887/1971*. London: Allen & Unwin.

Le Grand J (1982) *The Strategy of Equality*. London: Allen & Unwin.

Le Grand J & Robinson R (1984) *The Economics of Social Problems*. London: Macmillan.

Levitas R (ed) (1986) *The Ideology of the New Right*. London: Polity Press.

Lewis J & Hildrew P (1988) Nursing Strike 'Could Spread Through NHS'. *The Guardian*, 8 January 1988.

Lindblom C E (1959) The science of 'muddling through'. *Public Administration Review*, 19.

Lister J (1988) *Cutting the Lifeline*. London: Journeyman.

Littlewood R (1991) Gender, role and sickness: the ritual psychopathologies of the nurse. In: Holden P & Littlewood J (eds) *Anthropology and Nursing*. London: Routledge.

Lloyd D (1991) Lager lout? *Nursing Times*, 87:26 (26 June 1991).

Lukes S (1974) *Power: A Radical View*. London: Macmillan.

Lyall J (1986) Contracting out threatens good NHS relations. *Health Service Journal*, 6 January 1986.

Mackay L (1989) *Nursing a Problem*. Milton Keynes: Open University Press.

Maggs C (ed.) (1987) *Nursing History: The State of the Art*. Kent: Croom Helm.

Maggs C (1987) The unquiet revolution. *Nursing Times*, 83:47 (25 November 1987).

Marshall P (1991) Theorists not needed. *Nursing Times*, 87:23 (5 June 1991).

Mason J H N (1985) *Mayday Hospital Croydon 1885–1985*. Croydon: Croydon Health Authority.

Maxwell R (ed.) (1986) *Reshaping the NHS*. Berks: Policy Journals.

MHIWU (1931) *The History of the Mental Hospital and Institutional Workers' Union*. Manchester: MHIWU.

Menzies IEP (1970) *The Functioning of Social Systems as a Defence Against Anxiety*. London: Tavistock.

Miller G (1962) *Psychology*. Harmondsworth: Penguin.

Mitchell J (1984) *What is to be Done about Illness and Health?* London: Penguin.

Morgan K O (1992) *The People's Peace, British History 1945–1990*. Oxford: Oxford University Press.

Morgan L (1939) 2,000 Nurses Lose their Jobs: Latest Muddle. *News Chronicle*, 16 November 1939.

Morton A L (1989) *A People's History of England*. London: Lawrence & Wisehart.

Naughtie J (1986a) A kick up the coccyx. *Nursing Times*, 29 January 1986.

Naughtie J (1986b) When the projections fail to persuade. *Nursing Times*, 26 March 1986.

Naughtie J & Hildrew P (1988) Newton Backs Down Over Nurses' Money. *The Guardian*, 13 January 1988.

Navarro V (1979) *Class Struggle, The State and Medicine*. London: Martin Robertson.

Netherne Hospital Annual Reports 1905–1924.

NIHSM, BMA & RCN (1983) Public Expenditure In The NHS: Recent Trends and Outlook. Joint Report. London.

Nixon J (1982) The Home Office and race relations policy: co-ordinator and initiator? *Journal of Public Policy* 2:4.

Ollearnshaw S (1983) The Promotion of Employment Equality in Britain. In: Glazer N & Young K (eds) *Ethnic Policy and Public Policy*. London: Heinemann.

Owens G (1992) Training in the twenties. *Nursing Times*, 88:3 (15 January 1992).

Owens P & Glennerster H (1989) *Nursing in Conflict*. London: Macmillan.

Pelling H (1971) *A History of British Trade Unionism*, 2nd edn Harmondsworth: Penguin.

Pembrey S & Punton S (1990) The lessons of nursing beds. *Nursing Times*, 86:14 (4 April 1990).

Pettigrew A, McKee L & Ferlie E (1988) Understanding Change in the NHS. *Public Administration*, 66.

Pettigrew A, McKee L, Ferlie E (1989) Hints on how to ring the changes. *Health Service Journal*, 16 February 1989.

Pownall M (1988a) Working on. *Nursing Times*, 84:5 (3 February 1988).

Pownall M (1988b) That's The Way The Money Goes. *Nursing Times*. 84:43 (26 October 1988).

Pyne R H (1982) The General Nursing Councils. In: Allan P & Jolley M (eds) *Nursing, Midwifery and Health Visiting Since 1900*. London: Faber & Faber.

RCN (1974) *Raise the Roof!* London: RCN.

RCN (1988) Working to grade. *Newsline*, 13.

RCN (1993) *Handbook*. London: RCN.

Reid T (1993) Kill or cure? *Nursing Times*, 89:39 (29 September 1993).

Ritter S (1984) Does the team work? *Nursing Times*.

Ritter S (1985) Primary nursing in mental illness. *Nursing Mirror*.

Robb B (1967) Sans Everything: A Case To Answer. London: Nelson.

Robinson R (1989) New health care market. *British Medical Journal*, 298.

Rowden R (1993) The next decade. *Nursing Times*, **89**:43 (27 October 1993).

Royle J A & Walsh M (1992) *Watson's Medical Surgical Nursing and Related Physiology*, 4th edn. London: Baillière Tindall.

Salvage J (1985) *The Politics of Nursing*. London: Heinemann.

Salvage J (1989) *NDUs – Flagships of the Future*. London: King's Fund Centre.

Salvage J (1990) Treating the malaise in time. *Health Service Journal*, 18 January 1990.

Samuels B (1984) Let us end this madness. *Nursing Mirror*, **158**:6 (8 February 1984).

Seifert R (1992) *Industrial Relations in the NHS*. London: Chapman & Hall.

Sethi S & Dimmock S (eds) (1982) *Industrial Relations and Health Services*. London: Croom Helm.

Sherman J (1988) Strike Threat By Nurses At Eight Hospitals. *The Times*, 20 January 1988.

Simon P (1992) Professional Services. *Nursing Times*, **88**:23 (3 June 1992).

Smith P (1982) *A History of The RCN and Industrial Relations Within The Nursing Profession and NHS*. Unpublished dissertation.

Snell J (1988) Leading Lady. *Nursing Times*, **84**:45 (9 November 1988).

Snell J (1989) Quo Vadis? *Nursing Times*, **85**:32 (9 August 1989).

Staff Side of the Nursing and Midwifery Staffs Negotiating Council (1987) Evidence to the Pay Review Body for Nursing Staff, Midwives and Health Visitors.

Stevens T (1985) *In the National Interest*. Herne Bay: Mere Commodity Arts Ltd.

Taylor Gooby P (1986) Privatisation, Power and the State. *Sociology*, 20:2

Taylor Gooby P & Papadakis E (1987) *The Private Provision of Public Welfare*. Brighton: Wheatsheaf.

Thomas L H (1993) Comparing qualified nurse and auxiliary roles. *Nursing Times*, **89**:38 (22 September 1993).

Thompson E P (1968) *The Making of the English Working Class*. Harmondsworth: Penguin.

Thompson J (1990) No Vacancies. *Nursing Times*. **86**:21 (23 May 1990).

Tomlinson B (1992) *Report of the Inquiry into London's Health Service, Medical Education and Research*. London: HMSO.

Tonkin B (1988) Strong medicine. *Community Care*, 10 November 1989.

Townsend P & Davidson N (1982) *Inequalities in Health*. Harmondsworth: Penguin.

Trevelyan G M (1959) *A Shortened History of England*. Harmondsworth: Pelican.

Tschudin V (1985) Too much pressure. *Nursing Times*, **81**.

Tudor Hart (1971) The inverse care law. *Lancet*.

Turner T (1988) The Divided Unions. *Nursing Times*, **84**:10 (9 March 1988).

Turner T (1988a) Frustrations on the boil. *Nursing Times*, **84**:37 (14 September 1988).

Turner T (1992) After the resolution. *Nursing Times*, **88**:17 (22 April 1992).

Turner T (1993a) Cut to the quick. *Nursing Times*, **89**:43 (27 October 1993).

Turner T (1993b) Members' market. *Nursing Times*, **89**:39 (29 September 1993).

UKCC (1979) *How the UKCC Works For You*. London.

UKCC (1992) *Code of Professional Conduct for the Nurse, Midwife and Health Visitor*, 3rd edn. London: UKCC.

UKCC (1989) *Exercising Accountability*. London: UKCC.

UNISON (1993) *Driven to the Edge*. London.

Vousden M (1986) The Voice Of Pragmatism. *Nursing Times*, 18 June 1986.

Vousden M (1988) A Year To Remember. *Nursing Times*, **84**:51 (21 December 1988).

Vousden M (1989) User Friendly. *Nursing Times*, **85**:32 (9 August 1989).

Vulliamy D & Moore R (1979) Whitleyism and Health, The NHS and Its Industrial Relations. *Studies for Trade Unionists*, **5**:19.

Walker M (1992) *Let London Lead!* Unpublished paper.

Wallcraft J & Reid J (1992) *User Empowerment in Mental Health Services*. Banstead: COHSE/MIND.

Weber M (1947) The Theory of Social Organisation, New York: Free Press.

White M (1993) Are the Tories talking a lot of ball bearings? *Health Service Journal*, 23 September 1993.

White R (1978) *Social Change and the Development of the Nursing Profession*. London: Henry Kimpton.

White R (1985a) *Political Issues in Nursing Vol 1*. Chichester: John Wiley.

White R (1985b) *The Effects of the NHS on the Nursing Profession 1948–1961*. London: Kings Fund.

White R (1986) *Political Issues in Nursing Vol 2*. Chichester: John Wiley.

White R (1987) Health visitors: the willing horses. *Health Visitor*, 60.

Williams F (1987) *Critical Social Policy*, 20.

Wilson E (1983) *Feminism and Social Policy*.

Index

Numbers in italics refer to illustrations.
Numbers in **bold** refer to major references.

General Nursing Council (GNC), 30,
    53, 65, 105, 158, 159
  educational standards, 160
  replacement of, 163
General Strike, 1926: 68
Glasgow University, union member-
    ship study, 1988: 113
Goddard Report, 145
Gooch, Sally, 124, 239, 241, 265
'Good news unit', 241
Grades, 149
  clinical grading, **215–217**, 221,
    251–252
  key worker system, 247
  skill mix reviews, 251
  task allocation, 140
Grading, clinical *see* Clinical grading
Graduates in nursing, 245
Graham, Alistair, 123
Grand National Consolidated Trades
    Union, 35
'GRASP', 199
Green, David, 48, 94
Green Papers, on management, 173
Griffiths, Roy, 186
Griffiths Report, **186**, **189–191**,
    195–200, 202, **252**
  RCN campaign against, **191–192**,
    193
Group 81, COHSE, 114–115
Guardians, Poor Law institutions, 49
Guild of Nurses, 64, **65**, **66**, 69
Guillebaud Report, 172
Guy's Hospital, 104, 207, 253
  trust, 241

Halsbury Report, 81
Harman, Harriet, 206
Hart, Tudor, 170
'Hawthorne effect', 145
Haywood, Stuart, 175–176
Head Office, COHSE, 100–101
Headquarters, RCN, 100
Healey budgets, 84
Health and Safety at Work Act, 1974:
    86
Health care assistants, 247, 263

NVQs, 161, 244
Health visitors, 24, 25
  see also Infant mortality; Midwives
Health Visitors' Association (HVA),
    26, 124, 129, 131, 245
Heath Government, 84
  industrial legislation, 86, 110
Herbert, Elizabeth, 16
Hierarchy
  nursing, 48, 52, **136**, 137, 139,
    140–141, 151–152, 154, 194
  union, 43
Hillingdon Hospital, 58
Hirst, Daniel, 221
History of nursing, concealment of,
    2–3
Holistic approach, **142**, 143, 148
Horder Committee, 140
Hospital
  admission, 7, **9–10**, 11–12, 18
  closures, 84
  consumer choice, 231
  nursing, 13
Hospital for Sick Children, Great
    Ormond Street, 255–256
Hospital Matrons' Association, 56
Hospitals, centralization of, 79
Hospitals and Welfare Services Union
    (HWSU), 47, 72
Hospitals' Association, 29
Hough, Herbert, 45
Hubbard, Louisa, 21
Hunter, David, 175–176

Iatrogenic conditions, 171
Illich, Ivan, 171
Image
  of COHSE, 101
  of health visitor, 25
  of nurse, 1, **3**, 12, **14–15**, 31,
    135–136, 193, 263, 265
  of RCN, 102, 109
  see also Polemic, caricatured
Incentive bonus schemes (IBSs), 79,
    237
Independent Ladies' Tailors Union,
    32